The Clock Book

The Clock Book

By
WALLACE NUTTING

BEING A DESCRIPTION OF FOREIGN AND AMERICAN ANTIQUE CLOCKS,
AND A LIST OF THEIR MAKERS.   PROFUSELY ILLUSTRATED

Modern Books and Crafts, Inc.
P.O. Box 38
Greens Farms, Ct. 06438 U.S.A.

Facsimile Edition
Copyright 1975
By Modern Books & Crafts, Inc.
ISBN 0-913274-04-6

PRINTED IN THE UNITED STATES

EXPLANATION

MORE and better pictures have long been needed by those interested in clocks. Some of the volumes on clocks have been beautifully illustrated, with a moderate number of examples. These works, however, were foreign, were high in price, and most of them are no longer available.

The advantage of gathering in one volume a very great number of pictures, reproduced in the best manner, is obvious. The author should perhaps call himself rather a compiler. A few of the pieces here shown have previously appeared. A great many of the illustrations were made particularly for this work.

There are adequate books describing technically the mechanism of clocks. We therefore in this volume call attention mainly to the features of peculiar decorative interest.

We make no pretence at any sort of originality. Some of the pictures are taken from French works, which have previously served as a storehouse for compilations on clocks. These works will be credited through this volume.

We have excluded all but two or three of the clocks owned by the author, so as to secure a more impartial treatment.

An important part of this volume is the lists of makers which take the place of an index. The American list is larger by about 250 names than any previously issued. It has been very carefully and exhaustively prepared by Mrs. Homer W. Brainard of Hartford.

As to the foreign list, we have met a puzzling question. Britten, who is the great English authority, covers, in his fifth edition, about two hundred pages with the names of makers. Rather than to increase the size of our work to such an inordinate extent, we have thought fit to abbreviate his list in an old edition which contained practically all important foreign names, and have omitted therefrom most of those who are listed as watch makers only.

Lists of makers are of course common property to an extent, but it should be stated as a very important matter that dealers in clocks formerly, as now, have had their names placed on the dials, so that a great number of so-called makers were not so. In many instances it is impossible to know whether the name on a dial means a maker or a dealer. It was a highly intricate matter to produce a good clock, so that it is a fair presumption that the makers were not nearly so numerous as the dealers.

The arrangement of the book has been guided more by exigencies as to the shapes of clocks than by their merit or date. But in general the American subjects will be found in the earlier part of the book and the foreign subjects in the latter part.

Mr. Walter H. Durfee of Providence, whose extended experience has been drawn upon freely by the author, is most thankfully remembered.

The volume has been made uniform in size and style with the author's series on the States Beautiful.

WALLACE NUTTING

Framingham
Massachusetts

Clock Book

The Clock Book

· ·
·

TIME markers are the most apt indications of advance from savagery. To the savage, time is of no account. The importance of a civilized man closely approximates to the value and division of his time. We find, therefore, at the remotest period, scientific sun dials, and, in every remote period, water clocks. In a region where the sun usually shines, as it did in the earliest centers of civilization, the sun dial answered all purposes. When, however, we arrive in northern Europe, as for instance at London, where the sun sometimes shines, the ingenuity of man was stimulated to mark time otherwise than by the sun. It is, perhaps, for this reason that London, at once the foggiest and largest city, became the center of clock making.

With the discovery of the earth's rotundity and the discovery of the pendulum, though Galileo's credit for it is now challenged, there was an immense stimulus to the making of clocks. Navigation required the most accurate of all time pieces, a chronometer. The author remembers his delighted amazement when, crossing the ocean in a fog, the ship found itself within a few rods of the precise point calculated upon off the Scilly Isles.

Clocks and watches were at once seized upon by artists as their opportunity for elaborate decoration. One clock shown in this work is almost an epitome of universal history, together with a generous quantity of legendary lore, in the sculptures which appear on all sides and on the top.

The great English work on this subject is by Britten, which in the last edition is almost monumental in the fulness of its material. With the usual British tendency to regard their island as the be-all and end-all, they have given in this work scarcely a glance at the immense development of American clock and watch making. David Rittenhouse, for instance, has four lines, and in that short space the capital error is made of stating that he was a Swiss, residing here! The entire family of the Willards do receive a little fuller mention. These two instances are sufficient to indicate that American clocks, in which the chief interests of Americans lie, require fuller attention by us. The word "banjo," for instance, is not found in the last edition of Britten!

It was not until such men as Willard turned their genius to this subject that the citizen of small means could possess a clock. In the earlier times of Bagnall and Claggett, the great names of the pioneers in this country, much attention was paid to the cases, and the faces, following in these regards the English habit. But Willard and many of his compeers were intensely practical Americans, and Simon Willard is perhaps the finest exponent of American mechanical genius, combined with that practical turn of mind which sought to confer a benefit upon all his countrymen by providing at once a good and a cheap clock. The story is told of Willard that so great was the accuracy of his hand and eye that he habitually filed the teeth of his cog wheels without marking them! This incredible feat may perhaps stand alone in the annals of mechanics. It is said that when someone asked Willard why he didn't stamp his brass with markers, he replied that it was unnecessary, as his wheels were accurate. As the writer has one of his order clocks, which has run to within thirty seconds of accuracy for a month, it is obvious that no answer can be made to Mr. Willard's statement.

Following this pioneer, and emulating his idea of the greatest good for the greatest number, the Connecticut clock maker now marks time for the world. There are single makers in Connecticut who now turn out several millions of clocks annually. Their product goes literally everywhere. Its diffusion is one of the most hopeful signs for stability and progress. When the Arabs, the Indians, and the dwellers in the

THE CLOCK ON THE LENOX CHURCH

tropics want clocks, they make clear to the world that they are looking toward doing something with their hours. It is true they may in instances be following a fashion, just as the native waiter on table in a South Sea isle, when warned that company was coming and he must dress, astonished the guests by appearing in a necklace and a tall hat, being otherwise stark naked. Nevertheless a clock is the pioneer school teacher. It is the only article of furniture with a face and hands and voice. It is the first thing to interest a child. Quite spontaneously, numerous persons become collectors of clocks. We limit our field to clocks, passing over the fascinating and large field of watch design, because the public may not be ready for a work as exhaustive as both subjects would require. Also in this work, owing to the large size of the individual illustrations, we cannot show one half as many as we could wish. We recognize that although this work shows hundreds of examples, it is a mere primer on the subject.

Some sort of timepiece is now thought necessary even by the small boy, and the famous "dollar watch" has become a byword. The little alarm clock is as necessary and common as one's breakfast.

The connection between astronomy and mechanical markers of time is very close. In the most ancient time there was a mystical, or at least a misty, halo connected with astronomy, which was one with astrology. The devotees of the science were of a priestly caste and made much of their secret knowledge, doubtless in a political sense. It may be that America had an earlier place in the astronomical marking of time than has previously been accorded us by Europe. This very year discoveries among the architectural remains of the Mayas has enabled us to correlate their calendar accurately with our own, and to know that they had a means once a year at least of checking their time to the instant. All this happened six thousand years ago or so.

Astronomical clocks have been a favorite device wherever wealth and genius coöperated. Indeed, our ordinary clocks, which mark simply the hour, are very humble cousins of the intricate instruments some of which are shown in this work. The device of showing the moon's phases by a

CLOCK, BRITISH MUSEUM

moving disc over the dial, and the little slot under which moved the dial showing the days of the month, are about the only features left in our grandfather's clocks, of the elaborate contrivances of the Middle Ages.

In this work most of the data connected with the maker's name will be found alphabetically listed in the two catalogs closing the volume. In the numbers which follow we merely call attention to certain features of special interest, and to the owners' names where known.

The romance connected with American clock making would furnish a large chapter, filled with pathetic, amusing and sometimes amazing incidents. The elegant clocks provided by metropolitan dealers in these days, and the methods of their sales, are a far cry from the ancient time when a clock maker loaded the works of two or three clocks on a pack saddle and traveled about the country until he sold his wares. David Rittenhouse, it is true, exhibited a broader genius than was possessed by the Yankee clockmaker, inasmuch as he was our most eminent astronomer at that time, and in a social and political way was a large factor in the life of Pennsylvania and even of the nation. But the itinerant mender of clocks, or the original vendor, were strongly marked types. We well remember how, more than half a century since, the tinker and clock repairer and general exponent of mechanical genius went from house to house in the country and gave a new lease of life to the old tall clock which had become rheumatic through age or abuse.

If we are to consider American clocks as works of original art, we shall have little to say except about the attractive banjo cases or their variants. The American makers seem not to have made any important advance over the foreign designs of cases. In fact, the more elaborate metal designs were not attempted at all here. The earliest cases of wood are substantially English in type. The scroll or broken arch top and the Chinese Chippendale type of top were for the most part superseded in this country by an open fret applied to an arch. The great merit of American clocks has been their manufacture by simplified methods or designs so that they became available for all.

The immense importance of accurate time keepers for ascertaining longitude, at sea, appeared by the offer of the King of Spain in 1598, of a reward of a hundred thousand crowns for the inventor of such a chronometer. Other governments made similar efforts, but in vain. Thus it was a hundred years and more after the discovery of America that the first serious attention was paid to the problem. Mariners encountered many difficulties by not knowing where they were. Tedious and fatal delays and even many wrecks resulted from the lack of a chronometer. A pendulum was impractical at sea.

It was not until a hundred and seventy years after the inception of this effort that a good chronometer was invented. The names of Earnshaw, Arnold and Mudge are connected with the successful invention. Each of them was honored by monetary rewards from the government of England. The suspension of the chronometer by gimbals, in the same manner as compasses and lamps at sea, and fitted with the Arnold detent escapement gave the world a scientific and closely accurate marine timepiece. This invention is a monumental instance of the time, toil, and genius bestowed on a single purpose. How many travelers by water know that their journeys are made practical by accurate time keepers, and how many recognize their debt to the infinite study of other generations of men!

It was natural that Britain, being an island, and therefore necessarily a maritime power, should devote more attention than other nations to chronometers. The reflex stimulus upon clock making in general is obvious. But climate is another stimulus. Whenever the climate conduces to effective labor, as in the northern temperate zone, the value of time is proportionately recognized and its passage is measured. The relation of invention in general to the insular location of Britain is suggested as a curious study.

In America, when the notable clock makers flourished, around the period of the Revolution, the country was really maritime. It had not then set its face toward the great West. This fact, together with the stimulus to inventive genius furnished by patriotism, which always calls on men to make for themselves what they have previously imported, may in part account for the development of Rittenhouse, Willard, and their associates, rivals, and imitators.

ART IN CLOCK CASES

THE inspiration of the revival of learning and art passing through Italy, France, the Low Countries and England, seems, so far as clock cases are concerned, to have reached its highest development in France. The French people are peculiarly fitted by habit, pride and genius, to succeed in the development of small works of art often included in the somewhat dubious designation "bric-a-brac." The clock case was developed by the French in the finest forms of art, and made in many instances a thing of wonderful beauty.

As always, when we leave Greece, we find many a tendency to flamboyance and the bizarre and rococo, so in France there were many examples of clocks in questionable and even wretched taste. Yet apart from, and parallel with, the bad, the French produced so many examples in chaste and elegant taste, that we may pardon their failures.

Is it not true that, during the inception and growth of any art, when abundant and healthy emulation and exuberant love of creation is rife, many experiments are tried? The finest forms in any art are the selected products of many abortive or over-confident attempts. Thus in England certain furniture designers showed in style books some wretched designs, along with others which have steadily approved themselves as the best of their kind, for pure beauty and the power of satisfying the artistic sense.

After we throw to the void the overdone or slovenly examples of French taste in clocks, we conclude that neither England nor America — still less America — has produced much that is artistic in comparison with France. With the solitary exception of the Curtis style, we have contributed little to the outside of clocks. That exception is, however, of the highest importance, as it marks the highest adaptation of beauty to design in wall clocks in America. The simple banjo case, without its bracket, lacks conviction as to lines of beauty, though its approach thereto is close.

In our own days it has been worth while for the large manufacturers to employ good talent in the design of cases. Many happy results have been reached, though we are bound to say that the reproduction of old forms still seems to appeal rather more strongly than the new. The order, so brusquely given, to an artist, to design a "new" clock case, carries with it many conditions staggering to the designer. The fact is often overlooked that thousands of men, often men of education and genius, have for centuries given careful, even painful, attention to style in clock cases. The probabilities that a new style of merit can be readily evolved are not encouraging. There are only so many lines that are possible, with grace. The inevitable tendency is to distortion of line in order to achieve originality. It is easily possible to make a new style in a clock case, if we are satisfied with a bad one. But when an artist is limited as to time, as to the material he is to employ, as to the cost of his work, and most of all, as to the state of public taste, he is certainly not to be envied. It is a labor worthy of a miraculous genius. Hence we need not wonder at the unsatisfactory result. It is this consideration that has in our day led many makers to reproduce, as the safer effort, some of the more highly approved designs of the eighteenth century.

The tendency to follow fads is exemplified in clocks, in the highest degree. The old tall, hall, long or grandfather's clock, called indifferently by any of these names, was often destroyed or put away in the lumber room when shelf clocks came in. Of course the moving spirit was congenial to the shelf clock. Now, however, and for thirty years more or less, the old hall clocks are cherished by everybody.

CURIOUS EARLY CLOCKS

IN the British Museum is a clock shown by Britten, which we here reproduce. The date is 1589 and the maker Isaac Habrecht. He was one of the brothers who made the second clock at Strasbourg. This example shows the Three Fates, the cock of St. Peter, etc. The cock flaps its wings and crows. This device is continued to this day in jewel-like cases, from which a bird emerges on the touch of a spring, sings a song and quickly disappears through a trap door, which is closed behind it.

The clock tower at Rouen is perhaps the most artistic in its location, and the best known of any to travelers. Americans are familiar with this beautiful location, which offers a suggestion to American builders. Indeed, we have hints enough to which the wealth of America has not responded. The writer made photographs of this clock about twenty years ago, in connection with a beautiful angle of the wall near at hand with its fountain, but the public have preferred less artistic compositions, done by us.

We also illustrate from Britten the clock tower in the old palace yard of Westminster.

We are not greatly impressed with the various odd designs of the figure of Death, of the twelve Apostles, or of other allegorical figures on clocks. These subjects, however, have always been extremely popular, furnishing as it were a kind of perpetual motion Punch and Judy show. The curious old clocks of Europe, especially that of Strasbourg, which is at least the third in its location, have for long been pilgrimage points. Pure art in clock cases has been about the last thing to be considered.

An odd meridian clock from L'Horlogerie by Joseph Rambal is here shown. It indicated accurately the solar noon, and also approximately the mean solar noon. It was about the last thing in the sun dial, carrying that ancient indicator as far as was possible.

The briefest outline of time measures is all that this volume can attempt. Perhaps it will be worth while to point out the difference between true solar time and mean solar time. They agree on the 25th of December, the 15th of April, the 14th of June and the 31st of August, although the time varies slightly, the error being corrected at leap year. When the sun is actually at meridian, as we see it, it had already reached that point some quarter of an hour before, or will reach it about fifteen minutes after. This occurs from the other movements of the earth in addition to its diurnal revolution. True and mean time would agree at the equinoxes and on the summer and winter solstices, except that the earth moves faster in December, when it is nearer the sun, than it does in July, when it is farther from the sun. The earth's motion is also disturbed by the attraction of the moon and the planets.

A sun dial, therefore, is never correct, and the man whose watch is regulated by the sun has a very poor watch.

The standard of time as used by astronomers is called sidereal, and of course is more precise than sun time, the sidereal day being 23 hours, 56 minutes, 4.1 seconds. Thus it may be learned by noting a star in a certain position two nights in succession, whether or not a clock is gaining or losing, since it will appear in the same position as on the night before, but three minutes and fifty-six seconds earlier.

We hope soon to have the new scientific calendar, which has been planned, and for which we believe some society is attempting to win the world. The present cumbersome computation by leap years, to be omitted so often and never leaving us in a correct position, is not worthy of our scientific age. Thus the cycle of the sun, a period of twenty-eight years, a device worked out about the time of the Christian era, in order to obtain the Dominical letter, would no longer be required.

In fact, our entire computation is arbitrary. The time of the birth of the Savior is thought by many to have been in February. Of course, if there had existed any importance in fixing that event on a certain day, it would have been done.

The Greeks' calculation regarding the return of the full moon in nineteen years on the same day of the month as at the beginning of that period, by which they established the Golden Number, and the use of the Golden Number to establish the Epact, is a matter too abstruse and too far from our present practical purpose.

Similarly the shifting of Easter Day as between the Eastern and Western Church has always been an annoyance and even a cause for war.

Our arrangement of the hours into twenty-four has been found open to objection in these days, and certain great organizations and even certain nations reckon from one to twenty-four without a division into two twelve-hour periods.

The Japanese clock was ingeniously arranged to be corrected every two weeks in order to divide the hours of darkness and light, equally; that is, the length of the hour changed in the old system in Japan.

We have shown a water clock or two. There are also clocks guided by the burning of oil. But the principal method of marking time was of course the sun dial.

The making of the first clock, like that of most other early inventions, is now a matter too foggy in the mist of ages to speak of with any definiteness. The ancients are said to have had clocks, and in the seventh century there is a record of clocks on the Continent. In the tenth century one is recorded to have been set up in Magdeburg. It is not known, however, whether this was a true clock or a kind of sun dial.

The derivation of the word clock is itself somewhat doubtful, but at first the signification is that of a bell, indicating of course that at first the hours were marked by a bell rung by hand. Clocks came out of the Orient at the time of the Crusades, and we find them mentioned quite frequently on public buildings, usually churches, in the thirteenth and fourteenth centuries.

In America the town clock, with the town pump, shared as the two important active institutions, with the town crier, who also had his bell. The expense of a clock was such that in the earliest times a common clock, like the common pump, was made to do service for all the people of the village. The town paid for the clock and for its upkeep. Even as late as the days of Simon Willard we find him supplying clocks for public buildings. Of course the decline of the town clock in our days arises from the fact that every family has its own timepiece. We are not altogether certain that the ties that bound together an ancient village were not a great advantage by way of fellowship. We have become almost too much marked by individual independence.

THE DETECTION OF SPURIOUS CLOCKS

IT will have been noted that the banjo and other clocks in very elegant forms are now reproduced. This is as it should be. If we can, however, say a word which may prevent fraud against an unsuspecting buyer, we ought to do so. The banjo clock, being small and popular, is especially liable to forgeries. Almost invariably the banjo clocks so far produced have their backs thicker than the antique examples. It is of course easy to buy works for any clock which only a clockmaker can distinguish from the old. If the new clocks are made of old wood, as is often the case, the difficulty of detection is increased. One should notice, however, that worm holes, wherever they occur, never show as grooves on the surface of old wood. One sees only the end of the hole. Grooves indicate that a piece of old wood has been dressed longitudinally. The aging of new wood has now reached such a degree of success, that the best judges may be deceived. Wood may be aged a hundred years in a day by steaming. It may be aged by exposing it to sun and storm for a few months. It may be bleached or stained quickly. So true is this, that we can recommend no sure method of detecting fraud in a clock case. The most usual and obvious error made by the rogues who do these things is to ask more for a clock than a new one would be worth, and less for it than an old one would be worth. If a maker has the face to ask the full price he may deceive his customer. If, however, any article of furniture is offered for half the price at which it can be purchased, of the most reputable people, the presumption is entirely against it.

Style has something to do with the detection. It is seldom that the maker takes pains to reproduce with sufficient exactness to deceive a careful buyer. But the person who is buying a new clock for an old is not usually a careful buyer. The perfection of the moldings and the general marks of age are therefore not observed by him.

A very keen dealer once told the writer that he was guided by the smell! He averred that there was a certain mustiness observable on pulling out an old drawer or opening an old clock door, which could not possibly be imitated. We have attempted to verify articles by this method, and often, when we were free from colds, the results were satisfactory. After all is said and done, however, one must have the flair for antiques to know an old clock from a new one. If one thinks he possesses this flair, he is perhaps just as happy.

The glasses in shelf clocks are more often than not reproductions, even when the clocks are old. It is not at all likely that many clocks could go through the usage to which they have been subjected for more than a hundred years without breaking. There are specialists who do nothing but reproduce dials, and glasses. The rubbing away of new paint in part, or the treating of it, with chemicals, may give it an appearance of antiquity. This process of course requires a good deal of trouble, so that more often than otherwise, the new dials look new. Of course their reproduction is a perfectly legitimate process if they are not given the appearance of age. It is their sale as old that is blameworthy.

Our attention was lately called to a Simon Willard tall clock, on the works of which his name was said to be engraved. The engraving was obviously recent, and of course could deceive only a novice, since Willard did not practice engraving his works. In fact, as we point out later, his name did not ordinarily appear even on the dials of his banjo clocks. So many dials of clocks of all shapes and sizes have no name upon them, that the temptation of the unscrupulous to paint a name is obvious. This, however, is not so easy as it seems. It requires being done very deftly, or even a novice can detect the freshness of the work.

CHAMBER CLOCKS

THE term appears to distinguish household clocks from the great public timepieces or elaborate clocks made to satisfy wealthy tastes. They were one day, that is thirty hour, movements of brass, and were set on wall brackets and wound by pulling on the ropes or chains which restored the weights to their high positions. The terms "lantern" and "birdcage" are applied to these clocks, which became very popular in England, though in this country they were never common.

Previous to the introduction of these clocks, at the beginning of the seventeenth century, the sun dial was still in general use, so much so that the old brass plates of sun dials were often used for the doors on the sides of the clocks, and the engraving for a dial may still be found occasionally on the inside of a door. Of course the invention of the clock reduced to scrap the parts in a dealer's stock which had been prepared for sun dials.

Into these clocks the bob pendulum was introduced soon after its invention, about 1640. The pendulum improved the time-keeping quality. The long pendulum coming in about 1680 was in turn substituted for the short (bob) pendulum, and thus the "grandfather's" clock came into being, lacking only a case for protection. The earliest of these clocks had, generally, only the hour hand. It was possible, however, with one hand, on a finely divided dial such as was applied to many clocks of that time, to read the time to a minute.

The dates of these clocks are indicated roughly by their sizes. The early examples were very small, only three to five inches square, whereas those made nearer the close of the seventeenth century were almost double in dimensions.

When the dial was enlarged, so as to project some inches beyond the side of the frame, the clock was called a sheep's head.

While such clocks are usually assigned to the seventeenth century, they were made in large numbers early in the eighteenth century. Simple examples often had no case except a rude wooden cover, and were attached to the wall by a hook.   The term "bedpost" was often applied to these clocks, from the four legs.

The Friesland clock is the Continental type most nearly like the bird-cage clock.   The pendulum, even when short, was generally longer than the case and swung in a hole in the shelf on which the clock was placed.

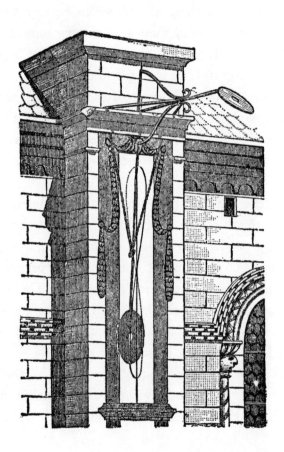

MERIDIAN CLOCK, L'HORLOGERIE

CLOCK TOWER, WESTMINSTER

Description of Illustrations

DESCRIPTION OF ILLUSTRATIONS

No. 1. A hall clock. Made by S. Taber. His exact date and place of business are unknown. An S. M. Taber was supposed to have been a maker at Providence in 1824.

The case is mahogany, inlaid. Date: about 1800–1810. It is a fine specimen. The same style of case was used by Simon Willard. Owner: Leonard M. Robinson, Providence, R. I.

No. 2. A Colonial hall clock made by Benjamin Willard, Grafton, Massachusetts, 1743–1803. The case is mahogany. Date: about 1790. The features are concave sunbursts in the door. A brass band runs around the two columns half way up, with plates below. It is very unusual. Owner: W. L. Mulligan, Springfield, Mass.

No. 3. A hall clock made by David Williams, Newport, R. I. The case is mahogany. Date: 1800–1810. Finely proportioned throughout. The fret is unusual. Owner: Dr. Emory M. Porter, Providence, R. I.

No. 4. A Colonial hall clock made by Caleb Wheaton, Providence, R. I., 1784–1827. The case is mahogany with a fret below the bonnet, inlaid. Date: about 1800. The fret follows the English Chippendale style. The brass ornaments are unusual. Owner: Mrs. Guy Metcalf Keating, Pinehurst, N. C.

No. 5. The dial of a Colonial chime clock, playing tunes. The clock chimes every three hours, at twelve, three, six, and nine. It has a different tune for each day of the week and a psalm tune on Sunday. It was owned by the late ex-governor Elisha Dyer, Providence, R. I. By Peregrine White (1774–   ).

No. 6. Calls for no explanation.

No. 7. An early Colonial hall clock made by William Claggett, 1730–1749, Newport, R. I. The case is mahogany. The clock is almost English in style. Most Claggett clocks have the dome top shown here. Owner: The Rhode Island Historical Society, Providence, R. I.

No. 8. A miniature hall clock, of late years called a grandmother clock. Made by Joshua Wilder, Hingham, Mass. The case is pine. Date: about 1790. It has time and alarm. The shield corners on the dial are common to this make. Owner: C. Prescott Knight, Providence, R. I.

No. 9. Showing the movement, time and alarm weight of dwarf or miniature hall clock pictured in No. 8. Most of these clocks have the movement put in from the back in this fashion, with a door in the back, running the full length of the clock.

No. 10. The dial of a William Claggett hall clock. He produced the finest dials of any Colonial maker. This example is owned by the heirs of William G. Russell, late of Providence, R. I.

No. 11. A dial by Fromanteel and Clarke. Date: 1710. The name appears on the outside edge of the dial circle. Below, on the dial, is " A. Fromanteel." He was one of the best early English makers. In the Pendleton Collection at the Rhode Island School of Design, Providence, R. I.

No. 12. Another William Claggett dial. It is very fine in workmanship, as was the former. This dial and case were buried at Kingston, R. I., during the Revolutionary War. All the Claggett movements were hand made. Owner: G. Winthrop Brown, Boston, Mass.

Nos. 13 and 14 show a hall clock movement made by Johannes A. Fromanteel, 1675, London. The alarm dial is on the side of the movement instead of in front. This plate shows a part of the movement. The wheel of the winding arbor is separate from the winding drum.

These are held together by movement plates. Very unusual. This movement is shown in the case on Plate No. 236.

No. 15. This plate shows in .greater detail the dial to the movement on plates Nos. 13 and 14. The clock is owned by Marsden J. Perry, Providence, R. I. This movement is shown in the case in plate No. 236.

No. 16. A Curtis girandole wall clock, made by Lemuel Curtis, Concord, Mass., 1810–1818. The case is pine and is painted white. The bracket, lower door, center panel and top ornament are of pine, gilded. It is a very rare clock. The glasses are unusual. The style of hands is peculiar to this maker. Owner: Mrs. L. F. O'Neil, Auburn, N. Y.

No. 17. Shows the movement, weight run, etc., of a striking shelf clock. The dial and center panel are removed, and the door is opened. Made by L. Curtis, Concord, Mass., 1810–1818. The case is mahogany. The style is very unusual. Owner: C. Prescott Knight, Providence, R. I.

No. 18. By Aaron Willard, Jr., Boston.

No. 19. A shelf clock after the "Massachusetts pattern." Made by John Sawin, Boston, Mass. The case is mahogany with painted glasses around the dial and in the lower panel. Date: about 1830. This style shelf clock seems to have been peculiar to Massachusetts makers. The dial is dished, the usual term for convex. Owner: Edwin P. Anthony, Providence, R. I.

No. 20. Square fretted top. A pattern used in Rochester, N. H., circa 1800.

No. 21. A dwarf or miniature hall clock, otherwise a grandmother clock. Made by J. Wilder, Hingham, Mass. Date: 1780–1800. Compare with No. 8. These miniature clocks are rare and this maker seems to have specialized on them. Owner: C. Prescott Knight, Providence, R. I.

No. 22. A shelf clock after the "Massachusetts pattern." The maker is unknown. The case is pine. Date: 1780–1790. It has a thirty-hour movement, and is very unusual and early for this style. Owner: Elisha C. Durfee, Providence, R. I.

No. 23. A shelf clock on the Massachusetts pattern. Made by E. Taber. The case is mahogany, inlaid. Date: about 1800. A feature of interest is the kidney dial, a good example. Owner: Mr. C. Prescott Knight, Providence, R. I.

No. 24. A wall clock by Simon Willard. The case is mahogany. Date: 1770–1780. A very rare clock. It has the thirty-hour movement and a brass dial. Owner: G. Winthrop Brown, Boston, Mass.

No. 25. A Connecticut shelf clock. Made by C. & N. Jerome, Bristol, Conn. The case is mahogany. Date: about 1830. It belongs to the heavy rolled late Empire style. It has an eight day brass movement, and an unusual dial of black and gold, pierced in the center to show movement. Owner: Dr. Charles H. Chetwood, Chatham, Mass.

No. 26. A pillar and scroll clock, made by Eli Terry, Plymouth, Conn. The case is mahogany. Mr. Durfee gives the date as uncertain, but Eli Terry's work dates between 1793 and 1818. This very popular clock had more artistic merit than most of the late designs. Many other makers imitated the style. A thirty hour movement of wood.

No. 27. A shelf clock of the Massachusetts pattern. Made by Aaron Willard, Boston, Mass. The case is of mahogany, inlaid, with French foot. Date: about 1800. Owner: C. Prescott Knight, Providence, R. I. It is a fine specimen with a kidney dial, and unusually good hands. Ogee feet are more usual.

No. 28. A lyre wall clock, made by L. Curtis, Concord, Mass. The case is mahogany, with a carved bottom bracket and center panel, also leaf ornament at the top. The precise date is uncertain. It is a fine example of the style. The movement is very rare. It strikes the hours on two piano wires. Owner: Mr. G. Winthrop Brown, Boston, Mass.

No. 29. A banjo clock, made by L. Curtis, Concord, Mass. The case is of mahogany. The front panels are of pine, gilded. The precise date is uncertain. The center glass is unusual. Curtis made few of this style of clock. Owner: Philip A. Johnson, Norwich, Conn.

No. 30. A banjo clock, made by William Grant, Boston, Mass. The case is of mahogany, the front panels of pine being gilded. The date is uncertain. It is about 1815–1825. A very good example. Owner: Robert C. Johnson, Norwich, Conn.

No. 31. A "spool" banjo, made by William Cummens. The case is mahogany with brass molding on the inside of the center and lower panels. Date: about 1815. The clock is larger than the ordinary banjo but in fine proportion. The spools under the side brasses are exceptional. Owner: C. Prescott Knight, Providence, R. I.

No. 32. A handsomely scrolled lyre clock, belonging to William E. Montague, Norristown, Pa.

No. 33. Needs no description.

No. 34. A hall clock by William Cummens. The case is of mahogany, inlaid on the lower panel. Date: uncertain, but about 1825. The clock has very fine moldings and good proportion. The base is missing. Owner: D. J. Steele, East Milton, Mass.

No. 35. A hall clock in the Pendleton collection, Rhode Island School of Design, Providence, R. I. The maker is unknown. The clock was bought in Frederick, Md. The case is of Virginia walnut, and the movement looks English. It runs eight days, and strikes the hour and the quarters.

No. 36. An alarm clock made by John Sawin, Boston.

No. 37. A shelf clock by Eli Terry of Plymouth, Conn. The case is mahogany. Date: about 1818. This is one of the first clocks made in this style, since it has the escape wheel in the front of the dial. Owner: Francis E. Bates, Oaklawn, R. I.

No. 38. A clock by Nath. Edwards, Acton, Mass. The photograph was furnished by Warren W. Creamer, Waldoboro, Maine. The case is of mahogany, inlaid. The height is 88 inches. The widest portion of the hood is 18½ inches, and that of the base 17¾ inches. The waist is 17⅝ inches.

No. 39. Made by Aaron Willard, Roxbury, Mass. The photograph was furnished by Warren W. Creamer, Waldoboro, Maine. The case is of mahogany with inlay. The height is 76 inches. The width of the hood is 18½ inches, the waist 13¾ inches, and the base 17 inches.

The dial is signed on the back with white enamel: "By William Prescott," who, it is understood, was a decorator of considerable note.

No. 40. A clock by David Wood of Newburyport. He made many shelf and tall clocks, but very few patent timepieces.

No. 41. Col. Isaac G. Reed's banjo clock, by Aaron Willard, Junior. It is in mahogany and gilt. The height including eagle is 36 inches. The width of the base is 10 inches, of the face 8½ inches. The eagle is 6 inches high and has a 6-inch spread of wings. It will be noticed that this clock has the word "Willard" on the upper glass. This method of using the word "for" before the name on the glass indicates that it was made to order or that it was a presentation clock. The photograph was furnished by Warren W. Creamer, Waldoboro, Maine.

Nos. 42, 43, 44, 45. English clock hands, hand made. From early hall clocks. About 1700. Photograph furnished by Walter H. Durfee.

No. 46. A plate to show the bridge and pendulum attachment of a Simon Willard banjo. From a clock owned by Mr. Harry Weeks, Framingham, Mass.

No. 47. An acorn clock, Forrestville Mfg. Co., Bristol, Conn., U. S. A. The mounting reminds one somewhat of the dainty mounting used for swinging dresser mirrors. It is a most interesting specimen. Owner: Mr. W. E. Montague, of Norristown, Pa.

No. 48. A wall clock by Joseph Ives, New York City. The case is rosewood. Date: 1818–1830. The clock has a very fine wagon spring movement, running thirty days. This movement was removed from the case and re-cased in the Connecticut shelf clock shown in plates Nos. 65 and 66. The movement now in the clock is shown in plate No. 100. Owner: C. Prescott Knight, Providence, R. I.

No. 49. A Connecticut shelf clock made by Jerome & Darrow, date about 1825–1830. The case is mahogany with black and gold stenciled columns and top. This is the most common style of its period. The painting on the lower glass is very good and in an unusually good state of preservation. It has thirty-hour wooden works. Owner: Richard E. Wheeler, Providence, R. I.

No. 50. A tower clock removed from a church in Morristown, N. J., and now in the Washington Headquarters Museum in that town. Of Colonial date.

No. 51. A banjo clock made by Aaron Willard. "Willard's Patent" on narrow glass. Owned by Mr. William E. Montague of Norristown, Pa.

No. 52. A regulator wall clock. Made by Aaron Willard. The case is mahogany. Date: early 19th century. This clock has a dished dial and a regular banjo movement. The case is plain, but very well made, similar to the English "act of Parliament" clock, and probably copied from it. Owner: Dr. Emory M. Porter, Providence, R. I.

No. 53. A lyre clock, the property of Mr. William E. Montague of Norristown, Pa. We regret the difficulty of bringing out the details more clearly of the picture on the lower door, as it is very quaint.

No. 54. A clock owned by Mr. William E. Montague of Norristown, Pa. A comparison of the shape of this clock with the conventional banjo form shows a change coming about eventuating in the elegant designs of Curtis.

No. 55. A clock by Z. Gates, the property of Mr. William E. Montague, of Norristown, Pa. Attention is called to the chariot picture and to the pleasant variant of design seen in the hands.

No. 56. A banjo clock, the property of Mr. William E. Montague of Norristown, Pa. There has been a good deal of discussion in relation to the ornaments at the tops of clocks. Claim has been made that the acorn was always used at the top. Others say that the eagle was frequently used. As nearly as we can ascertain the fact, both forms are original. We find the eagle on the mirror at a date before banjo clocks were made. "Patent" on glass.

No. 57. A "pillar and scroll" clock, made by Seth Thomas, Plymouth Hollow, Conn. Case: mahogany. Date: about 1820. A very fine specimen. The veneer under the three ornaments is of satinwood. The painting is original and very good. The glass is slightly curved, as was the case in all of the original glass, so that at the side it falls slightly back from the rabbet. This is one of the most desirable styles of Connecticut shelf clocks. Owner: Mrs. Harrison B. Huntoon, Providence, R. I.

No. 58. A shelf clock with square top. Owner, William E. Montague, Norristown, Pa. Made by Simon Willard, Boston. A simple but elegant example.

No. 59. A clock by David Rittenhouse. It is owned by William E. Montague of Norristown, Pa. The marked simplicity of the case is as attractive as it is unusual.

No. 60. A tall clock, the property of William E. Montague, Norristown, Pa. It has the blocks and outside finials at the extreme edge of the scroll top.

No. 61. A late Empire clock, made by Atkins & Downs, Bristol, Conn. It is of mahogany, with carved columns, feet and top. Date: about 1830. This style is about the height of the scroll and pillar clock. When so fully carved, this style is now sought for. Owner: Mrs. George L. Shattuck, Providence, R. I.

No. 62. An Empire shelf clock, made by Munger & Benedict, Auburn, N. Y. "A. Munger" on paster. This case is mahogany, with carved columns and feet, while the top is of plaster with a painting of Washington in the center, covered by glass.   The columns, instead of extending the full length of the case, stop half way followed by painted glasses of a stenciled design, inserted in the upper part of the clock. The same stencil design is carried out around the dial. Perhaps unique. The date, 1833, is engraved on the front side of the striking hammer. An eagle makes the pendulum bob. Owner: C. Prescott Knight, Providence, R. I.

No. 63.   Shows the interior of the clock in Plate No. 62.

No. 64.   Shows the interior of clock in Plate No. 25.

Nos. 65 and 66.   A clock showing a cart spring movement, pictured also in Plate No. 100. A late Empire clock with carved feet and finials and stenciled scroll.

No. 67.   A grandfather clock with mahogany case, made by Thomas Harland, of Norwich, Connecticut, about 1775–1800. It is now in the Metropolitan Museum, New York.

No. 68.   A grandfather clock owned by the Metropolitan Museum. It is of inlaid curly maple, and was made by N. Storrs, of Utica, N. Y., in the nineteenth century.

No. 69.   Metal clock, painted ornaments. Late. W. F. Hubbard, Hartford.

No. 70.   Curious small wall style $18\frac{1}{2}$ x $8\frac{3}{4}$ x $4\frac{1}{4}$. A Wag-on-the-Wall. Circa 1820.

No. 71.   Small metal style. Painted decoration. W. F. Hubbard, Hartford.

No. 72.   David Rittenhouse takes rank among the greatest Americans.

His life constitutes some of the most fascinating reading in our literature. He is said to have been the only American in his time capable of calculating the transit of Venus. He shares with Franklin that characteristic of the ideal American, a capacity to do a great many different things. He has been much neglected in the literature of American clocks. The beauty and quality of those clocks is unsurpassed. Rittenhouse was notable politically, socially, and mechanically. His achievements were monumental, though he was handicapped by serious illness. We wish our limits permitted at least a résumé of his manifold and honorable activities. His home in Norriton, a township from which Norristown is taken, has been beautifully restored. He is justly revered and honored in Pennsylvania and several of his clocks are shown in this work.

No. 73. An Aaron Willard clock with shields in the spandrels of the dial.

No. 74. A double Gothic steeple shelf clock, sometimes called a "double decker" steeple clock. Made by Birge & Fuller, Bristol, Conn. The case is mahogany. Date: about 1830–1835. It has an eight-day wagon spring movement. Made under the Joseph Ives patent. This sort of movement is generally found with this style of case. Owner: Dr. Emory M. Porter, Providence, R. I.

No. 75. A clock made by Thomas Claggett, Newport, R. I., about 1730–1749. The miniature case is of mahogany. Property of the Metropolitan Museum.

No. 76. A mahogany clock with marquetry panels. It was made in Connecticut, about 1803. Property of the Metropolitan Museum, New York.

No. 77. A lyre clock of good design. Formerly in the possession of the author. Present owner is unknown.

No. 78. A detail of a Simon Willard banjo escapement, to show the curved teeth of the wheel.

No. 79. A Samuel Bagnall clock, Boston, 1740–60. The case is of mahogany. Property of the Metropolitan Museum, New York.

No. 80. A lacquered clock by Edward Faulkner, London, 1710–1735. Owner: Mr. Henry Ford. The clock is in the Wayside Inn, South Sudbury, Mass., it having been sought out by Mr. Ford and returned to its position in the parlor, where it used to be many years ago.

No. 81. An American clock, mahogany on pine. The date is 1800–1825, and the maker is David Wood, Newburyport, Mass. It is the property of the Metropolitan Museum.

No. 82. A beautiful Simon Willard, owned by Willard E. Montague of Norristown, Pa., who has a very great collection of fine examples, both banjo and tall clocks.

No. 83. A very handsomely veneered clock of the better American tall clock type, with a good scroll. Property of John H. Halford, Norristown, Pa.

No. 84. A clock by Enos Doolittle of New Haven, Conn., 1772. It is owned in Plymouth, Mass. The concave sunrise carving on the door is carried out on the edge by raised molding all about the door.

No. 85. A wall regulator clock. Made by George D. Hatch, North Attleboro, Mass. The case is rosewood. The date is uncertain. An unusual style of case with a striking banjo movement. The same movement is sometimes found in the banjo clock with plain half round moldings and black and gold painted glasses. Owner: Dr. Emory M. Porter, Providence, R. I.

No. 86. A shelf clock by J. D. Custer, Norristown, Pa. (b. 1805, d. 1872). The design is quaint and the basket of flowers in the arch over the dial is effective. The design suggests in some degree the Connecticut pillar and scroll clock. Owned by William E. Montague, Norristown, Pa.

No. 87. A shelf clock in the Massachusetts pattern. Made by David Williams, Newport, R. I. The case is mahogany. Date: 1820–1830.

The kidney dial is excellent and well decorated. The hands are also fine. The top, with three blocks and brass urns, but without any frets, is out of the ordinary. This style was occasionally followed by Rhode Island makers. Owner: Benj. A. Jackson, Providence, R. I.

No. 88. A David Rittenhouse twenty-four hour clock. Owned by John H. Halford, Norristown, Pa.

No. 89. A pattern resembling a monument. Onion feet.

No. 90. A Benjamin Bagnall clock, Boston, 1725–1750. It is of black walnut on pine. There is beautiful fret work in the spandrels over the door arch. Property of the Metropolitan Museum.

No. 91. A Christopher Gould clock, London, about 1695. Beautiful burl walnut case. Owned by John H. Halford, Norristown, Pa.

No. 92. A curious clock of unknown origin, owned by the author. Its chief oddity is that the pendulum is in front of the dial. The picture of Father Time shows in somewhat fresh paint above. It may be late or a patched-up affair.

No. 93. A lantern clock, by Thomas Moore, Ipswich, England, about 1610. Owned by Mr. John H. Halford, Norristown, Pa.

No. 94. A clock owned by William E. Montague of Norristown, Pa. It is of an unusual but very handsome design, and has a three circle dial. Both the bombé waist and the outline of the top of the hood are extremely rare in tall clocks. Made by Griffith Owen, Philadelphia, 1811.

No. 95. "Benjamin Rittenhouse, Worcester, fecit" on dial. Owner: W. E. Montague. The case is very carefully made, with rosettes finishing the broken arch.

No. 96. A stenciled banjo clock. Made by Simon Willard & Sons, Boston, Mass. The case is mahogany. The stencil work is on the moldings, on the center and bottom panels, and bottom bracket. Date: about 1820–1825. A rare clock. The stencil ornamentation is in an almost perfect state. Owner: Dr. Emory M. Porter, Providence, R. I.

No. 97. A lyre clock by Sawin & Dyer, Boston. This beautiful example is by the maker who is supposed to have originated this form. The case is mahogany. In Metropolitan Museum, New York.

No. 98. A lyre wall clock, made by John Sawin. The case is of mahogany with a carved center panel. The eagle is of pine, gilded. Date: about 1830–1835. A fine example. Owner: Mrs. Emma A. Taft.

No. 99. A lyre clock, made by A. Chandler, Concord, N. H. The case is of mahogany with a carved center panel and finial. Date: about 1835–1840. In this style there is a bottom door. The Prince of Wales feather finial is rare. It is of course brought down from a much earlier date. The clock has a striking movement with a count wheel. Owner: Benj. A. Jackson, Providence, R. I.

No. 100. A Joseph Ives cart spring movement, which was re-fitted into the shelf clock shown in plates No. 65 and 66. Owner: C. Prescott Knight, Providence, R. I.

No. 101. A grandmother clock owned by P. H. Safford, Fitchburg, Mass. We show three clocks with this peculiar door. There is an inlay of brass just below the dial. The owners think it probable that the clock is by S. Mulliken. Cherry case, $43\frac{1}{2}$ by 10 inches. Dial $5\frac{1}{2}$ inches, silvered brass. Pallet arbor without suspension spring. Found in a New Hampshire attic.

No. 102. A receipt sent the author by Mr. W. G. A. Turner of Malden, Mass.

No. 103. A shapely clock belonging to Mrs. M. B. Cookerow of Pottstown, Pa. Made by Daniel Rose, Reading, Pa., 1820–1840. An unusual feature is the quarter columns on the lower panel. The writer should express his opinion with diffidence, but he is more fond of the broken arch scroll on the hoods of clocks than of the fret.

No. 104. English, with closed pediment. Carved modillions. A type rarely found in America.

No. 105. A clock of beautiful design, in the Old Garrison House, Trenton, N. J. The shell is particularly elaborate, there being a small obverse shell superimposed on a larger reverse shell.

No. 106. An English clock by John Winkley, date about 1760. It is owned by William G. A. Turner of Malden. The works are brass, engraved with the name of the maker. It has banjo works.

The clock is 27 inches high and 9 inches wide, and has a cherry case.

No. 107. A grandmother or miniature clock with a lower door. There is no name on the face of this clock nor inside the door. It is owned by Mrs. M. B. Cookerow, Pottstown, Pa.

No. 108. A grandmother or miniature clock owned by Mrs. M. B. Cookerow, Pottstown, Pa. The inscription on the dial reads " Hy. Bower."

Nos. 109, 110. This clock shown open and closed, is the same as shown in No. 106. The odd weight attached so as to gain a longer run is interesting. Owned by William G. A. Turner, Malden, Mass. The ornaments at the top are original.

No. 111. A picture supplied to the author by W. G. A. Turner, of Malden, Mass. He has an important clock collection. The clock label here shown considerably enhances the value of the clocks in which it is found, that is, the inside of the long door of the grandfather clock case.

No. 112. A label found in an Aaron Willard clock. One of the points of interest is the engraving of a shelf clock of English design in the oval at the top. One is led to wonder why an engraving of one of the author's own clocks was not used, unless he had this label done in England.

No. 113. A banjo shaped clock, belonging to the Essex Institute, Salem, Mass. The clock has an astronomical attachment, a twenty-four hour dial, and shows time in twenty-four places. It is by James Ferguson, London, 1710–1776. It was formerly owned by the station agent at Franklin, N. H. Hammond Collection.

No. 114. A shelf clock made by Simon Willard. It is from the Charles F. Williams collection, and is now the property of the Pennsylvania Museum.

No. 115. A "Boston Light" brass dial, with iron painted top. It is the dial of an Ephraim Willard clock. It is owned by William G. A. Turner, Malden, Mass.

No. 116. A shelf clock made by Aaron Willard, in the Charles F. Williams collection. Now the property of the Pennsylvania Museum.

No. 117. A "Gothic" clock. An example of one of the late clocks which had an amazing popularity under the name "cathedral clocks." The firm of Brewster & Ingraham, the name which appears on the face, did business in Connecticut in 1843–1848. It is during this time, therefore, that this clock must be dated. Elias Ingraham, the founder of the firm, designed the so-called sharp Gothic clock while he was on a sailing voyage to Caracas to introduce his clocks into South America. He whittled the design from a block of wood to beguile the tedium of the journey. The photograph was furnished by the E. Ingraham Company, Bristol, Conn.

No. 118. A clock made by Henry Flower, Philadelphia. The property of Mrs. C. Wheaton Vaughan of Philadelphia.

This is a very handsome specimen of cabinet work.

No. 119. A miniature tall clock, forty-eight inches high. We have no information as to its origin. It is owned by the Essex Institute, Salem, Mass.

No. 120. An astronomical clock now owned by the Essex Institute, Salem, Mass. "It shows the time all over the globe, and the position of the stars at all times." It has the balance escapement, and was made by the Universum Clock Company of Boston.

No. 121. An interesting clock by Seth Thomas, Plymouth Hollow, Conn., about 1860. The interest lies chiefly in the heavy scroll of the base, which is obviously precisely the same motive as that used on the Victorian veneered mahogany chests of drawers of the period. The columns, on the other hand, are brought down from the styles in use on mirrors about thirty years earlier. Owned by the Essex Institute.

No. 122. A Willard banjo clock with a barometer. This most rare example belongs to Mr. Harry Weeks, Framingham, Mass.

No. 123. A shelf clock, owned by the Essex Institute, Salem, Mass.

No. 124. A Gothic clock from a photograph furnished by the E. Ingraham Company, Bristol, Conn. For fuller description see No. 117.

No. 125. We have no information regarding this curious clock. The original dial has been removed. Property of the Essex Institute, Salem, Mass.

No. 126. A clock with balance escapement, made by Burnham Terry of Connecticut, and sold by J. J. and W. Beals, Boston. Owned by the Essex Institute, Salem, Mass.

No. 127. A four hundred day clock, made by the Boston Clock Company. Owned by the Essex Institute, Salem, Mass.

No. 128. A clock owned by the Essex Institute, Salem, Mass. It has the familiar sea fight design on the lower glass.

No. 129. A plate from which to print dials. The name is Preserved Clapp, New England. We show elsewhere a dial made from such an engraved plate. An interesting detail of the dial before us is that the reverse has been used for engraved music.

Of course the engraved plate derived from this clock was the American answer to a popular demand, since the price of an engraved dial would have been prohibitory, in a popular clock. Owned by the Essex Institute, Salem.

No. 130. "Father Time," made at Lakeport, California, from a type patented in 1808 by John Schmidt of London, a Dane, who was taken prisoner at Copenhagen and brought to England. He called it "The Mysterious Circulator of Chronological Equilibrium." This clock is now the property of the Essex Institute, Salem, Mass.

Nos. 131, 132. A Gothic clock shown with the doors opened and closed. The label reads in part, "Improved steel spring eight-day brass clocks, Birge & Fuller, Bristol, Conn." The glass is especially good.

No. 133. A grandfather clock, marked "D. H. Solliday, Sy. Town." It is owned by William E. Montague, Norristown, Pa. It was not originally with glass in lower door.

No. 134. A David Rittenhouse clock. Owner: W. E. Montague. Sold once for twenty cents, resold for a barrel of flour!

No. 135. A Simon Willard clock in a pine case, from which the front has been removed. It is a banjo movement, and the plain box case is original. Owned by Mr. Harry Weeks, Framingham, Mass.

No. 136. A handsome Simon Willard banjo clock, on which the picture in the lower glass is entitled "Telemachus." Owned by Mr. Harry Weeks, Framingham, Mass.

No. 137 is self-explanatory. Photograph furnished by Walter H. Durfee of Providence, R. I.

No. 138. A shelf clock by Ezekiel Jones, Boston. The feet and the picture are unusual.

No. 139. This letter is self-explanatory.

No. 140. A scrolled hood grandfather's clock.

No. 141. The Colonel William Terry clock, in the museum of the

Old Garrison House, at Trenton, N. J. It is by John Wood, Philadelphia, carefully made, in excellent style.

No. 142. A beautiful little shelf clock owned by Clarence H. Allen of Portland, Maine.

No. 143. A so-called lighthouse clock, owned by the Essex Institute.

No. 144. A Timothy Chandler clock, Concord, N. H. Date about 1800. In the broken arch top finished with a rosette we have a perfect copy of the highboy top and of the door-head of the mid-eighteenth century period, except that the latter did not have the side urns. Property of Essex Institute, Salem, Mass.

No. 145. A grandfather's clock by Hoadley, Plymouth, Conn. The clocks of this maker are very numerous, and they are usually in simple cases. Owned by the Essex Institute, Salem.

No. 154. A French clock, of ormolu and gilt bronze, with Sèvres porcelain mounts. It is the property of the Essex Institute, Salem, Mass.

No. 155. Probably an English clock. Owned by the Essex Institute. The odd motion of the pendulum, simulating the piston rod of a steam engine, glorifies our mechanical age. On the one side is the clock, on the other a barometer.

No. 156. A dry battery electric clock. It is owned by the Essex Institute, Salem, Mass.

No. 157. An Irish clock. By Thomas Cornwall, Dublin. Wedgwood medallions are seen in a remarkable row on the case. Property of the Essex Institute, Salem, Mass.

No. 158. A wag-on-the-wall, probably of German origin. It is owned by the Essex Institute, Salem, Mass.

No. 159. A wag-on-the-wall of German origin. Property of the Essex Institute, Salem, Mass.

No. 160. A "solar timepiece," made by Timby of Baldwinsville, N. Y. Now owned by the Essex Institute, Salem, Mass.

No. 161. A late type of shelf clock, by the Atkins Clock Co., Bristol, Conn. 1820–1870. Owned by the Essex Institute, Salem, Mass.

No. 162. A wag-on-the-wall, owned by the Essex Institute. The figure over the dial of a wingèd horse may be supposed to represent the flight of time.

No. 163. A wag-on-the-wall belonging to the Essex Institute, Salem, Mass.

No. 164. A Friesland clock owned by the Essex Institute. These hooded clocks, with pewter or brass filigree, all follow the same general type. The figures in the ornaments usually afford a hint of the date.

No. 165. A clock owned by the Essex Institute. The case seems much too plain for the works. Made by R. T. Manning, 1767.

No. 166. A wag-on-the-wall assembled by Mr. Hammond from parts of other clocks. It is the property of the Essex Institute, Salem, Mass.

No. 167. The author confesses to the unpardonable sin of having lost the data on this interesting clock.

No. 168. A lantern clock of English make. This is the same clock shown in nearly all previous American works on clocks or furniture. Date: 1650–1690. Owner: The writer.

No. 169. An attractive design is this clock owned by Clarence H. Allen of Portland, Maine. It has the appearance of one case superimposed upon another. In this connection the immense variety of styles of cases may be remarked upon. Clocks being of different shapes, some with long and some with short pendulums, afforded endless scope for design. Made by Simon Willard.

No. 170. A watchman's clock, with anchor escapement, by Aaron Willard. The property of the Essex Institute, Salem, Mass.

No. 171. A hall clock in English style. Data cannot now be found.

No. 172. An English shelf clock by Alexander Cumming, London (b. 1732, d. 1814).

No. 173. A two day mantel clock, with fusee movement. By Edward Smith, Dublin, Ireland. Date about 1810. It is probable that the plain lettering " Two days " on the dial was a supposed advantage in selling. Property of the Essex Institute, Salem, Mass.

No. 174. A clock belonging to the Essex Institute. Its origin is not known but is thought perhaps to be French. The scrolled design on the face is interesting.

No. 175. Probably Swiss, but possibly of German origin. A considerable number of such clocks are found. They represent an odd taste, appealing to fanciful minds. That is to say, the clock, being subordinated to the picture, is not the principal object of attention. Owned by the Essex Institute, Salem, Mass.

No. 176. A Swedish wall clock. O. I. Dahl, Artmark, Sweden. Owned by the Essex Institute.

No. 177. A clock belonging to the Essex Institute, Salem, Mass. It is of foreign origin.

No. 178. An English clock, with anchor escapement, one day. Date, 1792. Owned by the Essex Institute, Salem, Mass.

No. 179. A lacquered clock with a simple plain dome. Made by Thomas Wagstaff, London, 1766–1794. He was a Quaker, and American Quakers in London would often take clocks of his home with them. The molding of the base is not original. Owner: Mr. Harry Weeks, Framingham, Mass.

No. 180. The description accompanying this clock is recommended to be taken with a grain of salt. " Made in Bensburg, Prussia, early fourteenth century. Taken to Dalsband Co., Sweden. Found in the early sixteenth century in the ruins of a church abandoned 1347–8." From the Essex Institute collection.

No. 181. A Flemish clock with anchor escapement, one day, made by J. B. Vanderam, Braine l'Alleul, twelve miles south of Brussels. Property of the Essex Institute, Salem, Mass.

No. 182. A German clock, by Jacob Strausser, Nürnberg, 1737. It has a chime of fifteen bells. The case is of New England origin, and dates about 1800. Property of the Essex Institute.

No. 183. Philadelphia type. Finely carved hood, winged foliations. Pennsylvania Museum.

No. 184. A Japanese clock, about which we have no other information. It is owned by the Essex Institute, Salem, Mass.

No. 185. A "mysterious clock" of French origin. Owned by the Essex Institute.

No. 186. A lighthouse clock owned by the Rosenbach Company, Philadelphia.

No. 187. A grandfather clock finished in Chinese lacquer, made by William Claggett, Newport, R. I., date 1730–1749. Photograph furnished by Walter H. Durfee, Providence, R. I.

No. 188. A Japanese wall clock, in which the scroll design of the case is carried over to the wall board or bracket. Property of the Essex Institute.

No. 189. A Japanese clock. Property of the Essex Institute, Salem, Mass.

No. 190. A German sword clock, owned by the Essex Institute, Salem, Mass.

No. 191. A clock by W. Oakes, Oldham, England. It has the fusee anchor escapement. The design of the pedestal is suggestive of what might be done in this way. Owned by the Essex Institute.

No. 192. A clock from Medici palace, Via Servi, Florence, Italy. Property of the Essex Institute, Salem, Mass.

No. 193. An Italian clock, made by Archangelo Mayereffer of Rome, in 1794. Owned by the Essex Institute, Salem, Mass.

No. 194. The face of the General Wayne clock made by David Rittenhouse, and in the possession of William E. Montague, Norristown, Pa. The entire clock is shown elsewhere.

No. 195. A Norwegian product. The figures dance. Property of the Essex Institute. One should compare this clock with specimens from Spain, one of which we show, since the carving of the face suggests a common inspiration.

No. 196. Unique pattern. All guilded. $35 \times 13\frac{1}{2} \times 3\frac{1}{8}$. Face diameter $12\frac{1}{2}$. Early 19th Cent. Owned by Wallace Nutting.

No. 197. David Wood, Newbury Port. Inlaid on base with snail and fans.

No. 198. By David Wood, Newbury Port (sic), good design.

No. 199. A French fusee clock, property of the Essex Institute.

No. 200. A French fusee clock. The greater part of these clocks are on white stone bases, which have ball feet. Generally, it will be noted, the clock is raised on bell-shaped piers, but in some instances, as in No. 201, there is an arrangement for leveling. Property of the Essex Institute.

No. 201. Rare pattern. Bas relief Cupids. Above, a lyre motive. Beautiful design.

No. 202. By Ebenezer Belknap, Boston, A.D. 1823.

No. 203. "Grandmother" style, 48″ high. Cherry. Small waist, as usual in Pennsylvania.

No. 204. By Rueben Towe, Kingston, Massachusetts. 1812–20.

No. 205. A Peter Clark, Manchester, England. Garvan Collection. Light inlaid scrolls in spandrels.

No. 206. Mahogany. Probably by E. Taber.

No. 207. A German clock, dating from the sixteenth century. It is from the Charles F. Williams collection, and is the property of the Pennsylvania Museum.

No. 208. This clock was owned by Mary Willard Hazen. Present owner unknown.

No. 209. An English tall clock. Made by Daniel Quare, about 1700. The Charles F. Williams collection, property of the Pennsylvania Museum. Quare was a very celebrated English maker.

No. 210. A French clock of the sixteenth century. It is from the C. F. Williams collection, and is now the property of the Pennsylvania Museum.

No. 211. A shelf clock made by Thomas Parker of Philadelphia. The property of Miss Susan P. Wharton.

No. 212. An Italian clock of the 17th century. It is from the Charles F. Williams collection, and is now owned by the Pennsylvania Museum.

No. 213. French, of the sixteenth century. The C. F. Williams collection, property of the Pennsylvania Museum.

No. 214. American, with French works. Fine ogee feet. Good scroll. From Francis D. Brinton, West Chester.

No. 215. A Chippendale shelf clock. This rare specimen, very ornate, has three urns with flames, shells below and above the dial and on the knees, and ball feet. From the Hostetter Collection, Lancaster, Pennsylvania.

No. 216. A shelf clock of English style.

No. 217. A shelf clock, in English style.

No. 218. A clock similar to No. 157, the origin Swiss or German. Owner: Mr. William E. Montague, Norristown, Pa.

No. 219. A water clock owned by Mr. William B. Montague, Norristown, Pa. It is marked "Albert Davis, A. D. Norwich, 1671."

The water clock was one of the earliest forms known, having been in use, it is said, in classical times.

No. 220. Lighthouse clock. Invented by Simon Willard. Applied leaf. Among the great rareties.

No. 221. From Soltykoff's "Horlogerie," 1858, Plate XI. By Andreas Müller, in the reign of Ferdinand, brother and successor of Charles V.

No. 222. From Soltykoff's "Horlogerie," 1858, Plate VII. Dimensions in centimeters: 34 high, 23 across at the base, 13 across in the main part of the clock, and 7 deep. This shows the Annunciation, the Adoration of the Magi and various other scenes from the life of Christ. A very elegant example. Date, 1521.

No. 223. From Soltykoff's "Horlogerie," 1858, Plate XX. "The monogram G. G. proves that the beautiful piece belonged to Gaston of Orleans, son of Henry IV."

Nos. 224, 225. From Soltykoff's "Horlogerie," 1858, Plate I. Constructed by Louis David, period of Henry III. The plaque above is a satire of the Huguenot time against the papacy.

No. 226. An English hall clock, made by Edward East, London. The case is inlaid walnut. Date: about 1690. A very rare month movement. Beats 4.8 to the minute. Only 4 ft. 6 in. high. Note that the pendulum bob shows the extreme length of the pendulum. In the Wetherfield collection, England.

No. 227. An English hall clock, made by Thomas Tompion. The case is marquetry. Date: about 1690. A good style by a famous maker. A month movement. In the Wetherfield collection, England.

No. 228. An English mantel or bracket clock. The case is in red Chinese lacquer. Made by J. Smith & Sons, London, about 1810. Photograph furnished by Walter H. Durfee, Providence, R. I.

No. 229. From Soltykoff's "Horlogerie," 1858, Plate XVIII. This and the other plates reproduced from Soltykoff we believe will satisfy critical inspection. The originals are in steel. Soltykoff states that this piece carries neither signature nor date, but that he believes it to be German, of the period of Ferdinand of Austria, brother of Charles V.

No. 230. A Friesland clock owned by Mr. L. C. Flynt, Monson, Mass. It dates from the eighteenth century. They are somewhat more elaborate than the wag-on-the-wall clocks.

No. 231. A clock, probably from Spain. There is another in Madrid like it. This clock, in the possession of the author, came from New York City many years ago, and was supposed to be of Knickerbocker origin. It may have come from the Spanish Netherlands. In the back is a zither and musical attachment. Two tunes are played.

No. 232. A shelf clock concerning which the author's records are missing.

No. 233. An English bracket or mantel clock. The case is of mahogany, inlaid. Owner: G. Winthrop Brown, Boston, Mass.

Nos. 234, 235. A clock by Benjamin Bagnall, Charlestown, Mass. The case is of burl veneer on pine. Date: about 1730. One of the earliest of American hall clocks, distinctively English in style. Owner: John M. Miller, Providence, R. I.

No. 236. An English hall clock, very early. The movement dial and parts are shown in Plates No. 13, 14 and 15.

No. 237. An English hall clock by George Peacock. The case is marquetry. Date: about 1700. The floral design of marquetry is good. The owner is unknown.

No. 238. An Empire shelf clock, maker unknown. The case is mahogany. Date: about 1825–1830. The clock has an imported repeating movement, striking every fifteen minutes and the hour. It is very rare. The case is of American make. Owner: Warren R. Fales, East Providence, R. I.

No. 239. An English bracket or mantel clock, made by John Martin, London. The case is inlaid with brass mountings. Date: about 1700. A very rare clock. In the Wetherfield collection, England.

No. 240. An English mantel clock by Daniel Quare. The case is ebony, brass mounted. Date: 1700. The works have three trains and a quarter chime on six bells. This maker invented a repeating watch. In Wetherfield collection, England.

No. 241. A mantel clock made by T. G. Moore, Worthington, England. The case is mahogany with brass frets under the dial and brass ogee feet. Date: about 1830. Owner: unknown.

No. 242. A mantel clock made by Mummery, Dover, England. The name is not given in the fifth edition of Britten. The case is mahogany with brass inlay, beautifully done. Date: about 1830. The clock is a fine specimen throughout. Owner: Stephen O. Metcalf, Providence, R. I.

No. 243. An English mantel clock by Stephen Rimbeault, London. The case is ebony. Date: 1760–1780. The clock has sixteen hammers, chimes at three quarters, and plays at the hour. Musicians in the arch of the dial play with the tune. Owner: Marsden J. Perry, Providence, R. I.

No. 244. Original bottom glass. "S. Willard Patent." One of the rarest "time pieces."

No. 245. A hall clock by Charles Gretton, London, England. The case is marquetry. Date: about 1795. A good example of a very early eight day English striking hall clock. In the Wetherfield collection, England.

No. 246. A hall clock by Joshua Willson, London. The case is marquetry. Date: about 1705. The inlay in this case is remarkable. The proportions are good. In Wetherfield collection, England.

No. 247. A very fine English Chippendale wall clock. Owner: Benj. M. Jackson, Providence, R. I.

No. 248. A hall clock by Esaye Fleureau, London. The case is marquetry. Date: about 1810. The marquetry is in the Arabesque design. In Wetherfield collection, England.

No. 249. A hall clock by Jonathan Lounds, London. The case is marquetry. Date: about 1705. The case shows good treatment in the scroll of the inlay. In Wetherfield collection, England.

No. 250. The finest Rittenhouse example. In the Pennsylvania Museum.

[1]   [2]

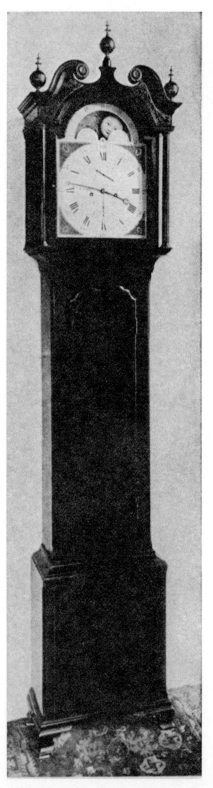

[3]   [4]

DIRECTIONS FOR PUTTING UP THE TIMEPIECE.

Drive a brad in the wall where it is to be placed and Suspend the Timepiece upon it. Open the lower Door which is unfastened by turning the button a little forward with the key. Loosen the pendulum by which the Timepiece may be plumbed, observing that it hangs free of the case and in a line with the point where it was confined: then screw it to the wall with two screws thro' the back. Put the pendulum in motion. The weight is already wound up. Set it with the minute hand which may be moved backwards or forwards. To make the TIMEPIECE go faster raise the pendulum ball by the screw at the bottom, to make it go slower lower the ball with the same screw.

These Timepieces are an improvement upon all others, as they go by a Weight instead of a Spring, and the pendulum being of a longer calculation than in any other small Pieces, renders it more accurate and has proved to keep better time. The President of the United States having granted a Patent for them, they are made by licence from the Patentee, by Aaron Willard Jun.r Washington St. Boston.

near Roxbury,
MASSACHUSETTS.

[6]

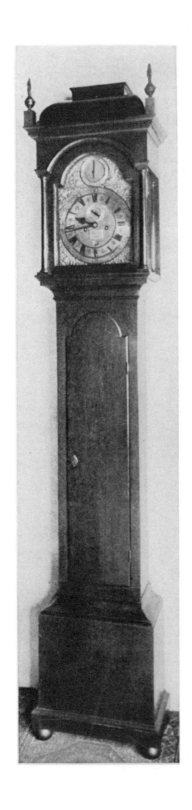

[7]   [8]

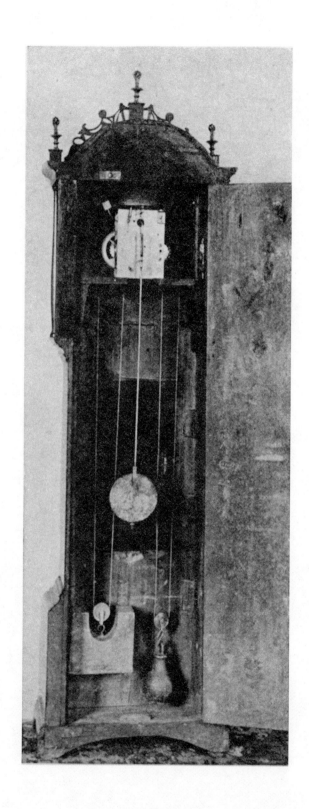

[20]   [21]

[23]

[24]

[26]

[25]

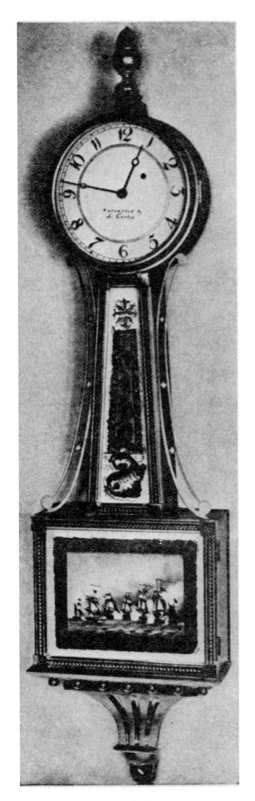

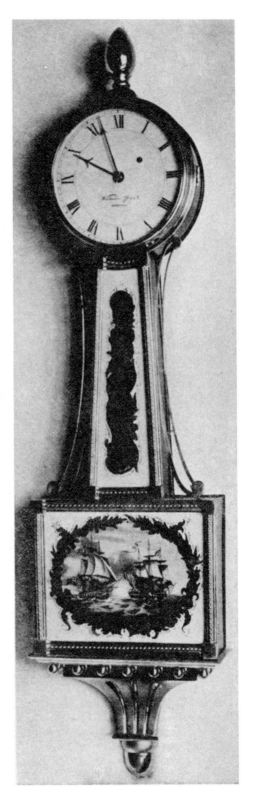

[29]   [30]

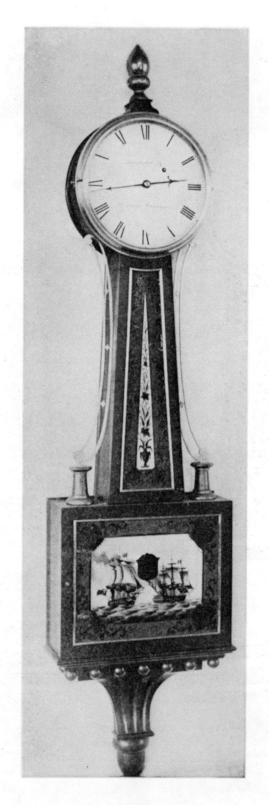

SIMON WILLARD,

BEGS leave to inform the publick, that he has opened a Shop in ROXBURY-STREET, nearly opposite the road that turns off to PLYMOUTH, where he carries on the Busines of

Clock Making

in all its branches.——Gentlemen may be supplied at said shop on the most reasonable terms, with CLOCKS of different constructions, to run either a day, eight days, one month, or a year, with once winding up ; common eight-day repeating Clocks, Spring Clocks of all sorts, among which are, common spring table, spring chime, and spring tune Clocks, which will play different tunes every hour ; also large tune clocks which run with weights, will play every hour, repeat the quarters, &c.——Also, may be had, said WILLARD's new constructed Astronomical TIME KEEPER, ascertaining the 60th or 20th part of a minute, by a second hand from the centre of the large circle, made upon a most simple plan, in which the friction and influence of the oil is almost annihilated, and has proved to keep time with the greatest accuracy, with a new constructed pendulum, from the centre of the ball, shews the different degrees of expansion of the bars, and answers, in some degree, as a thermometor, &c. those that oscilate half seconds are portable, and are easily moved to any part of the room, or where it is convenient for to make observations ; to the pedestal of which is affixed (without obstructing the movement) a perpetual calender, newly engraved, which shews at one view, the day of the month, the true and comparative time of the sun's rising and setting forever ; as well as the age, increase, decrease, rising and setting of the moon, time of high water, &c. the whole globe with its rotation every twenty-four hours, shewing the longitude, latitude, the hour and minute upon the most noted places on the globe.—Such gentlemen or ladies as will favour the said Willard with their commands in the above business, may depend on having their work done in the neatest manner, and may be supplied with MEHOGANY CASES in the newest taste.—Those who live at a distance may have Clock Work sent them, with direction how to manage and set them up, without the assistance of the Clock-Maker.

Watch Work

of all sorts is done in the neatest manner, and carefully cleaned and regulated, with Crystals, Keys, Seals, Chains, Springs, &c. &c. Also, is made by said WILLARD, and COMPANY, a new invented

Roasting Jack,

in which is containe. a compleat apparatus of Kitchen Dripping-Pan, Spit, Skewers and Baster, &c. which is so constructed with tin plates as to reflect back upon the meat all the heat the tin receives, which occasions the saving of almost one half of that important article fire-wood ; it is also recommended for its being portable, which can be placed to any small fire-place, in any room, and which is made upon so simple a plan that it is not subject to get out of repair, and the friction upon every part being so trifling, that it will continue for longer duration than any mechanical performances of that kind is known to do.

Roxbury, February 24 1784.

N. B. The above JACKS may be had of Col. PAUL REVERE, directly opposite Liberty-Pole, Boston.

Copied from

T.HOMAS'S MASSACHUSETTS SPY, Or WORCESTER GAZETTE

Thursday, March 11, 1784

[34]

[35]

[36]   [37]

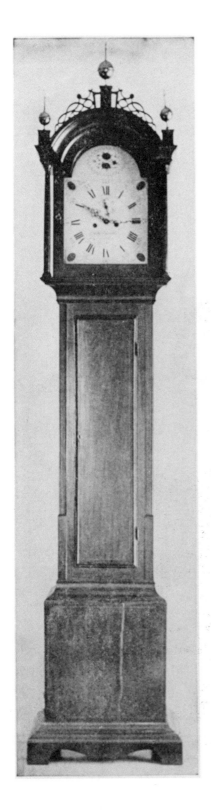

[38]   [39]

[40]   [41]

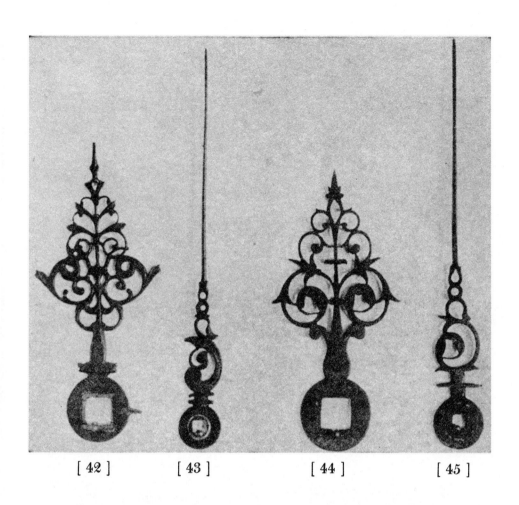

[42]   [43]   [44]   [45]

[46]

[50]

[49]

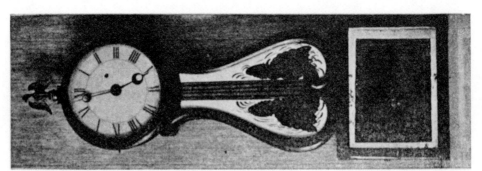

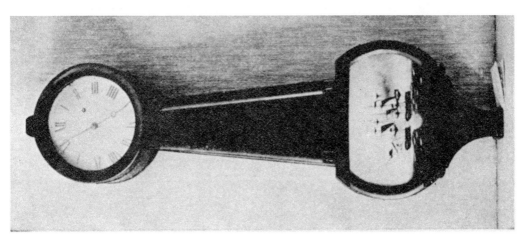

[58]

[57]

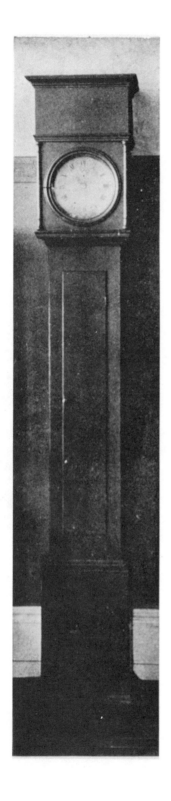

[59]   [60]

[61]   [62]

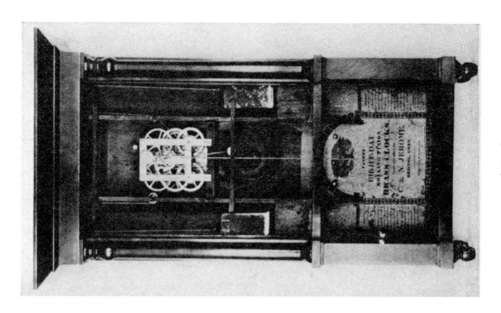

[64]

[63]

[66]

[65]

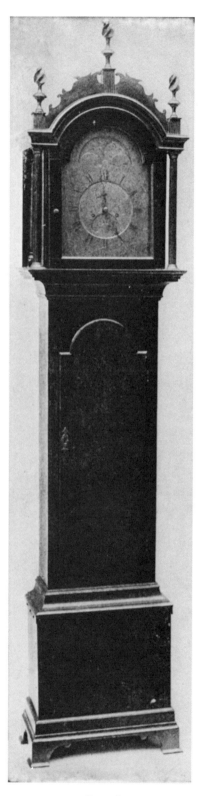

[67]   [68]

[71]

[70]

[69]

Dav. Rittenhouse

[73]   [74]

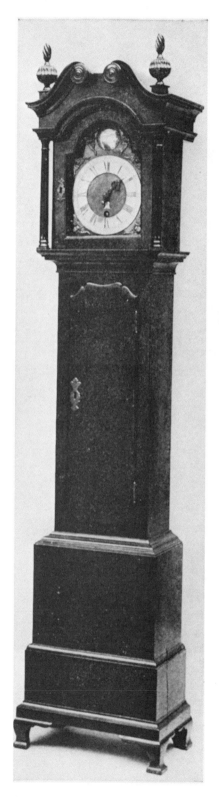

[75]   [76]

[78]

[77]

[79]   [80]

[81]   [82]

[83]   [84]

[86]

[85]

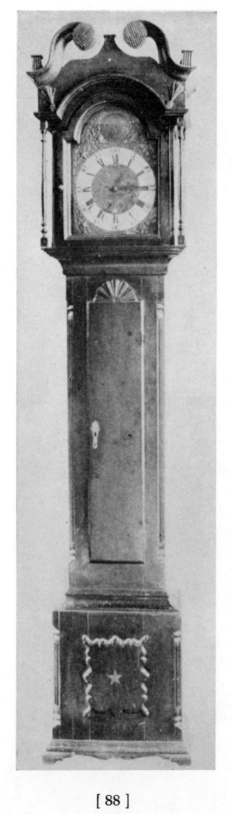

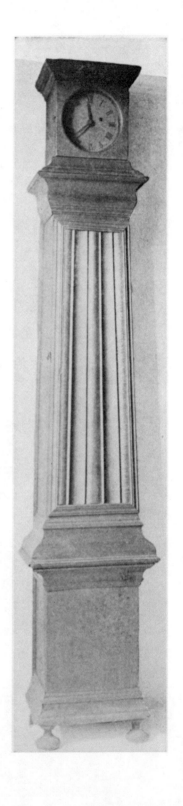

[88]

[89]

[90]   [91]

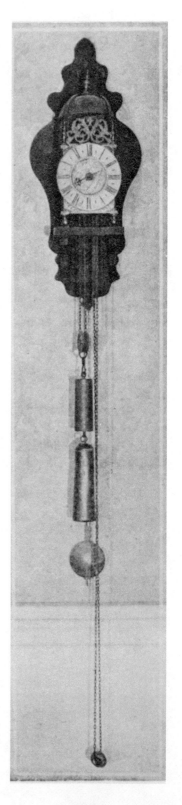

[92]   [93]

[94]　　　　　　　　　　　　[95]

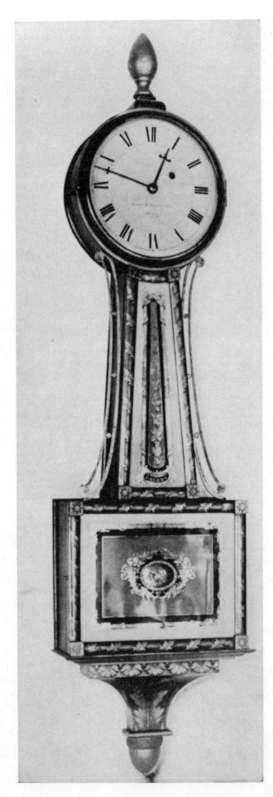

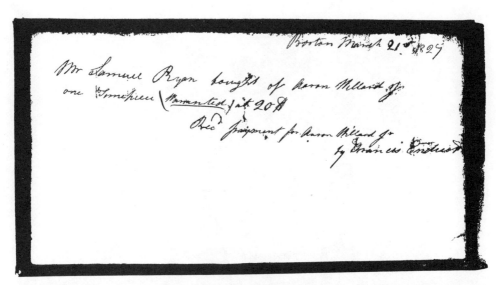

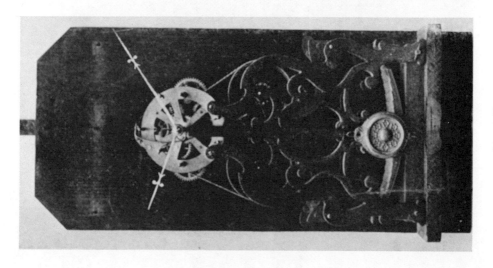

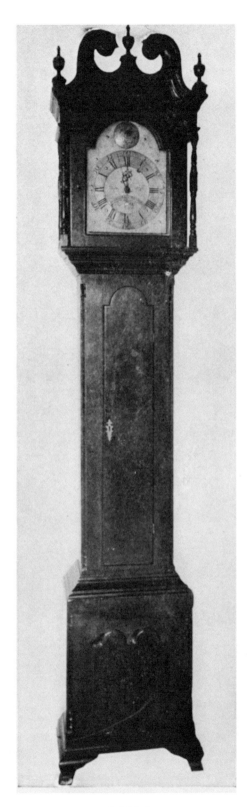

[103]

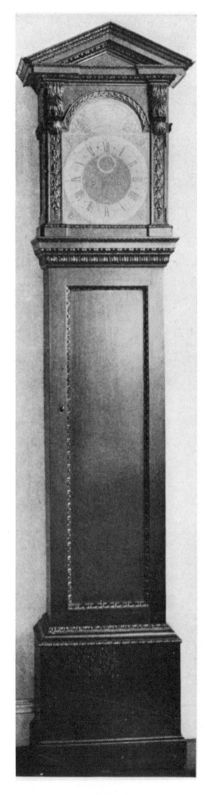

[104]

[106]

[105]

[107]   [108]

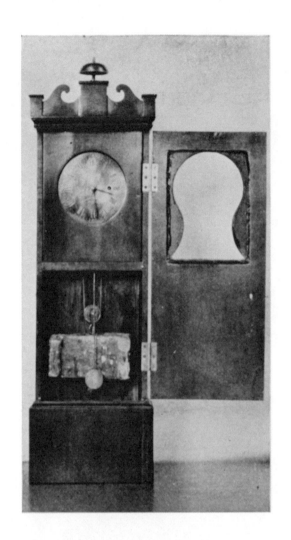

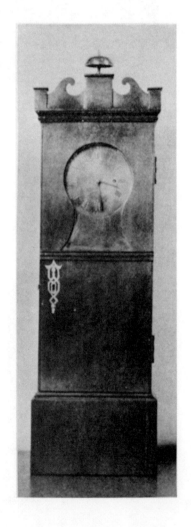

[109]   [110]

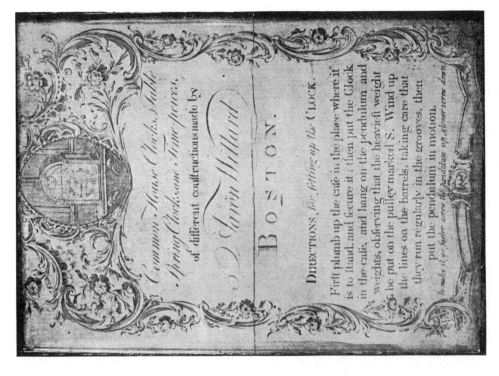

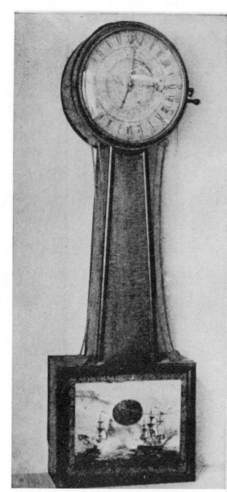

[113]   [114]

[116]   [117]

[118]

[119]

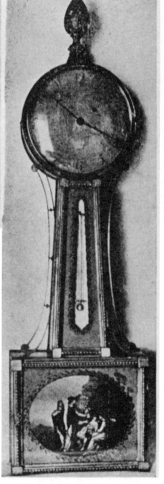

[121]   [122]

[123] [124]

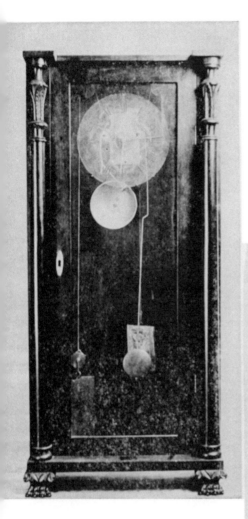

[127]   [128]

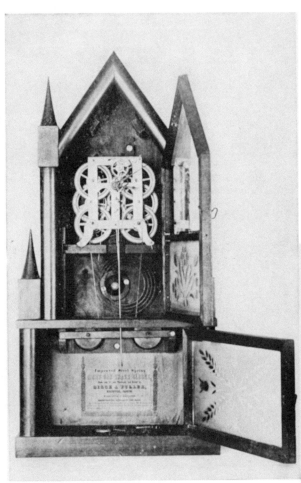

[131]   [132]

[133]

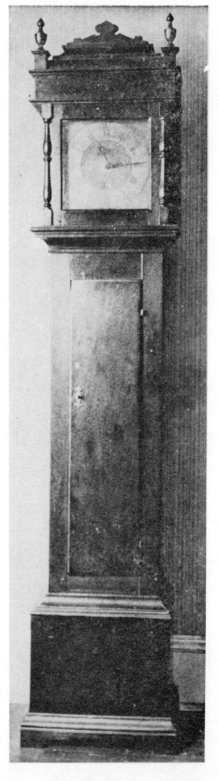

[134]

[135]   [136]

BENJAMIN WILLARD,
CLOCK and WATCH-MAKER.

BEGS leave to inform his friends, and former cuſtomers, that after eight years abſence from this county, he has again begun his buſineſs at his farm in GRAFTON, eight miles from Worceſter, where he carries on CLOCK and WATCH-MAKING in all their various branches. He would inform the publick, that he has for thoſe many years paſt, been with the beſt approved clock and watch-makers on the continent, in order to obtain further knowledge in the different branches of ſaid buſineſs. The publick are often greatly impoſed on, by employing unſkilful workmen ; and many good watches as well as clocks have been almoſt entirely ruined by thoſe pretenders to this art. Said Willard lets no work go out of his hands but ſuch as he will warrant. He is determined to work on the moſt reaſonable terms ; and as he lives on a farm, and his expences are much leſs than if he lived in a ſeaport, he can afford to work cheaper ; it is alſo neceſſary, that his buſineſs (to do it well) ſhould be carried on in retirement. In order the better to accommodate the publick, he has engaged with Mr. Thomas to receive and forward all commands left at his printing-office ; all watches wanting repair, left with him, will be ſafely forwarded to me at Grafton, on Thurſdays, and on the week following will be returned, finiſhed, to ſaid office, where thoſe who left them may receive them, warranted ; and, the expence for repairing, not more than one half as much as commonly charged by watch-makers in ſea-ports.—Said Willard informs thoſe who have purchaſed clocks of him before the war, (as the laſt finiſhed and ſold two hundred and fifty three eight-day clocks, chiefly in this State,) that thoſe which want repair, if any, he is ready to repair, and warranted once gratis, if there is any fault in their making, &c. &c. He alſo makes the

New Invented CLOCK-JACK,

for roaſting meat ; ſaid jacks may be had of Meſſrs. S. and S. SALISBURY, merchants, in WORCESTER. This jack was invented by Mr. Simon Willard, who obtained a patent from the General Court for an excluſive right. Said Simon Willard has authoriſed me to make ſaid jacks, which are very uſeful and much approved of by thoſe who have experienced them.—They are much cheaper than imported jacks and more durable.—Country produce will be taken in payment for his work.—Said Willard alſo makes

All kinds of TIN-WARE,

which he ſells wholeſale and retail.

☞ Wanted by ſaid Willard, two or three active, ſprightly BOYS, about fourteen years of age, as apprentices.

Dr. Sir:

Dec.r 7.th 1792

In my Accounts for the Year 1778 as settled by Committee of Assembly, and printed, you will see how the 35,000 Dollars was disposed of. Whether there was any receipts with the Extracts I can't say, for I think all the Vouchers are in your hands. It seems likely that there was one or two receipts, for my receipt for the money is dated March 98.th And I find three Entries of payments on the 24.th and 27.th.

I am Dr Sir
most respectfully
Your very humble serv.t
Dav.d Rittenhouse

Comptroller Gen.l

[139]

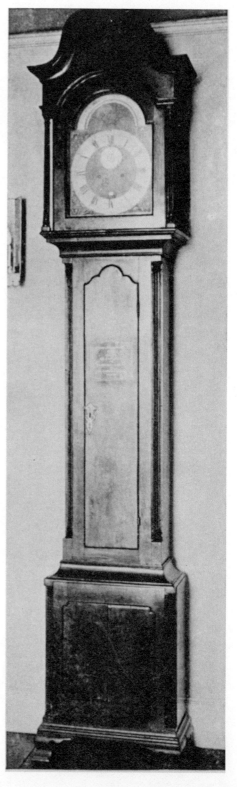

[140]   [141]

[143]

[142]

[144]   [145]

[154]

[155]

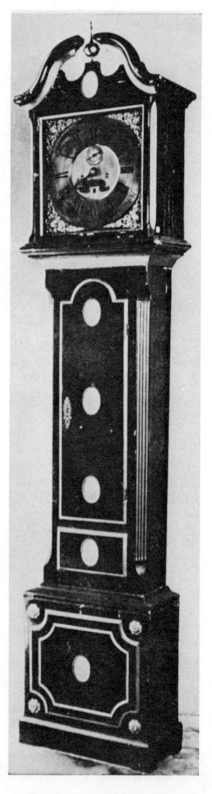

[156]   [157]

[158]   [159]

[162]

[163]

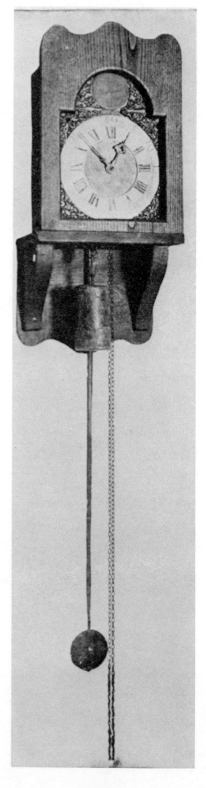

[164]   [165]

[167]   [168]

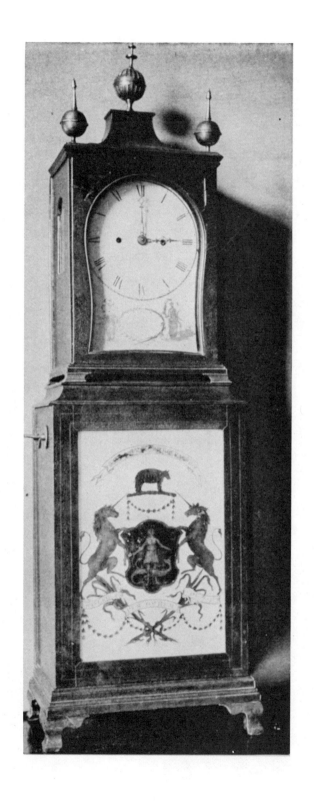

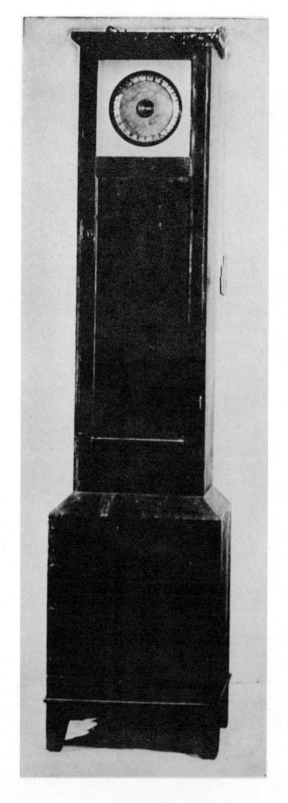

[170]   [171]

[173]

[172]

[174]

[175]

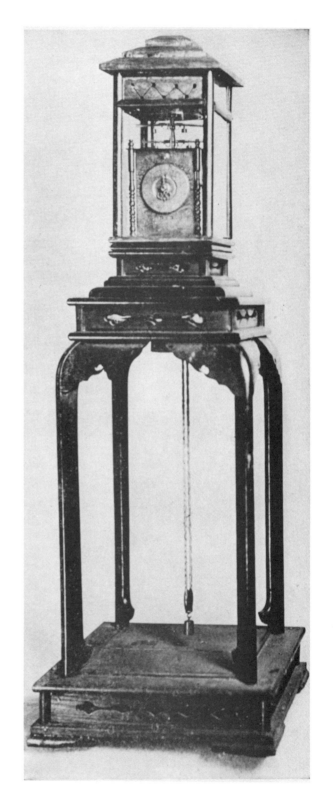

[176]   [177]

[178]

[179]

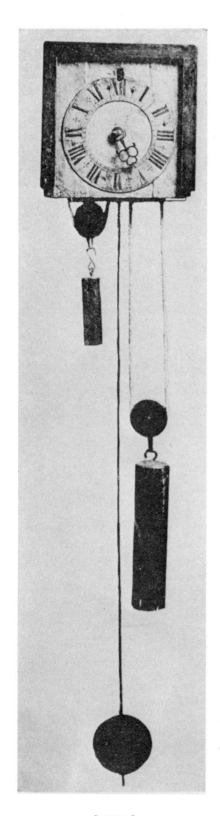

[180] [181]

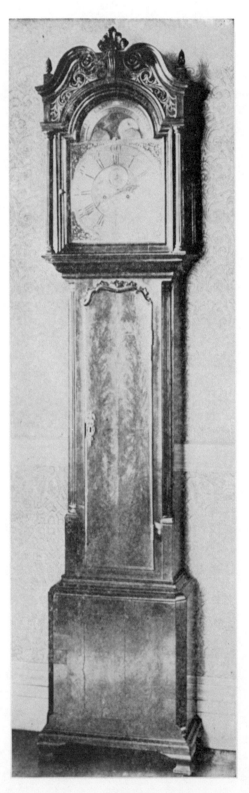

[182]   [183]

[186]
        [187]

[188]   [189]

[190]   [191]

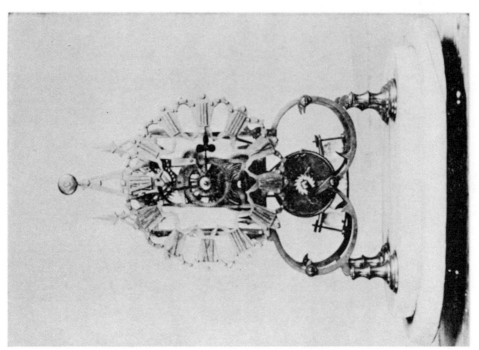

[201]   [202]

[203]   [204]

[206]   [207]

[208]   [209]

[212]

[211]

[213]

[214]

[217]

[216]

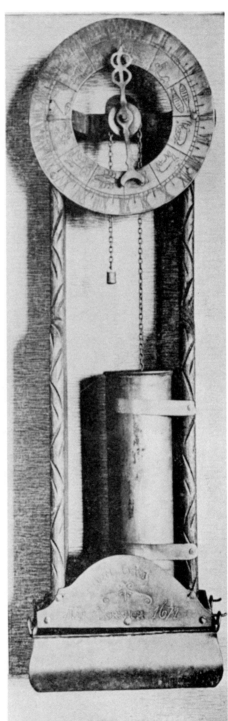

[218]   [219]

[224]

[225]

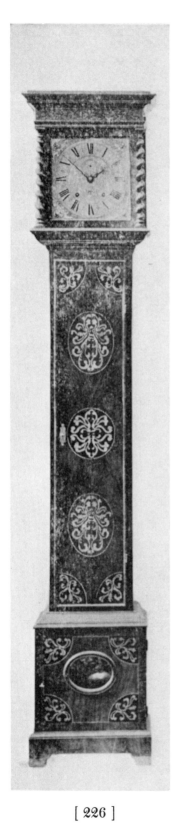

[226]   [227]

[233]

[232]

 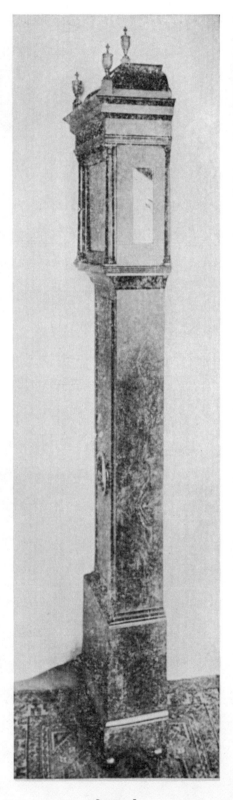

[234]   [235]

[236]

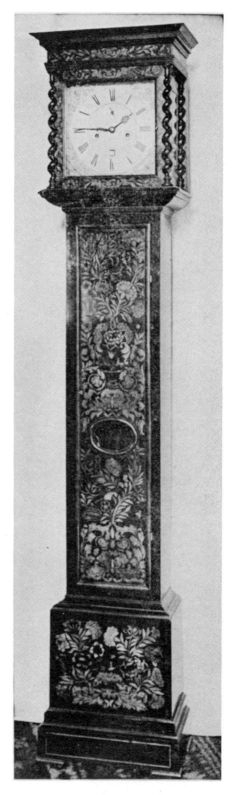

[237]

[242]

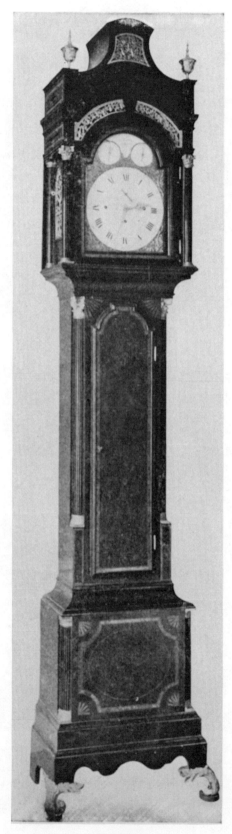

[245]   [246]

[248]   [249]

[*Dates signify date at which the maker flourished. Sometimes double dates include lifetime.*]

Abbott, Moses, Sutton, N. H. (about 1820).

Adams, Jonas, Rochester, N. Y. (1834).

Adams, Nathan, Boston, Mass. (1796–1825).

Adams, Thomas F., Baltimore, Md. (1804).

Adams, William, Boston, Mass. (1823).

Agar, Edw., New York City (1761).

Aikinson, Peabody, Concord, Mass. (1790). Apprentice of Levi Hutchinson.

Aird, David, Middletown, Conn. (1785).

Alden & Eldridge, Bristol, Conn. (1820).

Allebach, Jacob, Philadelphia, Pa. (1825–40).

Allen, James, Boston, Mass. (1684).

Allen, Jared T., Rochester, N. Y. (1844).

Allen, John, New York City (1798).

Almy, James, New Bedford, Mass. (1836).

Alrichs, Jacob, Wilmington, Del. (1797–1857).

Alrichs, Jonas, Wilmington, Del. (1780–93).

Alrichs, Jacob & Jonas, Wilmington, Del. (1793–97).

Altmore, Marshall, Philadelphia, Pa. (1832).

Amant, Fester (or Peter), Philadelphia, Pa. (1793).

Anderson, David D., Marietta, Ohio (1821–24).

Andrews, F. C., Bristol, Conn.

Andrews, L. & F., Bristol, Conn. (Prior to 1840).

Andrews, N. & T., Meriden, Conn. (1832).

Ansonia Brass & Clock Co., Ansonia, Conn. (1855).

Anthony, L. D., Providence, R. I. (1849).

Ash, Lawrence, Philadelphia, Pa.

Ashby, James, Boston, Mass. (1769). "Watch-maker and finisher from London, near the British Coffee House in King street, Boston, Begs leave to Inform the Publick, that he performs the different Branches of that Business in the Best and Completest Manner at the Most Reasonable Rates."

Ashton, Philadelphia, Pa. (1797).

Atheaton, Otis, New York City (1798).

Atkins & Allen, Bristol, Conn. (1820).

Atkins & Downs, Bristol, Conn.

Atkins, Eldridge G., Bristol, Conn. (1830).

Atkins, Ireneus (or Irenus), Bristol, Conn. (1830–60). Made first-rate 30-day brass clock, movement for which was invented by Joseph Ives.

Atkins, Merritt W., Bristol, Conn. (1856).

Atkins, Rollin, Bristol, Conn. (1826).

Atkins & Son, Bristol, Conn. (1870).

Atkinson, M. & A., Baltimore, Md. (1804).

Attmore, Marshall, Philadelphia, Pa. (1832).

Austin, Isaac, Philadelphia, Pa. (1785–1805).

Austin, Orrin, Waterbury, Conn. (1820). Had factory on Beaver Pond Brook in which he made parts of clocks.

Avery, ——, Boston, Mass. (1726). Made the clock which hangs in the Old North Church of Paul Revere fame.

Avery, John, Jr., Preston, Conn. (1732–94). "One of the members of the Avery family who had inventive genius, he was a self-taught silver-smith and clock-maker."

Babbitt, H. W., Providence, R. I. (1849).

Babcock, Geo. W., Providence, R. I. (1838–53). Made banjo clocks.

Babcock & Co., Philadelphia, Pa. (1832).

Bachelder, Ezra, Danvers, Mass. (1793–1840).

Bacon, John, Bristol, Conn. (1830).

Badollet, Paul, New York City (1798).

Bagnall, Benjamin, Charlestown, Mass. (1712–40).

Bagnall, Benjamin (son of Benjamin 1st), Boston, Mass. (1770). Had a shop at Cornhill near the Town House.

Bagnall, Samuel (son of Benjamin 1st), Boston, Mass. (1740–60). He also had a shop in Boston.

Bailey & Brothers, Utica, N. Y. (1847).

Bailey & Ward, New York City (1832).

Bailey, William, Philadelphia, Pa. (1832–46). In directory 1819 & 20, Bailey, William, Jr.

Bailey, see Bayley.

Baker, George, Providence, R. I. (1824–49).

Balch, Benjamin (Balch & Son), Salem, Mass. (1837).

Balch, Charles Hodge, Newburyport, Mass. (Born 1787). In 1817 he was appointed superintendent of the town clocks.

Balch, Daniel, Newburyport, Mass. (1760–90). He took care of the town clock, 1781–83, and perhaps longer.

Balch, Daniel (Son of Daniel 1st), Newburyport, Mass. (1782–1818).

Balch, James (Balch & Son), Salem, Mass. (1837).

Balch & Lamson (James Balch & Charles Lamson), Salem, Mass. (1842).

Balch, Moses P., Lowell, Mass. (1832).

Balch, Thomas H. (Son of Daniel 1st), Newburyport, Mass. (1790–1818).

Baldwin, Anthony, Lancaster, Pa. (1810–30).

Baldwin, George (brother of Anthony), Sadsburyville, Pa. (1808–32).

Baldwin, Jabez (brother of Jedediah), Boston, Mass. (1812 and earlier). Apprentice of Thomas Harland. Successor to William Cleveland in Salem; later established the firm of Baldwin & Jones in Boston.

Baldwin, Jedediah (brother of Jabez), Hanover, N. H. (1780). Apprentice of Thomas Harland.

Baldwin, Jedediah, Rochester, N. Y. (1834).

Baldwin & Jones, Boston, Mass. (1812).

Baldwin, S. S. & Son, New York City (1832). "Dealers in Clocks, Watches, Jewelry, Silver Ware, etc."

Banks, Edward P., Portland, Me. (1834).

Banstein, John, Philadelphia, Pa. (1791).

Barber, James, Philadelphia, Pa. (1846).

Barker, B. B., New York City (1786–1802).

Barker, William, Boston, Mass. (1823).

Barnes & Bacon, Bristol, Conn. (1840).

Barnes & Bailey, Berlin, Conn. (1831).

Barnes, Thomas, Bristol, Conn. (b. 1773, d. 1855). E. C. Brewster sold clocks in the South for Thomas Barnes about 1815–17.

Barnes, Timothy, Litchfield, Conn. (1790).

Barnes, Timothy, Kirkland (village of Clinton), N. Y.

Barnhill, Robert, Philadelphia, Pa.

Barrow, Samuel, Philadelphia, Pa.

Barrows, James M., Tolland, Conn. (1832). "Manufacturer of Silver Spoons, and Dealer in Watches and Jewelry."

Barry, Standish, Baltimore, Md. (1804).

Bartholomew & Barnes, Bristol, Conn.

Bartholomew & Brown, Bristol, Conn. (1822–37?).

Bartholomew, E. & G., Bristol, Conn. (about 1820).

Bartholomew, Hills & Brown, Forestville, Conn. (1835–). Built factory and thus began settlement of this village. Made wooden clocks. This factory, after passing through several intermediate hands, became nucleus of E. N. Welch Mfg. Co.

Barton, Benjamin, Alexandria, D. C. (1832).

Bassett, N. B., Albany, N. Y. (1813).

Bateson, John, Boston, Mass. (1720). He died in 1727, and left in his shop an eight-day clock movement valued at £25 10s. and a silver repeating watch valued at £90.

Batterson, James, Boston, Mass. (1707–30). In Oct., 1707, James Batterson, "lately arrived from London," opened a store in Boston for the sale of watches and clocks.

Battles, A. B., Utica, N. Y. (1847).

Baugh, Valentine, Abingdon, Va. (1820–30).

Baur, John N., New York City (1832).

Bayley (or Bailey), Calvin (brother of John & Lebbeus), Hanover, Mass. (1800).

Bayley (or Bailey), John (brother of Calvin & Lebbeus), Hanover, Mass. (1770–1815). "One of the most skillful mechanics of his time." Many of his clocks in Hanover and surrounding towns still keeping good time (1910).

Bayley (or Bailey), John (son of John 1st), Hingham, Mass. (1815–20).

Bayley (or Bailey), Joseph, Hingham, Mass. (1808).

Bayley (or Bailey), Lebbeus (brother of John and Calvin), ——, Me. (about 1800).

Bayley, Simeon C., Philadelphia, Pa. (1794).

Beach & Byington, Plymouth, Conn. (1849).

Beach & Hubbell, Bristol, Conn. (1869).

Largely engaged in manufacturing the movements of brass marine clocks.

Beach, Miles, Hartford, Conn. (1799). "Silversmith and jeweller. Clocks, watches, swords and hangers, copper kettles."

Beal, J. J. & Son, Boston, Mass. (1849).

Beard, Duncan, Appoquinemonk, Del. (1755–97).

Belk, William, Philadelphia, Pa. (1796).

Belknap, Ebenezer, Boston, Massachusetts (1823).

Bell, James, New York City (1804).

Bell, John, New York City (1734).

Benedict & Burnham Co., Waterbury, Conn. (1850–55). (See Waterbury Clock Co.). In 1850 they joined Chauncey Jerome in a joint-stock company in New Haven, — the Jerome Mfg. Co. After a year or two Mr. Burnham and others sold out to the Jeromes.

Benedict, S. W., New York City (1829).

Benjamin, Barzillai, New Haven, Conn. (1823). "Gold and Silver watches, Duplex or vertical movements, warranted for one year."

Bentley, Eli, West Whiteland Township, Chester Co., Pa.

Berry, James, New York City (before 1793).

Berwick, Abner, Berwick, Me. (1820).

Bessonet, John P., New York City (1793).

Bevans, William, Norristown, Pa. (1816 and earlier).

Biddle, Owen, Philadelphia, Pa.

Biegel, Henry W., Philadelphia, Pennsylvania (1813).

Bigger & Clarke, Baltimore, Md. (1784).

Bigger, Gilbert, Baltimore, Md. (1799).

Bill, Joseph R., Middletown, Conn. (1841).

Billon, Charles, Philadelphia, Pa. (1813).

Billon & Co., Philadelphia, Pa. (1797).

Billow, Charles, & Co., Boston, Mass. (1796).

Bingham & Bricerly, Philadelphia, Pa. (1778–99).

Birdsey, E. C. & Co., Meriden, Conn. (1831).

Birge & Fuller, Bristol, Conn. (1830–35).

Birge, Gilbert & Co., Bristol, Conn. (1835).

Birge, John, Bristol, Conn. (1830–37). First was wagon builder. Afterward purchased the patent of the rolling-pinion eight-day brass clocks, bought an old factory, and began to manufacture these clocks. Sent peddlers south and west with them. Continued clock business and farming till a few years before his death.

Birge, Mallory & Co., Bristol, Conn. (1830).

Birge, Peck & Co., Bristol, Conn. (1830–56).

Birnie, Lawrence, Philadelphia, Pa.

Bisbee, J., Brunswick, Me. (1798–1825).

Bishop & Bradley (James Bishop and L. B. Bradley), Plymouth, Conn. (1825–30).

Bissell, David, East Windsor, Conn. (1832). "Watch and Clock Maker and Dentist."

Bixler, Christian, Easton, Pa. (about 1750).

Bixler, Christian, Easton, Pa. (1785–1830).

Blakeslee, Jeremiah, Plymouth, Conn. (1841–49). With Myles Morse.

Blakeslee, Marvin & Edward, Heathenville (near Plymouth), Conn. (1832).

Blakesley (or Blakeslee), Milo, Plymouth, Conn. About 1824 he was employed by Eli Terry, Jr., and some time afterwards became a partner with Terry.

Blasdell, David, Amesbury, Mass. (1741).

Blasdell, Isaac, Chester, N. H. (1762–91). Son of David Blasdell of Amesbury. Probably Isaac Blasdell's were the first clocks made in New Hampshire.

Blasdell, Richard (probably son of Isaac), Chester, N. H. (about 1788).

Boardman, Chauncey, Bristol, Conn. (1813). Began making clocks about 1813 in North Forestville (village in Bristol). Began to make brass clocks 1838, and continued this until his failure, 1850.

Boardman & Dunbar, Bristol, Conn. (1811).

Boardman & Wells (Chauncey Boardman and Joseph A. Wells), Bristol, Conn. (1815). Soon after 1820 they built a factory in North Forestville, one of the most important of that time.

Bode, William, Philadelphia, Pa. (1796).

Bogardus, Everardus, New York City (1698).

Bond, William, Boston, Mass. (1800–10).

Bonfanti, Joseph, New York City (1823). He advertised for sale German and French clocks.

Bonnaud, ——, Philadelphia, Pa. (1799).

Boss & Peterman, Rochester, N. Y. (1841). "We strive To Excel. Dealers in Watches and Jewelry. Try us before purchasing elsewhere. We feel warranted in saying that all watch and clock work entrusted to our care will be executed better than at any other establishment in this city."

Botsford, S. N., Hamden (Whitneyville), Conn. (1856).

Boughell, Joseph, New York City (1787).

Bower, Michael, Philadelphia, Pa. (1790–1800).

Bowman, Joseph, Lancaster, Pa. (1821–44).

Bowne, Samuel, New York City (1751). Advertised "Japanned and Walnut cased Clocks."

Brace, Rodney, North Bridgewater (now Brockton), Mass. (18–). Several years since (1800), Rodney Brace came from Torrington, Conn., and commenced the manufacture of small wooden clocks, with Isaac Packard. They sent them to all parts of the country in wagons, and were among the first to introduce small clocks.

Bradley & Barnes, Boston, Mass. (1856).

Bradley & Hubbard, Meriden, Conn. (1854).

Bradley, Nelson, Plymouth, Conn. (1840).

Bradley, Richard, Hartford, Conn. (1825–39). Watch repairer.

Bradley, Z., & Son, New Haven, Conn. (1840).

Brandegee, Elishama, Berlin, Conn. (1832). "Manufacturer of Cotton Thread, Clocks of all descriptions, and Dealer in American Goods."

Brandt & Mathey, Philadelphia, Pa. (1799).

Brandt, Brown & Lewis, Philadelphia, Pa. (1795).

Brasher, Abraham, New York City (1757).

Brasier, Amable, Philadelphia, Pa. (1795–1820).

Brastow, Adison & Co., Lowell, Mass. (1832).

Brearley, James, Philadelphia, Pa. (1793–1811).

Breckenridge, J. M., Meriden and New Haven, Conn. (born 1809, died 1896).

Brewer, Isaac, Philadelphia, Pa. (1813).

Brewer, William, Philadelphia, Pa. (1785–91).

Brewster, Elisha C., Bristol, Conn. (1833–62). Born 1791; died 1880. Traveled in South selling clocks for Thomas Barnes of Bristol. For a few years carried on business of clock worker in Plainville. Then came to Bristol and engaged in painting clocks, dials and glass. In 1833 he bought clock factory and business of Charles Kirk, employing him to conduct the same until about 1838. In connection with Shaylor Ives he invented a new spring for clocks and manufactured the first spring clocks made in this coun-try. In 1843 he formed partnership with Elias and Andrew Ingraham, which continued till 1848, when he bought them out; afterward associated with himself William Day and Augustus Norton, later buying them out and carried on the business alone until 1862, when he retired. He had a branch house in London, England, for the sale of his goods, conducted for about four years by Epaphroditus Peck, and twenty years by his son, N. L. Brewster.

Brewster & Ingraham, Bristol, Conn. (1843–48).

Brinckerhoff, Dirck, New York City (1756). "At the Sign of the Golden Clock."

Bronson, I. W., Buffalo, N. Y. (1825–30).

Brooks, B. F., Utica, N. Y. (1847).

Brown, David, Providence, R. I. (1834–50).

Brown, Gawen, Boston, Mass. (1750–76).

Brown, J. C., Bristol, Conn. (1827–55). In 1835 William Hills, J. C. Brown, Jared Goodrich, Lora Waters, and Chauncey Pomeroy built a factory where the Welch Co. now is (1885). Mr. Brown bought out the rest of the firm, and in 1853 built what is still called the J. C. Brown shop. Upon his failure this passed to Mr. Welch, and from him to the E. N. Welch Mfg. Co.

Brown, Joseph R., Providence, R. I. (1849).

Brown & Kirby, New Haven, Conn. (1840).

Brown, Laurent, Rochester, N. Y. (1841).

Bryant, Thomas, Rochester, N. Y. (18–).

Bullard, Charles, Boston, Mass. (born 1794, died 1871). Was apprentice and successor of the English artist who painted glass fronts and dials for Simon Willard.

Burdick, M. H., Bristol, Conn. (1849).

Burkelow, Samuel, Philadelphia, Pa. (1791–99).

Burnap, Daniel, East Windsor and Andover, Conn. (1780–1838). Born 1760 in Coventry (now Andover), Conn. Learned his trade from Thomas Harland of Norwich. In 1776 he was in East Windsor, Conn. Shortly before 1800 he came back to Andover and worked there till 1838. His clocks had tall cases, brass works, and silvered dials beautifully engraved, often also moon phases, calendar attachments, and chimes. The workmanship is very fine. He was also a silversmith.

Burr, C. A., Rochester, N. Y. (1841). "Wholesale and retail Dealer in Watches, Clocks, Jewelry, etc. Has on sale Gold, Silver, Duplex, Anchor, Independent Sec'ds, Patent Lever, Lepine and Vertical Watches, French, Mantel, Wood, Brass 30 hour and 8 day clocks."

Burr, Ezekiel & William, Providence, R. I. (1792).

Burritt, Joseph, Ithaca, N. Y. (1831).

Bush, George, Easton, Pa. (1812–37).

Butler, N., Utica, N. Y. (1803).

Byington & Co., L., Bristol, Connecticut (1849).

Calendar Clock Co., The, Glastonbury, Conn. (1856).

Cain, C. W., New York City (1836).

Cairns, John, Providence, R. I. (1784).

Cairns, John, 2d, Providence, R. I. (1840–53).

Camp, Hiram, nephew of Chauncey Jerome, New Haven, Conn. (1829–93). Entered clock-making business of his uncle, at Bristol, 1829. In 1845 went to New Haven. When the Jerome Mfg. Co. failed it was succeeded by The New Haven Clock Co., and Hiram Camp was its president, for about forty years.

Campbell, Charles, Philadelphia, Pa. (1795–99).

Campbell, R. A., Baltimore, Md. (1832).

Campbell, William, Carlisle, Pa. (in 1765), Philadelphia, Pa. (in 1799).

Canby, Charles, Wilmington, Del. (1815–50).

Capper, Michael, Philadelphia, Pa. (1799).

Carrell, John and Daniel, Philadelphia, Pa. (1791–93).

Carver, Jacob, Philadelphia, Pa. (1785–99).

Cary, James, Jr., Brunswick, Me. (1806–50). Apprentice of Robert Eastman, 1805, and partner, 1806–09. Cary had as apprentice, in 1830, Aaron L. Dennison.

Case & Birge (Erastus and Harvey Case, and John Birge), Bristol, Connecticut (1830–37).

Case, Dyer, Wadsworth & Co., Augusta, Ga. (1835). Seth Thomas made the cases and movements for them. They merely put the parts together at Augusta, and sold them.

Case, Erastus (brother of Harvey), Bristol, Conn. (1830–37).

Case, Harvey (brother of Erastus), Bristol, Conn. (1830–37).

Case & Robinson, Bristol, Conn. (1856).

Castan, Stephen, & Co., Philadelphia, Pa. (1819).

Cate, Col. Simeon, Sanbornton, N. H. (18–?).

Chadwick, Joseph, Boscawen, N. H. (1810–31).

Chandlee, Benjamin, Baltimore, Md. (1817).

Chandlee, John, Wilmington, Del. (1795–1810).

Chandler, Abiel, Concord, N. H. (1829–58). Son and successor to Maj.

Timothy Chandler. He was also a maker of mathematical instruments.

Chandler, Major Timothy, Concord, N. H. (1785–1840). Came on foot from Pomfret, Conn., 1783. Hired a man named Cummings, who was apprentice to Simon Willard, and set up clock-making in Concord.

Chapin, Aaron, & Son, Hartford, Conn. (1825–38).

Chase, Timothy, Belfast, Maine (1826–40).

Chaudron, P., Philadelphia, Pa. (1799).

Chaudron, S., & Co., Philadelphia, Pa. (1811).

Cheeny, J., East Hartford, Conn. (1790).

Cheney, Asahel, Northfield, Mass. (1790).

Cheney, Benjamin, brother of Timothy, East Hartford (now Manchester), Conn. (about 1745–80). They were among the first clockmakers in New England. Their clocks had tall, carved, cherrywood cases, and wooden works. In their shop John Fitch, inventor of the steamboat, was apprentice.

Cheney, Benjamin (son of Elisha), Berlin, Conn.

Cheney, Elisha (son of Benjamin), Middletown and Berlin, Conn. (about 1800–35). First made screws for the pistol factory of his brother-in-law, Simeon North, in Worthington Parish. When North's business was moved to Middletown, Cheney engaged in manufacture of clocks, first tall cased clocks, afterwards mantel clocks.

Cheney, Olcott (son of Elisha), Middletown and Berlin, Conn. (about 1820–50). He worked with his father until about 1835, then bought his father out, and carried on the business for a number of years. While he lived in Berlin, his shops were just over the Middle-town line; the Cheney clocks were therefore marked "Middletown."

Cheney, Russell (son of Benjamin and brother of Elisha), East Hartford, Conn., and Thetford, Vt. Learned the family trade of clockmaking and became a skilful workman, but probably did not stay in the business.

Cheney, Timothy (brother of Benjamin), East Hartford (now Manchester), Conn. (about 1776–95).

Chester, George, New York City (1757).

Child, John, Philadelphia, Pa. (1813–35).

Child, True W., Boston, Mass. (1823).

Chollet, John B., Philadelphia, Pa. (1819).

Church, Joseph, Hartford, Conn. (1825–38).

Church, Lorenzo, Hartford, Conn. (1846).

Clagget, H., Newport, R. I. (1726–40).

Clagget, Thomas (brother of William), Newport, R. I. (1730–49).

Clagget, William (brother of Thomas), Newport, R. I. (1720–49).

Clark, Benjamin, Wilmington, Del. (1837–50).

Clark, Benjamin, Philadelphia, Pa. (1790–1819).

Clark, Benjamin & Ellis, Philadelphia, Pa. (1813).

Clark, Daniel, Waterbury, Conn. (1814–20). Zenas Cook, Daniel Clark, and William Porter owned a clock factory in Waterbury in 1814.

Clark, Edward, Philadelphia, Pa. (1797).

Clark, Ellis, Philadelphia, Pa. (1811–45).

Clark, Ephraim, Philadelphia, Pa. (1780–1810).

Clark, Herman, Plymouth Hollow (now Thomaston), Conn. (1807).

Clark, Jesse, W. & C., Philadelphia, Pa. (1811).

Clark, Joseph, Danbury, Conn. (1800).

Clark, Joseph, New York City (1768).

Clark, Sylvester, Salem Bridge (now Naugatuck), Conn. (1830).

Clarke, Charles, Philadelphia, Pa. (1806–11).

Clarke, George G., Providence, R. I. (1824).

Clarke, Gilbert & Co., Winsted, Conn. (1842).

Clarke, Lucius, Winsted, Conn. (1841). In 1841 he purchased business left after death of Riley Whiting, and associated with himself William L. Gilbert, — Clarke, Gilbert & Co.

Clarke, John, New York City (1770–90).

Clarke, John, Philadelphia, Pa. (1799).

Claton, C., Philadelphia, Pa.

Clements, Moses, New York City (1749).

Cleveland, Benjamin Norton, Newark, N. J. (Born, 1767; died, 1837).

Cleveland, William, Salem, Mass. (1780). Apprentice of Thomas Harland. Was ship owner, watchmaker and merchant.

Cleveland, William (nephew of other William), Worthington, Mass., Salem, Mass., and Norwich, Conn. Resided first at Norwich, Conn., where he learned the trade of silversmith, watch- and clockmaker from Thomas Harland. Soon after marriage (1793) he set up in business at Worthington, Mass. He removed to Salem, Mass., where he remained in business a few years, thence went to New York. Returned to Norwich, 1812, and died there, 1837. He was grandfather of President Grover Cleveland.

Coe, Russell, Meriden, Conn. (1856).

Cole, James C., Rochester, N. H. (1812–). Served apprenticeship with Edward S. Moulton, and established the same business (1812), adding that of watchmaker and jeweler.

Cole, Shubael (son of James C. Cole), Great Falls (now Somersworth), N. H. (18–?).

Conant, Elias, Bridgewater, Mass. (1776–1812).

Conant, Elias, Lynn, Mass. (1812–15).

Conant, W. S., New York City (about 1820).

Conrad, O., Philadelphia, Pa. (1846).

Cook, E., Rochester, N. Y. (1824).

Cook, Zenas, Waterbury, Conn. (1811–20). Bought part of clock factory in 1811. Zenas Cook, Daniel Clark, and William Porter were proprietors of clock factory built on Great Brook, Waterbury, in 1814.

Cooper, T., Olneyville, R. I. (1849).

Corey, P., Providence, R. I. (1849).

Corliss, James, Weare, N. H. (1800). "It is said he stole the trade by peeking into Emery's windows nights."

Cornell, Walter, Newport, R. I.

Couper, Robert, Philadelphia, Pa.

Cox & Clark, New York City (1832). "Importers and Dealers in Lamps, etc.; also French China and Mantel Clocks, Silver Ware, etc."

Cozens, Josiah B., Philadelphia, Pa. (1819).

Cranch, Richard, Boston and Braintree, Mass. (1771–1789). "Before the war carried on business near the Mill-Bridge in Boston." Sold all kinds of watch- and clockmakers' Tools.

Crane, Simeon, Canton, Mass. (?)

Crane, William, Canton, Mass. (1780).

Crehore, Charles Crane, Boston, Mass. (Born, 1793; died, 1879). Made clock cases for Simon Willard, Jr., and Benjamin F. Willard, also some for Simon Willard, Sr., and many other clockmakers.

Critchet, James, Candia, N. H. (about 1800).

Crocker, Orsamus, East Meriden or Bangall,

Conn. (about 1831). More than 70 years ago (1906), he built a factory here for making clocks, but the business proved a failure.

Cross, James, Rochester, N. H. (18–?).

Crow, George, Wilmington, Del. (1740–70).

Crow, John, Wilmington, Del. (1770–98).

Crow, Thomas, Wilmington, Del. (1770–1824).

Crow, Thomas, Philadelphia, Pa. (1795).

Crow, Thompson, Wilmington, Del.

Crowley, John, Philadelphia, Pa. (1813).

Crowther, William, New York City (1820).

Cummens (or Cummings), William, Roxbury, Mass. (1788–1834). Apprentice of Simon Willard; then engaged in clockmaking business. Had a son William, who assisted him.

Cure, Lewis, Brooklyn, N. Y. (1832).

Currier, Edmund, Salem, Mass. (1837).

Curtis & Dunning.

Curtis, Lemuel, Concord, Mass. (1814–18), Burlington, Vt. (1818–57). In 1816 took out a patent on an improvement on the Willard timepiece. Moved to Burlington, Vt., 1818 or 1820, and died there 1857. Curtis modeled his clocks on the Willard timepiece, but used more ornament and more pleasing proportions. One feature of the Curtis clock is the circular pendulum box.

Curtis, Solomon, Philadelphia, Pa. (1793).

Custer, Jacob D., Norristown, Pa. (Born, 1805; Died, 1872). He began the manufacture of "grandfather clocks" about 1831. In 1842 he commenced the manufacture of clocks to propel the lights in lighthouses.

Daft, Thomas, New York City (1786).

Daft, Thomas, Philadelphia, Pa.

Daggett, T., Providence, R. I. (1849).

Dalziel, John, New York City (1798).

Dana, George, Providence, R. I. (1805). He and Thomas Whitaker bought out Nehemiah Dodge.

Dana, Payton, Providence, R. I. (1849).

Dana, Peyton and Nathaniel, Providence, R. I. (1800).

Darrow, Elijah, Bristol, Conn. (1822–30). In 1824 joined Chauncey and Noble Jerome.

Davidson, Barzillai, Norwich, Conn. (1775). Worker in gold and silver, and offered for sale handsome assortments of jewelry and timekeepers.

Davidson, Barzillai, New Haven, Conn. (1825). Made a clock with wood works for New Haven Meeting House, $260, 1825.

Davis & Babbitt, Providence, R. I. (1810).

Davis, David P., Roxbury, Mass. (1847–56). In partnership with Edward Howard.

Davis, John, New Holland Patent, Pa. (1802–05).

Davis, John, Philadelphia, Pa.

Davis, Peter, Jaffrey, N. H.

Davis, Samuel, Pittsburgh, Pa. (1815).

Davis, William, Boston, Mass. (1683). He came from England to pursue his trade, and David Edwards became surety for Davis and his family, that they would not become charges upon the town.

Dawson, Jonas, Philadelphia, Pennsylvania (1813).

De Forest & Co., Salem Bridge, Conn. (1832).

Delaplaine, James K., New York City (1786–1800).

Deloste, Francis, Baltimore, Md. (1817).

Demilt, Thomas, Philadelphia, Pa. (19th century).

Demilt, Thomas, New York City (1798–1818).

Demilt, Thomas & Benjamin, New York City (1802–18).

Dennison, Aaron L., Roxbury and Waltham, Mass., and Birmingham, England (1850–95). A pioneer of American watchmaking. In 1850 he and Edward Howard started a watch factory at Roxbury. In 1854 they removed to Waltham. When this factory was sold, 1857, Dennison remained as superintendent for a while. After several changes, this developed into the present Waltham Watch Co. Dennison subsequently settled in England, and devised machinery for making watch cases at Birmingham.

Derby, Charles, Salem, Mass. (1846–50).

Derby, John, New York City (1816).

De Riemer & Mead, Ithaca, N. Y. (1831).

De Saules & Co., New York City (1832).

Deverell, John, Boston, Mass. (1789–1803).

Dexter, Joseph W., Providence, R. I. (1824).

De Young, Meichel, Baltimore, Md. (1832).

Dix, Joseph, Philadelphia, Pa.

Dobbs, Henry M., New York City (1794–1802).

Dodge, Ezra W., Providence, R. I. (1824).

Dodge, George, Salem, Mass. (1837).

Dodge, Nehemiah, Providence, R. I. (1794–1824). In 1799 was associated with Mr. Stephen Williams for short time. Later had Gen. Josiah Whitaker as partner. On retirement sold to George Dana and Thomas Whitaker.

Dodge, Seril, Providence, R. I. (1788). Apprentice of Thomas Harland.

Dominick, Friedrich, Philadelphia, Pa.

Doods, Joseph.

Doolittle, Enos, New Haven, Conn. (1772–).

Doolittle, Isaac, New Haven, Conn. (1748–1810).

Doty, John F., Albany, N. Y. (1813).

Douglass, John, New Haven, Conn. (1800–20).

Douty, Henry, Philadelphia, Pa.

Dowdney, Burrows, Philadelphia, Pa.

Dowle, Robert, New York City (1793).

Dowling, G. R. & B., Co., Newark, N. J. (1832).

Downs, Anson, Bristol, Conn. (1830).

Downs, Ephraim, Bristol, Conn. (1811–43). Began clockmaking in Waterbury, Conn., 1811, working for Lemuel Harrison. Later he made at least two horseback trips to Cincinnati, O., making clocks there for Lumas Watson, 1816–21. In 1822 he settled at "Ireland," later Hoadleyville, now Greystone, working at clocks with Seth Thomas, Eli Terry and his brother-in-law, Silas Hoadley. He began business for himself here, but in 1825 removed to Bristol. From "Down's Mill" Yankee clocks went to N. Y., N. J., Penn., O., Mo., La., Miss., and elsewhere. The "looking-glass" clock was a favorite. He alone of all the Bristol clockmakers neither failed nor made assignment in the "hard times" of 1837. He retired from business 1842–3.

Droz, Charles A., Philadelphia, Pa. (1813).

Droz, Humbert, Philadelphia, Pa. (1797).

Droz, Humbert A. L., Philadelphia, Pa. (1811).

Droze & Sons, Philadelphia, Pa. (1813).

Drysdale, William, Philadelphia, Pa. (1819–51).

Dubois & Folmar, New York City (1816).

Ducommun, A. L., Philadelphia, Pa. (1797).

Dudley, Benjamin, Newport, R. I. (1840).

Duffield, Edward, Philadelphia, Pa. (1741–47), Lower Dublin, Pa. (1747–1801). A particular friend of Benjamin Franklin.

Duffield, Edward, West Whiteland Township, Chester County, Pa.

Dunbar, Butler, Bristol, Conn. (1810–30). About 1810 he was associated with Dr. Titus Merriman, making clocks. He finally went to Springville, Pa.

Dunbar, Jacobs & Warner, Bristol, Conn. (1849).

Dunbar & Merriman, Bristol, Conn. (1810–).

Dunheim, Andrew, New York City (1775).

Dunlap, Archibald, New York City (1802).

Dunning & Crissey, Rochester, N. Y. (1847).

Dunning, J. L. Associated somewhat with Lemuel Curtis.

Dupuy, John, Philadelphia, Pa. (1770).

Dupuy, Odran, Philadelphia, Pa. (1735).

Durgin, F., Andover, N. H.

Dutch, Stephen, Jr., Boston, Mass. (1800–10).

Dutton, David, Mount Vernon, N. H.

Dyar, Warren, Lowell, Mass. (1831).

Dyer, Joseph, Concord, Mass. (1815–20). He was a journeyman with Lemuel Curtis, and when the latter moved to Burlington, Vt., Dyer carried on the business alone. Later he went to Middlebury, Vt.

Easterley, John, New Holland, Pa. (1825–40).

Eastman, Abel B., Belfast, Me. (1806–21). Earliest clockmaker in Belfast. Came here in 1806 from Concord, N. H.

Eastman, Abel B., Haverhill, Mass. (1816–21).

Eastman & Cary, Brunswick, Me. (1806–09). About 1809 Eastman sold out to Cary.

Eastman, Robert, Brunswick, Me. (1805–08). James Cary, Jr., was his apprentice. In 1806 Eastman took Cary as partner (Eastman & Cary). About 1809 Eastman sold out to Cary.

Eaton, John H., Boston, Mass. (1823).

Eberman, John, Lancaster, Pa. (1780–1820).

Edson, Jonah, Bridgewater, Mass. (1815–30).

Edwards, Abraham, Ashby, Mass. (1794–1840). A self-taught clockmaker.

Edwards, Samuel, Gorham, Me. (1808–). Came from Ashby, Mass., about 1808, and for many years carried on manufacture of wooden clocks.

Eliot, William, Baltimore, Md. (1799).

Elliot, Hazen, Lowell, Mass. (1832).

Elsworth, David, Windsor, Conn. (1780–1800).

Elvins, William, Baltimore, Md. (1799).

Embree, Effingham, New York City (1785–94).

Emery, Jesse, Weare, N. H. (1800). Made the first clocks here.

Ent, Johann, Philadelphia, Pa.

Ent, John, New York City (1758). Advertised as follows: " John Ent, Clock and Watch-maker, at the sign of the Dial, has moved to the house of Mr. John Wright, Watch-maker, in Bayard street, where he continues to make and repair in the newest manner, All Sorts of Clocks and Watches, whether repeating, horizontal, or the plain kind. Gentlemen and Ladies that are pleased to honor him with their Employ may depend on the greatest care and Dispatch imaginable."

Essex, Joseph, Boston, Mass. (1712).

Eureka Shop, The, Bristol, Conn. (before

1837). "Built by a large partnership."

Evans, David, Baltimore, Md. (1770–73). "At the Sign of the Arch, Dial and Watch, Gay street."

Evans, Thomas, New York City (1766).

Evans, William M., Philadelphia, Pa. (1813–19 or longer).

Eyre, Johann, Philadelphia, Pa.

Fahrenbach, Pius, Boston, Mass. (1856).

Fales, G. S., New Bedford, Massachusetts (1827).

Fales, James, New Bedford, Mass. (1810–20).

Fales, James, Jr., New Bedford, Mass. (1836).

Farnham, S. S., Oxford, N. Y. (1842).

Farnum, Henry & Rufus, Boston, Mass. (1780). Apprentices of Thomas Harland.

Farr, John C., Philadelphia, Pa. (1832). "Watches, Jewelry and Silver Ware."

Favre, John James, Philadelphia, Pa.

Fellows, James K., Lowell, Mass. (1832).

Fellows, Read & Olcott, New York City (1829). "Importers of Fancy Hardware, Watches, Jewelry, Watch Materials, Tools, etc."

Fellows, Storm & Cargill, New York City. (1832). "Watches, Jewelry and Fancy Goods."

Ferrigo, or Perrigo.

Ferris, Benjamin, C. & W., Philadelphia, Pa. (1811).

Ferris, Tiba, Wilmington, Del. (1812–50).

Fessler, John, Fredericktown, Md. (1782–1820).

Fessler, John, Jr., Fredericktown, Md. (1820–40).

Feton, J., Philadelphia, Pa. (1828–40).

Field, Peter, New York City (1802). Watch and clockmaker.

Field, Peter, Jr., New York City (1802–25).

Fiffe, H.

Filber, John, Lancaster, Pa. (1810–25).

Fish, Isaac, Utica, N. Y. (1846).

Fisk, William, Boston, Mass. (Born, 1770; Died, 1844). Made nearly all Simon Willard's clock cases in 1800–38, also made them for Aaron Willard, and other clockmakers.

Fite, John, Baltimore, Md. (1817).

Fitz, ——, Portsmouth, N. H. (about 1769).

Fix, Joseph, Reading, Pa. (1820–40).

Fletcher, Charles, Philadelphia, Pa. (1832). "Imports Watches, Jewelry, Mantel Clocks. . . ."

Fletcher, Thomas, Philadelphia, Pa. (1832). Manufactory of Jewelry and Silver Ware, and Furnishing Warehouse. Extensive assortment of Watches . . . Mantel Clocks. . . .

Fling, Daniel, Philadelphia, Pa. (1811).

Flower, Henry, Philadelphia, Pa. (1753).

Folmar, Andrew, New York City (1810).

Foot, Charles J., Bristol, Conn. (1856).

Forbes, Wells, Bristol, New Hampshire (about 1840).

Forestville Manufacturing Co., Bristol (village of Forestville), Conn. (about 1830).

Foster, John C., Portland, Me. (1834). "Horography, Watches, Clocks and Timekeepers of all escapements cleaned and adjusted."

Foster, Nathaniel, Newburyport, Mass. (1818–28). In 1818 he opened a store on State St., where he carried on "the clock and watch making business in all its branches." He had charge of the town clocks from April, 1818, until 1828, and perhaps later.

Fowell, J. & N., Boston, Mass. (1800–10).

Francis, Basil & Alexander Vuille, Baltimore, Md. (1766).

Frary, Obadiah, Southampton, Mass. (1745–75). Made some good brass clocks for families, and a few for meeting-houses.

Friend, Engell, New York City (1825). "Clock maker and brass founder."

Friend, George, New York City (1820). "Clockmaker and brass founder."

Frost, Jonathan, Reading, Mass. (1856).

Frost & Mumford, Providence, R. I. (1810).

Frost, Oliver, Providence, R. I. (1800).

Gaines, John, Portsmouth, N. H. (1800).

Galbraith, Patrick, Philadelphia, Pa. (1795–1811).

Galpin, Moses, Bethlehem, Conn. (before 1821). Not a maker, but a peddler, though he put his name on clocks he bought from others. Chauncey Jerome, with five or six others, trusted Galpin with a large quantity of clocks, and he took them to Louisiana to sell in fall of 1821. In the course of the winter he was taken sick and died there. One of his peddlers came home without one dollar in money. The creditors tried to get something from his property but were not successful. Chauncey Jerome lost $740.

Galt, Peter, Baltimore, Md. (1804).

Galt, Samuel, Williamsburg, Va. (1751).

Gardiner, B., New York City (1832). "Furnishing Warehouse, Manufacturer of Silver Ware, and Importer of Lamps . . . Clocks. . . ."

Gardiner, John B., Ansonia, Conn. (1857).

Garrett, Benjamin, Goshen, N. Y. (1820).

Garrett, Philip, Philadelphia, Pa. (1819).

Garrett & Sons, P., Philadelphia, Pa. (1832). "Importers of Watches . . . Manufacturers of Jewelry, Silver Spoons, Spectacles, etc."

Gates, Zaccheus, Charlestown, Mass. (1831).

Gaw, William P., Philadelphia, Pa. (1819).

Gaylord, Homer, Norfolk, Conn. (until 1812). Homer Gaylord made clocks on his father's farm in Norfolk until 1812, when a freshet tore away the dam, after which he moved to Homer, N. Y.

Geddes, Charles, Boston, Mass. (1773).

Gelston, George S., New York City (1832). "Manufacturer and Importer of Fine Jewelry, Watches and Fancy Goods. Orders left with Hugh Gelston, Baltimore, punctually attended to."

Gelston, Hugh, Baltimore, Md. (1832). "Importer of Watches, Jewelry, etc."

Gerding & Siemon, New York City (1832). "Importers of . . . Mantelpiece Clocks. . . ."

Gerrish, Oliver, Portland, Me. (1834). "Clocks, watches and jewelry repaired."

Gibbons, Thomas, Philadelphia, Pa.

Gilbert, Jordan & Smith, New York City (1832). "Dealers in Combs, Cutlery, Jewelry, Silver Spoons, Spectacles, Thimbles, Needles, and a Variety of Fancy Goods."

Gilbert Manufacturing Co., The, Winsted, Conn. (Incorporated 1866–1871 to date). After reorganization in 1871, called The Wm. L. Gilbert Clock Company. Still doing business.

Gilbert, William L., Winsted, Conn. (1823–66). In 1841 or '42 he joined Lucius Clarke, the firm name being Clarke, Gilbert & Co. Later it became W. L. Gilbert, and in 1866 was incorporated as The Gilbert Manufacturing Co. In 1871 reorganized as The Wm. L. Gilbert Clock Co. Still doing business.

Gill, Caleb, Hingham, Mass. (1785).

Gill, Leavitt, Hingham, Mass. (1785).

Giraud, Victor, New York City (1847).

Glover, William, Boston, Mass. (1823).

Goddard, George S., Boston, Mass. (1823).

Godfrey, William, Philadelphia, Pa. (1750–1763).

Godschalk, Jacob, Philadelphia, Pa.

Goff, Charles.

Goodfellow, William, Philadelphia, Pa. (1793–99).

Goodfellow, William, Philadelphia, Pa. (1813).

Goodfellow, William, & Son, Philadelphia, Pa. (1796–99).

Goodhue, D. T., Providence, R. I. (1824).

Goodhue, Richard S., Portland, Me. (1834).

Gooding, Henry, Boston, Mass. (1810–30).

Gooding, Joseph, Dighton, Mass., and Bristol, R. I.

Goodrich, Chauncey, Bristol (village of Forestville), Conn. (1856).

Goodwin, Horace, Jr., Hartford, Conn. (1831–41 or longer). "Keeps constantly on hand for sale watches, jewelry, fancy goods, etc."

Gorden, Smyley, Lowell, Mass. (1832). "He was a maker of clock cases, and put his name on them."

Gordon, Thomas, Boston, Mass. (1759). "From London, opposite the Merchant's Coffee House, sells all kinds of Timepieces."

Gould, Abijah, Rochester, N. Y. (1834).

Govett, George, Philadelphia, Pa. (1813–31).

Grant, William, Boston, Massachusetts (about 1815).

Graves, Alfred, Willow Grove, Pa. (1845).

Green, John, Carlisle, Pa.

Green, John, Philadelphia, Pa. (1794).

Greenleaf, David, Hartford, Conn. (1799). Watchmaker and jeweler.

Greenough, N. C., Newburyport, Mass. (1848).

Gridley, Timothy, Sanbornton, N. H. (1808–). He established a wooden clock manufactory, introducing two men from Conn., Messrs. Peck and Holcomb, to take charge of the business. Col. Simeon Cate bought out the clock business of Mr. Gridley. Mrs. James Connor painted and lettered the faces of the clocks for them.

Griffin, Henry, New York City (1793–1818).

Griffith, Owen, Philadelphia, Pa.

Griswold, Daniel White, Manchester, Conn. (Born, 1767; died, 1844.) Made a number of clocks, though his regular business was that of trader between Boston and New York.

Groppengerser, J. L., Philadelphia, Pa. (1840).

Grotz, Isaac, Easton, Pa. (1810–35).

Gruby, Edward L., Portland, Me. (1834).

Guild, Jeremiah, Cincinnati, O. (1831).

Guile, John, Philadelphia, Pa. (1819).

Guinard, F. E., Baltimore, Md. (1817).

Haas & Co., John, New York City (1825). "Musical clockmakers."

Hall, John, Philadelphia, Pa. (1811–19).

Hall, Seymour & Co., Unionville, Conn. (about 1820).

Ham, George, Portsmouth, N. H. (1810).

Ham, Supply, Portsmouth, N. H. One of the ancient and honorable clock and watch makers of Portsmouth. He owned a clock made by "J. Windmill, London," which bears this inscription of its owners: 1677, George Jaffrey; 1720, George Jaffrey, Jr.; 1749, George Jaffrey, 3rd; 1802, Timothy Ham; 1856, Supply Ham; 1862, Francis W. Ham.

Hamlen, Nathaniel, Augusta, Me. (1795–1820).

Hamlin, William, Providence, R. I. (1797).

Hampton, Samuel, Chelsea, Mass. (1847).

Hanks, Benjamin, Litchfield, Conn. (1778–1785). "Benjamin Hanks came from Mansfield, Conn., to this Town [Litchfield] in 1778, remaining only until 1785, when he returned to Mansfield. While here he was a clock and watch maker, and contracted for and put up the first clock in the city of New York, on the old Dutch Church, Nassau and Liberty Streets. This clock was unique, having a windmill attachment, his own patent, for winding itself up."

Harden, James, Philadelphia, Pa. (1819).

Harland, Thomas, Norwich, Conn. (1773–1807). His advertisement stated that he made "horizontal, repeating, and plain watches in gold, silver, metal or covered cases; spring, musical and plain clocks; church clocks and regulators. Watch-wheels and fusees of all sorts and dimensions cut and finished upon the shortest notice, neat as in London, and at the same prices." He also taught apprentices from all parts of New England, the most famous of whom was Eli Terry. In 1790 ten or twelve hands were constantly employed, and it is stated that he made annually 200 watches and 40 clocks. His prices varied from £4 10s to £7 10s.

Harrison, James (brother of Lemuel), Waterbury, Conn. (1790–1830). Built a clock factory on Little Brook in 1802.

Harrison, John, Philadelphia, Pa.

Harrison, John Murray.

Harrison, Lemuel (brother of James), Waterbury, Conn. (1800). He and his brother made clocks by hand before 1800. Ephraim Downs worked for him in 1811.

Hart, Alpha (brother of Henry), Goshen, Conn. (1820).

Hart, Eliphaz, Norwich on the Green, Conn. (1812). Worker in gold and silver, and offered for sale handsome assortments of jewelry and time-keepers.

Hart, Henry (brother of Alpha), Hart Hollow, Goshen, Conn.

Hart, Judah, Norwich at the Landing, Conn. (1812). Worker in gold and silver, and offered for sale handsome assortments of jewelry and time-keepers.

Hart, Orrin, Bristol, Conn. (1840).

Hart & Wilcox, Norwich, Conn.

Harwood, George, Rochester, N. Y. (1839). "Clocks, warranted to keep good time. 20 cases just received from Connecticut, which will be sold by the case or singly as low as any warranted clocks can be sold in this city."

Haselton & Wentworth, Lowell, Mass. (1832).

Hatch, George D., N. Attleboro, Mass. (1856).

Hawxhurst (or Hauxhurst) & Demilt, New York City (1790).

Hawxhurst, Nathaniel, New York City, (1786–98).

Hayes, Peter B. (or P.), Poughkeepsie, N. Y. (1831). "Dealers in Watches, Clocks. . . ."

Heath, Reuben, Scottsville, N. Y. (1791–1818). He was a clockmaker and repairer, and sold clocks of other makers.

Hedge, George, Buffalo, N. Y. (1831).

Heffords, ———, Middleboro (Titicut), Mass. Famous for clocks of superior

quality, which he invented and manufactured.

Heilig, Jacob, Philadelphia, Pa. (1770–
1824).

Heilig, John, Germantown, Pa. (1824–
30).

Hendrick, Barnes & Co., Forestville, Conn.
(1845). Went into the old Ives shop,
and there made the first marine clocks
ever made.

Hendricks, Uriah, New York City (1756).
Was by trade a watchmaker. "At his
store next door to the Sign of the
Golden Key in Hanover Square has
imported two fine repeating eight day
clocks which strike every half hour and
repeat."

Hepton, Frederick, Philadelphia, Pa.
(1785)

Hequembourg, C., New Haven, Conn.
(1818). Was in business many years.
Sold gold and silver watches with gold
or enamelled dials, and repaired clocks
and watches.

Heron, Isaac, New York City (1769–80).
"Isaac Heron, watchmaker, facing
Coffee House Bridge, has a musical
clock noble and elegant, also a neat
and extraordinary good chamber repeating clock."

Herr, William, Jr., Providence, R. I.
(1849).

Hicks, Willet, New York City (1790).

Hildeburn, Samuel, Philadelphia, Pa.
(1819).

Hildeburn & Watson, Philadelphia, Pa.
(1832). "Manufacturers of Jewelry
and Watch Case Makers, and Importers of Watches and Fancy Goods."

Hildeburn & Woodworth, Philadelphia, Pa.
(1819).

Hildreth, Jonas, Salisbury, Vt. (1805).

Hill, D., Reading, Pa. (1820–40).

Hill, Joakim, Flemington, N. J. (1800).
Made long-case clocks of excellent
workmanship, and charged a good price
for them.

Hiller, Joseph, Salem, Mass. (1770).
"1770. Joseph Hiller, moved from
Boston, has taken a shop opposite the
Court House, on the Exchange."

Hilldrop (or Hilldrup), Thomas, Hartford,
Conn. (1774–1794). Watch-maker,
jeweler and silversmith from London.

Hills, Amariah, New York City (1845).

Hitchcock, H., Lodi, N. Y. (about 1800).
"Seals, keys, chains, clocks and watches
for sale by H. Hitchcock, Lodi, N. Y."

Hitchcock, Samuel R., Humphreysville, N.
Y. (1810).

Hoadley, Samuel & Luther, Winsted (town
of Winchester), Conn. (1807–13).
In 1807 Samuel and Luther Hoadley
with Riley Whiting opened works at
Winsted, Conn., for making wood
clocks. Luther died 1813, Samuel
entered army, retiring from business.

Hoadley, Silas, Plymouth, Conn. (1808–
49). Learned the carpenter's trade
from his uncle, Calvin Hoadley.
Worked for Eli Terry, and in 1809
formed partnership with Eli Terry and
Seth Thomas at Greystone. Terry
withdrew 1810, Thomas 1812. Hoadley continued to make clocks here till
1849, when he retired.

Hodges & North, Wolcottville (now Torrington), Conn. (1830).

Hodgson, William, Philadelphia, Pa.
(1785).

Hoffner, Henry, Philadelphia, Pa. (1791).

Holbrook, George, Brookfield, Mass.
(1803). He made the clock and bell
which were placed on the meeting-
house of Leicester, Mass., Jan. 13,
1803.

Holbrook, ——, Medway, Mass. (about 1830). Made clock for Unitarian meeting-house in Keene, N. H., a few years after 1829.

Hollinshead, Jacob, Salem, Mass. (1771).

Hollinshead, Morgan, Moorestown, N. J.

Hollingshead, Morgan, Philadelphia, Pa.

Holman, Salem, Hartford, Conn. (1816).

Holway, Philip, Falmouth, Mass. (1800).

Homer, William, Moreland, Pa. (1849).

Hood, Francis, New York City (1810).

Hood, John, Philadelphia, Pa.

Hooker & Goodenough, Bristol, Conn. (1849).

Hopkins & Alfred, Harwinton, Conn. (1820), Hartford, Conn. (1827). They make excellent clocks, wood works.

Hopkins, Asa, Litchfield (parish of Northfield), Conn. (1820 and earlier). In 1813 he obtained a patent on an engine for cutting wheels.

Hopkins, Henry P., Philadelphia, Pa. (1832). "Dealer in Watches, Clocks. . . ."

Horn, Eliphalet, Lowell, Mass. (1832).

Horn, E. B., Boston, Mass. (1847).

Hotchkiss & Benedict, Auburn, N. Y. (about 1820). Makers of shelf clocks.

Hotchkiss, Elisha, Burlington, Conn. (about 1815).

Hotchkiss & Field, Burlington, Conn. (1820).

Hotchkiss, Hezekiah, New Haven, Conn. (1748).

Hotchkiss & Pierpont, Plymouth, Conn. (1811–). "Had been selling long clocks without the cases, in New Jersey." C. Jerome.

Hotchkiss, Robert & Henry, Plymouth, Conn. ("Prior to 1846").

Hotchkiss, Spencer & Co., Salem Bridge (now Naugatuck), Conn. (1832).

"Manufacturer of Buttons and Eight Day Brass Clocks."

Howard & Davis, Boston, Mass. (1847–56).

Howard, Edward, Roxbury, Mass. (1840–82). Apprenticed to Aaron Willard, Jr. Started business for himself, 1840. David P. Davis became his partner, 1847, and they made clocks and scales. In 1849, Aaron L. Dennison joined them, and a watch factory was started at Roxbury. In 1854 they moved to Waltham, and watches made there were marked "Dennison, Howard & Davis." In 1857 the Waltham factory was sold to Royal E. Robbins. Howard returned to Roxbury, and 1861 started the Howard Clock & Watch Company. He retired 1882.

Howard, Thomas, Philadelphia, Pa. (1789–91).

Howe, Jubal, Boston, Mass. (1833).

Hoyt, George A., Albany, N. Y. (1830).

Hoyt, James A., Troy, N. Y. (1837).

Hubbard, Daniel, Medfield, Mass. (1820).

Hubbell, L.

Huckel, Samuel, Philadelphia, Pa. (1819).

Huguenail, Charles T., Philadelphia, Pa. (1799).

Humbert, Dross, Philadelphia, Pa. (1795).

Hunt, ——, New York City (1789).

Hurtin & Burgi, Bound Brook, N. J., (1766).

Hutchins, Abel, Concord, N. H. (1788–1819). Apprentice of Simon Willard. Was in partnership with his brother Levi.

Hutchins, Levi, Concord, N. H. (1786–1819). Apprentice of Simon Willard. Learned art of repairing watches in Abington, Conn. About 1786 established business of brass clock-making. In 1788, his brother Abel became partner.

Hyman, Samuel, Philadelphia, Pa. (1799).

Ingersoll, Daniel G., Boston, Mass. (1800–10).

Ingraham, Elias, Bristol, Conn. (1835–85). Designer of the "Sharp Gothic" and other styles of clock cases. Originally a cabinet maker. Made clock cases 1827–35 for George Mitchell, and learned clockmaking in his factory. In 1835 bought a shop in Bristol and began making clocks. In 1843 he and his brother formed a partnership with Elisha C. Brewster. Brewster & Ingraham was succeeded by E. & A. Ingraham, and the latter by E. Ingraham & Co., 1856. A joint stock company was formed 1881, and his descendants still carry on the business.

Ingraham, E. & A., Bristol, Conn. (1848–55).

Ingraham & Co., E., Bristol, Conn. (1856–81) Joint stock company formed 1881 and now called The E. Ingraham Co.

Ives & Birge, Bristol, Conn. (about 1843).

Ives Brothers (five in number), Bristol, Conn. (1815–20 also 1822–37).

Ives, Charles G., Bristol, Conn. (about 1810–20). Made wood clocks.

Ives, Chauncey, Bristol, Conn. (1827–36).

Ives, C. & L. C., Bristol, Conn. (1832). "Manufacturers of Eight Day Patent Brass and Thirty Hour Wood Clocks." About 1830 Chauncey and Lawson C. Ives built a factory in Bristol for making 8 day brass clocks — the kind invented by Joseph Ives. Business was carried on successfully for a few years, but in 1836 was closed up.

Ives, Ira, Bristol, Conn. (about 1815–37).

Ives, Joseph, Bristol, Conn. and New York City (1811–25). " Joseph Ives made wood movements as early as 1811. In 1818 he invented a metal clock, with iron plates and brass wheels, and began its manufacture. This clock was large and clumsy and never became very successful."

Ives, Lawson C., Bristol, Conn. (1827–36).

Jacks, James, Philadelphia, Pa.

Jackson, Joseph H., Philadelphia, Pa. (1802–10).

James, Joshua, Boston, Mass. (1823).

Jeffreys, Samuel, Philadelphia, Pa.

Jencks, John E., Providence, R. I. (1800).

Jenkins, Harman, Albany, N. Y. (1817).

Jenkins, Ira, Albany, N. Y. (1813).

Jerome, Chauncey, Plymouth, Bristol and New Haven, Conn. (1816–60). Author of " American Clock Making," published 1860. Worked for Eli Terry winter of 1816; then began making clocks by himself. In 1821 moved to Bristol. In 1824 firm of Jeromes & Darrow formed (Chauncey and Noble Jerome and Elijah Darrow). A little later Chauncey Jerome got up the " Bronze Looking Glass Clock." Did well with this until the panic of 1837. In 1838 he invented and began making the one-day brass clock, which drove out all wood clocks. By 1840 his business was very large. In 1842 began sending clocks to England. In 1844 moved his business to New Haven. His product was so good that many small manufacturers used Jerome labels for their poorer clocks. In 1850 a joint stock company was formed in New Haven — The Jerome Manufacturing Company. In 1855 the company failed and Jerome was ruined. P. T. Barnum was connected with this company during the last six months of its existence. The real difficulty was the previous indebtedness of the Terry & Barnum Co., which was assumed by the Jerome Mfg. Co. Jerome spent his last years almost in obscurity and died in very straitened circumstances.

Jerome, Chauncey & Noble, Richmond, Va., also Hamburg, S. C. (1835–1836). They made the cases and parts at Bristol, Conn., packed and shipped them to Richmond, and took along workmen to put them together there.

Jeromes & Darrow, Bristol, Conn. (1824–31). "Manufacturers of Fancy Thirty Hour and Eight Day Wood Clocks."

Jerome & Grant, Bristol, Conn.

Jerome Mfg. Co., New Haven, Conn. (1850–55). (See Chauncey Jerome.)

Jerome, Noble, Bristol, Conn. (1820–40). Brother of Chauncey, and in business with him.

Jewell, Jerome & Co., Bristol, Conn. (1849). Town clocks.

Job, John, Philadelphia, Pa. (1819).

Jocelyn, Nathaniel, New Haven, Conn. (1790).

Johnson, Addison, Wolcottville (now Torrington), Conn. (1825). Pillar and scroll clocks, handsome cases and good works.

Johnson, Chauncey, Albany, N. Y. (1829). "Musical, ornamental and common clocks."

Johnson, Simon, Sanbornton, N. H. (1830–60). "A very superior quality of clocks has been produced from this establishment by the senior Mr. Johnson, and latterly by the Johnson Brothers."

Johnson, William S., New York City (about 1830).

Jonckheere, Francis, Baltimore, Md. (1817).

Jones, Abner, Weare, N. H. (1780). Made large old-fashioned 8-day brass clocks that sold for $50 each.

Jones, Ball & Poor, Boston, Mass. (1847).

Jones, Edward K., Bristol, Conn. (1825).

Jones, Ezekiel, Boston, Mass. (1823).

Jones, George, Wilmington, Del. (1810–37).

Jones, George, Jr., Wilmington, Del. (1814).

Jones, Jacob, Baltimore, Md. (1817).

Jones, Samuel, Baltimore, Md. (1817).

Joseph, Isaac, Boston, Mass. (1823).

Joslyn, James, New Haven, Conn. (1798–1820).

Joyce, Robert, New York City (1794).

Kedzie, J., Rochester, N. Y. (1847).

Kelly (or Kelley), Allen, Sandwich, Mass. (1810–30).

Kelly, Ezra, New Bedford, Mass. (1823–45).

Kelly, John, New Bedford, Mass. (1836).

Kemble, William, New York City (1786).

Kemlo, Francis, Chelsea, Mass. (1847).

Kennard, John, Newfields, N. H. (19th century). Was brass-worker and clockmaker. Henry Wiggin, Jr., made cases for his clocks.

Kennedy, Patrick, Philadelphia, Pa. (1795–99).

Kenney, Asa, West Millbury, Mass. (about 1800).

Kepplinger, Samuel, Baltimore, Md. (1800).

Kerner & Paff, New York City (1796). "Musical clocks with figures and cuckoo clocks."

Ketcham & Hitchcock, New York City (1818).

Kimball, John, Jr., Boston, Mass. (1823).

Kincaird, Thomas, Christiana Bridge, Del. (1775).

Kinkead, James.

Kippen, George, Bridgeport, Conn. (1822). Kept a great variety of goods, and made and repaired clocks and watches.

Kirk, Charles, Bristol, Conn. (1823–33). In 1833 he sold his clock factory and business to Elisha C. Brewster, but conducted it for him until about 1838.

Kirk, Charles, New Haven, Conn. (1847). Brass marine clocks.

Kline, B., Philadelphia, Pa. (1841).

Kline, John, Philadelphia, Pa. (1820).

Kline, John, Reading, Pa. (1820–40).

Knowles, John, Philadelphia, Pa.

Kohl, Nicholas, Willow Grove, Pa. (1830).

Koplin, Washington, Norristown, Pa. (1850).

Kumbell, William, New York City (1775–89).

Labhart, W. I., New York City (1810).

Ladomus, Lewis, Philadelphia, Pa. (1846).

Lamb, Cyrus, Oxford, Mass. (1832). Probably not a regular clock-maker. He was a mill-wright, and a skilful mechanic. It is said that he had in his shop at the time of the fire (Jan. 7, 1832) a remarkable clock of his own designing which it was supposed would run for several years with one winding.

Lamione, A., Philadelphia, Pa. (1811).

Lamson, Charles, Salem, Mass. (1850) (with James Balch).

Lane, James, Philadelphia, Pa. (1813).

Lane, J., Southington, Conn.

Lane, Mark, Southington, Conn. (1831). "Manufacturer of Eli Terry's Patent Clocks."

Langdon, Edward, Bristol, Conn. (19th century). In company with S. Emerson Root for a time.

Lanny, D. F., Boston, Mass. (1789).

Laquaine, Philadelphia, Pa.

Larkin, Joseph, Boston, Mass. (1841–47).

Latimer, James, Philadelphia, Pa. (1819).

Launay, David, New York City (1801). "Had for sale at his watchmaking shop a highly finished clock which decorated the library of the late King of France."

Laundry, Alexander, Philadelphia, Pa.

Launey, David F., New York City (1793 and 1802).

Lawrence, George, Lowell, Mass. (1832).

Lawson, William H., Waterbury, Conn.

Leach, Caleb, Plymouth, Mass. (1776–90).

Leach & Bradley, Utica, N. Y. (1832). "Dealers in Jewelry, Manufacturers of Silver Ware."

Leavenworth, Mark, Waterbury, Conn. (1810–30).

Leavenworth & Co., Mark, Waterbury, Conn. (1832).

Leavenworth & Sons, Albany, N. Y. (1817).

Leavenworth, William, Waterbury, Conn. (1802–15). Made clocks on Mad River about 1802. Col. Wm. Leavenworth was in the business in 1810, but failed, and moved to Albany, N. Y.

Leavitt, Dr. Josiah, Hingham, Mass. (1772). He made a clock which was placed in the attic story of the Old Meeting House (1772 or 73), and the dial appeared in a dormer window facing the street. Dr. Leavitt afterward removed to Boston, where he became somewhat noted as an organ-builder.

Lee, William, Charlestown, S. C. (1717).

Lefferts, Charles, Philadelphia, Pa. (1819).

Lefferts & Hall, Philadelphia, Pa. (1819).

Le Huray, Nicholas, Jr., Philadelphia, Pa. (1832). "Clocks, Watches and Jewelry."

Leigh, David, Pottstown, Pa. (1849).

Lemist, William King, Dorchester, Mass. (1812). Apprentice of Simon Willard about 1806 or 1808. Died 1820, in shipwreck.

Leslie & Price, Philadelphia, Pa. (1793–99).

Leslie, Robert, Philadelphia, Pa. (1745–91). "Robert Leslie, Clock and Watchmaker, on the north side of Market between Fourth and Fifth St., Philadelphia. Having obtained Patents for several Improvements on Clocks and Watches, begs leave to inform his friends and the public that he is now ready to execute any work on the said constructions; which may be applied to Clocks and Watches already made or new ones, and on trial have been found superior to any heretofore brought into common use. He has so simplified the repeating part of a watch as to enable him to make it at two-thirds of the common price which will not only be an advantage in the first purchase, but ever after as it can be cleaned when necessary for two-thirds less than the common price. He has also simplified the striking parts of clocks, which enables him to reduce the price one-fourth, and repairs at the lowest prices, horizontal, repeating, plain and other watches, and musical, chiming and plain clocks, with punctuality and dispatch, and warrants all work done in his shop. An assortment of Clock- and Watch-makers Tools and Materials for sale on Reasonable Terms. Two Journeymen and an Apprentice wanted." Gazette of the United States, Philadelphia, 1791.

Lester, Robert, Philadelphia, Pa. (1791–98).

Le Tilier, John, Philadelphia, Pa.

Levi, Isaac, Philadelphia, Pa.

Levy, Michael, Philadelphia, Pa. (1813).

Lewis, Erastus, New Britain (later Waterbury), Conn. (about 1800).

Lewis, Levi, Bristol, Conn. (1811–20).

Liebert, Henry, Norristown, Pa. (1849).

Limeburner, John, Philadelphia, Pa. (1791).

Lind, John (or Johannes), Philadelphia, Pa. (1791).

Lister, Thomas, Halifax, British North America (1760–1802). He was a maker of very choice long-case clocks, and in many of them which are still found going are the following lines, generally pasted on the door of the body:

" Lo! here I stand by thee
To give thee warning day and night;
For every tick that I do give
Cuts short the time thou hast to live.
Therefore, a warning take by me,
To serve Thy God as I serve thee:
Each day and night be on thy guard,
And Thou shalt have a just reward."

Little, Peter, Baltimore, Md. (1799).

Lockwood & Scribner, New York City (1847).

Lohse & Keyser, Philadelphia, Pa. (1832). " Importers of . . . Clocks. . . ."

Lord & Goddard, Rutland, Vt. (1797–1830).

Lorton, William B., New York City (1810–25). " Manufacturer and wholesale dealer in American clocks in all their variety."

Lovis, Capt. Joseph, Hingham, Mass., (1775–1804).

Low & Co., John J., Boston, Mass. (1832). " Importers of Watches. . . ."

Lowens, David, Philadelphia, Pa. (1785).

Ludwig, John, Philadelphia, Pa. (1791).

Lufkin & Johnson, Boston, Mass. (1800–10).

Lukens, Isaiah, Philadelphia, Pa. (1790–1828).

Lukens, Seneca, Horsham Meeting, Pa. (1830).

Luscomb, Samuel, Salem, Mass. (1773). Made clock put in tower of East Meeting House, 1773.

Lyman, G. E., Providence, R. I. (1849).

Lyman, Roland, Lowell, Mass. (1832).

Lynch, John, Baltimore, Md. (1804–32). "Manufacturer of Silver Work, and Clock and Watch Maker."

McClure, John, Boston, Mass. (1823).

M'Cormick, Robert, Philadelphia, Pa.

McDowell, James, Philadelphia, Pa. (1794–99 or later).

McDowell, James, Jr., Philadelphia, Pa. (1805–25).

Macfarlane, John, Boston, Mass. (1800–10).

M'Harg, Alexander, Albany, N. Y. (1817).

McIlhenny, Joseph E., Philadelphia, Pa. (1819).

McIlhenny & West, Philadelphia, Pa. (1819).

M'Keen, H., Philadelpha, Pa. (1832).

McMyers, John, Baltimore, Md. (1799).

Mackay, Crafts, Boston, Mass. (1789).

Manning, Richard, Ipswich, Mass. (1748–60).

Manross, Elisha, Bristol (village of Forestville), Conn. (1827–49). He occupied the Joseph Ives shop in Forestville. In 1845 he built a factory near the railroad.

Manross (two brothers), Bristol, Conn. (1860). Made movements of brass marine clocks.

Marache, Solomon, New York City (1759).

Marand, Joseph, Baltimore, Md. (1804).

Marble, Simeon, New Haven, Conn. (1817).

Marks, Isaac, Philadelphia, Pa. (1795).

Marquand & Bros., New York City (1832). "Importers and Dealers in Watches and Jewelry, Manufacturers of Silver Ware, Clocks and Watches Repaired."

Marsh, George, Bristol, Conn.

Marsh, George C., Wolcottville (now Torrington), Conn. (1830).

Marsh, Gilbert & Co., Farmington, Conn. (1820).

Masi & Co., F., Washington, D. C. (1833). "Manufacturers of Jewelry, Dealers in Watches. . . ."

Masi, Seraphim, Washington, D. C. (1832). "Dealer in Watches, Clocks. . . ."

Mason, H. G., Boston, Mass. (1844–49).

Mathey, Lewis, Philadelphia, Pa. (1797).

Matlack, White, Philadelphia, Pa.

Matlack, White C., New York City (1769–75).

Matlack, William, Philadelphia, Pa.

Matthewson, J., Providence, R. I. (1849).

Maurepas, ——, Bristol, Conn. (1855).

Maus, Frederick, Philadelphia, Pa. (1785–93).

Mayer, Elias, Philadelphia, Pa. (1832). "Manufacturer of Jewelry; keeps Watches and Materials."

Maynard, George, New York City (1702–30).

Mead, Adriance & Co., Ithaca, N. Y. (1832). "Dealers in Watches, Clocks. . . ."

Mead, Benjamin, Castine, Me. (1800–10).

Meeks, Edward, Jr., New York City (1796). "Makes and has for sale 8 day clocks and chiming timepieces."

Melcher, ——, Plymouth Hollow (now Thomaston), Conn. (about 1790).

Melly, "Brothers Melly," New York City (1829). "All kinds of watches and clocks."

Mendenhall, Thomas, Philadelphia, Pa.

Mends, Benjamin, Philadelphia, Pa.

Mends, James, Philadelphia, Pa. (1795).

Menzies, James, Philadelphia, Pa. (1800 and later).

Merchant, William, Philadelphia, Pa.

Merriam, Silas, ——, Conn. (1790).

Merriman & Bradley, New Haven, Conn. (1825).

Merriman, Titus, Bristol, Conn. (1810–30). About 1810 he was associated with Butler Dunbar making clocks.

Mery (or Merry), F., Philadelphia, Pa. (1799).

Meyer, J. A., New York City (1832). " Importer of . . . Clocks. . . ."

Meyers, John, Fredericktown, Md. (1793–1825).

Millard, Squire, Warwick, R. I. Maker of hall clocks.

Miller, Aaron, Elizabethtown, N. C. (?) (1747).

Miller, Abraham, Easton, Pa. (1810–30).

Miller, Edward F., Providence, R. I. (1824).

Miller, Pardon, Providence, R. I. (1824–49).

Miller (or Millar), Thomas, Philadelphia, Pa. (1832). " Watch and Jewelry Store."

Milne, Robert, New York City (1798–1802).

Mitchell & Atkins, Bristol, Conn. (1830).

Mitchell, George, Bristol, Conn. (1827–40)

Mitchell, Henry, New York City (1786–1802).

Mitchell, Hinman & Co., Bristol, Conn. (1831). " Manufacturers of Clocks, and Dealers in Buttons, etc."

Mitchell & Mott, New York City (1793–1802).

Mitchell, Phineas, Boston, Mass. (1823).

Mitchelson, David, Boston, Mass. (1774). " Watches, Plain, Skeleton and Horizontal, in Gold, Silver and Pinchbeck cases, in particular a great variety of Silver Watches for 10 dollars to 10 guineas, some of which show the day of the month, and others with Seconds are very suitable for Physicians, like-wise Spring and Pendulum Eight Day Clocks, also an assortment of Tools and Materials used by Clock and Watch-Makers."

Monroe & Co., E. & C. H., Bristol, Conn. (1856).

Monroe, John, Barnstable, Mass.

Montgomery, Robert, New York City (1786).

Moolinger, Henry, Philadelphia, Pa. (1794).

Morgan, Elijah, Poughkeepsie, N. Y. (1832). " Dealer in Watches, Clocks. . . ."

Morgan, Theodore, Salem, Mass. (1837).

Morgan, Thomas, Baltimore, Md. (1774).

Morgan, Thomas, Philadelphia, Pa. (1779–93).

Morrell, Benjamin, Boscawen, N. H. (1816–45).

Morrell & Mitchell, New York City (1816–20).

Morris, William, Grafton, Mass. (1765–75).

Morse & Co. (Myles Morse & Jeremiah Blakeslee), Plymouth Hollow (now Thomaston), Conn. (1841–49). Made clocks with brass works, 1-day time and wire gong.

Morse, Elijah (son-in-law of William Crane), Canton, Mass. (1819–).

Morse, Henry (son-in-law of William Crane), Canton, Mass. (1819–).

Morse, Miles (or Myles), Plymouth, Conn. (1849). With Jeremiah Blakeslee before 1849. Myles Morse and Gen. Thomas A. Davis of New York City built a clock factory on West Branch of Naugatuck, Plymouth, Conn., 1850–55.

Mosely, Robert E., Newburyport, Mass. (1848).

Mott, Jordan, New York City (1802–25).

Advertised, 1810, as follows: " Jordan Mott (of the late firm of Mott & Morrel), at his store No. 247 Pearl street, has on hand an extensive assortment of *Clocks*, *Gold* and *Silver Watches*, *Jewellery* and *Silver Ware*."

Moulton, Edward S., Rochester, N. H. (1807–).

Moulton, Francis, Lowell, Mass. (1832).

Moulton, Thomas M., Dunbarton, N. H. Made very fine long-case clocks.

Mowroue, Francis, New York City, N. Y. (1816).

Mulliken, Jonathan (son of Samuel), Newburyport, Mass. (1774–82). In 1774, bought land and buildings in Newburyport, where he made and sold watches and clocks.

Mulliken, Joseph, Newburyport, Mass. (died 1804).

Mulliken, Nathaniel, Lexington, Mass. (1751–89). His shop was burned by the British.

Mulliken, Samuel, Newbury (now Newburyport), Mass. (1750–56). Removed to Newbury 1750. Built house and shop where he made and repaired hall clocks until his death in 1756.

Mulliken, Samuel, Jr., Newburyport, Salem, and Lynn, Mass. (1781–1807). Probably grandson of Samuel, son of John, nephew of Jonathan. Born 1761. Served apprenticeship with Jonathan Mulliken; then opened shop on State St. In 1783 he married Jonathan's widow. Several years later he removed to Salem, and then to Lynn. Was postmaster of Lynn 1803–07. " Samuel Mulliken will barter clocks for English and West India goods and country produce."

Munger, A., Auburn, N. Y. (1825). Made shelf clocks with pillars and looking-glass.

Munger & Benedict, Auburn, N. Y. (1833).

Munger & Pratt, Ithaca, N. Y. (1832). " Dealers in Clocks, Watches. . . ."

Munroe, Daniel, Concord, Mass. (1800–08), and Boston, Mass. (1808–). Brother of Nathaniel and in business with him in Concord.

Munroe, Daniel, Jr., Boston, Mass. (1823).

Monroe, Nathaniel (brother of Daniel), Concord, Mass. (1800–1817), Baltimore, Md. (1817–). Served apprenticeship with Abel Hutchins. In business with brother Daniel, 1800–1808, and with Samuel Whiting, 1808–1817. Also had an extensive brass foundry where he made bells, clock movements, etc.

Monroe & Whiting (Nathaniel Munroe and Samuel Whiting), Concord, Mass. (1808–17). Did a large business, chiefly eight-day clocks, with brass works, and had seven or eight apprentices and journeymen.

Neiser (or Neisser), Augustine, (1737–80). He emigrated from his birthplace, Moravia, to Georgia in 1736; moved to Germantown, Pa., in 1739.

Nettleton, Heath & Co., Scottsville, N. Y. (1800–18). " Riley Whiting's model improved Clocks, cased and sold by Nettleton, Heath & Co., Scottsville, N. Y."

Nettleton, W. K., Rochester, N. Y. (1834).

Newberry, James, Philadelphia, Pa. (1819).

Newell, Thomas, Sheffield, Mass. (1810–20).

New Haven Clock Co. (1855–) Successor to the Jerome Mfg. Co. See Hiram Camp. Other men in this concern (1860) were: Hon. James English, H. M. Welsh, John Woodruff, Philip Pond (left two or three years before),

Chas. L. Griswold (left), L. F. Root.

Nicholls, George, New York City (1728–50).

Nichols, Walter, Newport, R. I. (1849).

Nicolet, Joseph Marci, Philadelphia, Pa. (1797).

Nicolette, Mary, Philadelphia, Pa. (1793–99).

Ninde, James, Baltimore, Md. (1799).

Noble, Philander, Pittsfield, Mass.

Nolan & Curtis, Philadelphia, Pa. Dial painters.

Nolen, Spencer, Philadelphia, Pa. (1819). Clock dial manufacturer.

North, Norris, Wolcottville (now Torrington), Conn. (1820).

Northrop, R. E., New Haven, Conn. (about 1820).

Northrop & Smith, Goshen, Conn. (about 1820).

Norton, Samuel, Hingham, Mass. (1785).

Norton, Thomas, Philadelphia, Pa. (1811).

Noyes, Leonard W., Nashua, N. H. (1830–40).

Nutter, E. H., Dover, N. H.

Oakes, Frederick, Hartford, Conn. (1828). Watch-maker and goldsmith.

Oakes, Henry, Hartford, Conn. (1839). Henry Oakes & Co., dealers in watches, jewelry, cutlery, combs, fancy goods.

O'Hara, Charles, Philadelphia, Pa. (1799).

Oliver, Griffith, Philadelphia, Pa. (1785–93).

Oliver, Welden, Bristol, Conn. (about 1820). Made shelf clocks, wood works, one-day time, bell strike.

Olmstead, Nathaniel, New Haven, Conn. (1826). Watches, jewelry and silverware. Clocks and watches made and repaired.

O'Neil, Charles, New Haven, Conn. (1823).

"Clock and watch repairer, informs his friends and the public he is at work at Messrs. Merriman and Bradley and solicits their patronage."

Orr, Thomas, Philadelphia, Pa. (1811).

Orton, Preston & Co., Farmington, Conn. (about 1815).

Osgood, John, Boston, Mass. (1823).

Osgood, John, Haverhill, N. H. Was an early jeweler, also manufactured the old-fashioned high clocks.

Owen, Griffith, Philadelphia, Pa. (1813).

Oyster, Daniel, Reading, Pa. (1820–40).

Packard, Isaac, North Bridgewater (now Brockton), Mass. (18–). Associated with Rodney Brace.

Packard, J., Rochester, N. Y. (1819).

Packard & Scofield, Rochester, N. Y. (1918). "Perpetual Motion." "Packard and Scofield, Watch-makers, have at their shop, next door south of 'The Telegraph,' a handsome assortment of Gold, Silver and Plated ware which will be sold at a moderate profit, for no man can live by the loss. Clocks and watches of every description repaired and warranted to keep in motion merely by winding every day."

Paine & Heroy, Albany, N. Y. (1813).

Palmer, John, Philadelphia, Pa. (1795).

Park, Seth, Park Town, Pa. (1790).

Parke, Solomon, Philadelphia, Pa. (1791–1819).

Parke & Co., Solomon, Philadelphia, Pa. (1799).

Parker, Gardner, Westborough, Mass. (17–). Before the Revolutionary War, Gardner Parker was making clocks.

Parker, Isaac, Deerfield, Mass. (1780).

Parker, Thomas, Philadelphia, Pa. (1785–1813).

Parker & Co., Thomas, Philadelphia, Pa. (1819).

Parker, Thomas, Jr., Philadelphia, Pa. (1819).

Parmelee (or Parmilee), Ebenezer, Guilford, Conn. (1726–40). In 1726, he made a clock for the church in Guilford, which was used until 1893. It is now set up in the attic of the Henry Whitfield House, and is still in running order. In 1740 he made a clock with brass works for the New Haven Meeting House.

Parmier, John Peter, Philadelphia, Pa. (1793).

Parry, John J., Philadelphia, Pa. (1795–1813).

Patton, Abraham, Philadelphia, Pa. (1799).

Patton, David, Philadelphia, Pa. (1799).

Patton & Jones, Baltimore, Md. (1798).

Payne, Lawrence, New York City (1732–55).

Pearsall & Embree, New York City (1786).

Pearsall, Joseph, New York City (1786–98).

Pearson, William, Jr., New York City (1775).

Pease, Isaac T., Enfield, Conn. (1818).

Peck, Benjamin, Providence, R. I. (1824).

Peck, Edson C., Derby, Conn. (1827).

Peck, Elijah, Boston, Mass. (1789).

Peck & Co., Julius, Litchfield, Conn. (1820).

Peck, Moses, Boston, Mass. (1789).

Peck, Timothy, Litchfield, Conn. (1790).

Peckham & Knower, Albany, N. Y. (1814). "Have for sale 7 Willard's Patent Timepieces and 8 day clocks warranted of the best workmanship."

Perkins, Robinson, Jaffrey, N. H.

Perkins, Thomas, Philadelphia, Pa. (1785–99).

Perkins, Thomas, Pittsburgh, Pa. (1815).

Perrigo, see Ferrigo.

Perry, Marvin, New York City (1769–80). "Repeating and Plain Clock and Watchmaker from London, where he has improved himself under the most eminent and capital artists in these branches, has opened shop in Hanover Square at the Sign of the Dial. He mends and repairs, musical, repeating, quarterly, chiming, silent, pull, and common weight clocks."

Perry, Thomas, New York City (1749–75). "Thomas Perry, watch-maker, from London, at the sign of the Dial, in Hanover Square, makes and cleans all sorts of clocks and watches in the best manner, and at a most reasonable rate."

Peters, James, Philadelphia, Pa. (1832). "Clock and Watch-maker, also Gold and Silver Ware."

Phillips, Joseph, New York City (1713–35).

Pierret, Matthew, Philadelphia, Pa. (1795).

Pierson, Henry S., Portland, Me. (1834).

Pinkard, Jonathan, Philadelphia, Pa.

Pitkin, Levi, East Hartford, Conn. (1795). "Jeweler, silversmith and clock-maker." Some of his clocks, made before 1799, may still be found in East Hartford houses.

Pitkins (four brothers), East Hartford, Conn. (1826–41 or later). In 1826 John O. Pitkin and Walter Pitkin commenced to manufacture silverware. In 1836 Henry Pitkin and James F. Pitkin commenced to manufacture watches. Theirs was the first watch made in America. Both industries were in the same building; their products were sold at the store of the Pitkins (H. & J. F.) in Hartford.

Pitman & Dorrance, Providence, R. I. (1800).

Pitman, Saunders, Providence, R. I. (1780).

Pitman, William R., New Bedford, Mass. (1836). "Manufacturers of gold and silverware, clocks and watches repaired and warranted."

Platt, ——, New Milford, Conn. (1793).

Platt, A. S., Bristol, Conn. (1849–56).

Platt & Blood, Bristol, Conn. (1849).

Platt, G. W. & N. C., New York City (1832). "Manufacturers of Silver Thimbles, Spectacles and Spoons; also Dealers in Jewelry, Silver Ware and Fancy Goods."

Pomeroy, Chauncy, Bristol, Conn. (about 1835).

Pomeroy, Noah, Bristol, Conn. (1849–78). In 1849 he bought out Chauncy Ives. Made clock movements only. Sold out to Hiram C. Thompson, 1878.

Pomeroy & Parker, Bristol, Conn. (1855).

Pond, Philip, Bristol, Conn. (1840).

Pope, Joseph, Boston, Mass. (1788).

Pope, Robert, Boston, Mass. (1786).

Porter, Daniel, Williamstown, Mass. (1799). Three of his clocks are still running in or near Williamstown. They are eight-day clocks, with brass works and handsome cases.

Porter, William, Waterbury, Conn. (1814–20). Zenas Cook, Daniel Clark and William Porter owned a clock factory in Waterbury in 1814.

Potter, Ephraim, Concord, N. H. (1775–90).

Potter, H. J., Bristol, Conn. (1849).

Potter, J. O. & J. R., Providence, R. I. (1849).

Praefelt, John, Philadelphia, Pa. (1797).

Pratt, Daniel, Jr., Salem, Mass. (1839).

Pratt, D., & Sons, Boston, Mass. (1849).

Pratt, Phinehas, Saybrook, Conn.

Pratt, William, & Brother, Boston, Mass. (1847).

Price, Isaac, Philadelphia, Pa. (1799).

Price, Joseph, Baltimore, Md. (1799).

Price, Philip, Philadelphia, Pa. (1819).

Prince, Geo. W., Dover, N. H.

Prince, Isaac, Philadelphia, Pa. (1791–95).

Proctor, Cardan (or Carden), New York City (1747–75).

Proctor, William, New York City (1737–60).

Pulsifer, F. L., Boston, Mass. (1856).

Quandale, Lewis, Philadelphia, Pa. (1813).

Quimby, Phineas, Belfast, Me. (1830–50).

Quimby, William, Belfast, Me. (1821–50). Succeeded Abel B. Eastman.

Quincy, Henry, Portland, Me. (1834). "Clocks, Watches, Jewelry, shell combs, all kinds of fancy articles repaired."

Rapp, William D., Philadelphia, Pa. (1831). Norristown, Pa. (1837).

Raulet, Samuel, Monmouth, Me. (1800).

Rea, Archelaus, Salem, Mass. (1789).

Read, Wm. H. J., Philadelphia, Pa. (1832). "Clock and Watch-maker. Everpointed Pencils, Spoons, . . . for sale."

Reed, Ezekiel, North Bridgewater (now Brockton), Mass. (Previous to 1800).

Reed, Simeon, Cummington, Mass. (about 1770).

Reed, Stephen, New York City (1802–32). "Store of Watches and Clocks; Jewelry and Silver Ware."

Reed, Zelotus (son of Simeon), Goshen, Mass. (about 1796).

Reed & Son, Isaac, Philadelphia, Pa. (1832). "Watch-makers and Importers. Manufacturers of Jewelry, etc."

Reeves, David S., Philadelphia, Pa. (1832).

Reiley, John, Philadelphia, Pa. (1785–95).

Rice, Joseph T., Albany, N. Y. (1813–31).

Rice, Phineas, Charlestown, Mass. (1830).

Rich, John, Bristol, Conn. (1820).

Richards, B & A., Bristol, Conn. (1820).

Richards & Co., Gilbert, Chester, Conn. (1832). "Manufacturers of Patent Clocks."

Richards & Morrell, New York City (1809–32).

Richardson, Francis, Philadelphia, Pa. (1736).

Richmond, Franklin, Providence, R. I. (1824–49).

Richmond, G. & A., Providence, R. I. (1810).

Richter, Joseph, Baltimore, Md. (1817).

Riggs, William H. C., Philadelphia, Pa. (1819).

Riley, John, Philadelphia, Pa. (1799).

Ritchie, George, Philadelphia, Pa. (1785–93).

Rittenhouse, David, Norristown, Pa. (1751–70), Philadelphia, Pa. (1770–77). Established his trade of clockmaking in Norristown, 1751. Moved to Philadelphia, 1770. Was also a famous astronomer, and made mathematical instruments. Was Treasurer of Pennsylvania, 1777–89; Professor of Astronomy in Pennsylvania University, 1779–82; Director of U. S. Mint at Philadelphia, 1792–95; President of American Philosophical Society, 1790–96.

Roath, R. W., Norwich, Conn. (1832). "Manufacturer of Ever Pointed Pencil Cases and Window Springs; Dealer in Watches. . . ."

Roberts & Co., E. (Sons of Gideon), Bristol, Conn. (1815–30).

Roberts, Gideon, Bristol, Conn. (1780–1804). Pioneer of Clockmaking in Bristol. "He made the columns and pinions on a small foot-lathe, cut

out the wheels with his jack-knife and hand-saw, and painted the dial-face on a piece of white paper which he afterward pasted upon the clock. When he had finished a few, he mounted his horse, with the clocks fastened about him, and started out to peddle them. Many clocks made by him are known to have done good service for many years. He made clocks in this rude way several years, and handed down the business to his sons. Very little is known as to the number of clocks made by this family or the length of time they continued in the business.

Roberts, Jacob, Easton, Pa. (1810–30).

Roberts, John, Philadelphia, Pa. (1799).

Rockwell, Samuel, Providence, R. I. (1750–54). Neither born nor deceased here, and had left before 1763. Four fine tall clocks have been located, with "Samuel Rockwell, Providence" across face.

Rode, William, Philadelphia, Pa. (1785–95).

Rogers, Isaac, Marshfield, Mass. (1800–28).

Rogers, James, New York City (1822–78).

Rogers, Samuel, Plymouth, Mass. (1700–1804).

Rogers, Wm., Boston, Mass. (1860).

Rogers, William, Hartford, Conn. (1837). "Dealer in watches, and timepieces of every description repaired in the best manner."

Rohr, John A., Philadelphia, Pa. (1811).

Root, S. Emerson, Bristol, Conn. (born, 1820; died, 1896). Orphaned when young, came to Bristol and lived with his uncle, Chauncey Ives. When a young man, engaged in clock business, at first with Edward Langdon, then alone. He was the inventor of the paper clock dial with brass sash.

Rose, Daniel, Reading, Pa. (1820–40).

Roth, N., Utica, N. Y. (1840).

Rouse.

Russell, George, Philadelphia, Pa. (1832). "Clock and Watch-maker; also Dealer in Watches, Jewelry and Silver Ware."

Russell, Major John, Deerfield, Mass. (1765). Son of John Russell, "set up his trade of watchmaker," 1765.

Rutter, Moses, Baltimore, Md. (1804).

Sadd, Thomas, East Windsor, Conn. (1750).

Sadtler, P. B., Baltimore, Md. (1804).

Samuels & Dunn, New York City (1844). Sold clocks with spurious labels (Chauncey Jerome).

Sandell, Edward, Baltimore, Md. (1817).

Sands, Stephen, New York City (1772–86).

Sanford, Eaton, Plymouth, Conn. (1760–76).

Sanford, Ransom, Plymouth, Conn. (1840). Made brass pinions and barrels for Seth Thomas clock movements.

Sanford, Samuel, Plymouth, Conn. (1845–77).

Sargeant, Jacob (brother of Joseph), Hartford, Conn. (about 1790–1838). One of the first jewelers and silversmiths in Hartford; also made clocks.

Sargeant, Joseph (brother of Jacob), Springfield, Mass. (1800).

Savoye, N., Boston, Mass. (1832).

Sawin & Dyer, Boston, Mass. (1800–20).

Sawin, John, Boston, Mass. (1823–63). Apprentice of Aaron Willard; in clockmaking business in Boston; fre-

quently employed by Simon Willard, Jr., & Son, to make clocks for them. "Manufacturer of all kinds of clocks for Church, Gallery, Bank, Ins. office, Factory, Watch-Clocks and common House Clocks, 33 Cornhill."

Sawin, John, Chelsea, Mass. (1847).

Sawyer, C. & H. S., Colebrook, Conn. (1849).

Saxton & Lukens, Philadelphia, Pa. (1828–40).

Sayre, John, New York City (1800).

Sayre & Richards, New York City (1805).

Schreiner, Charles W., Philadelphia, Pa. (1813).

Schriner, Martin, Lancaster, Pa. (1790–1830).

Schriner, M. & P., Lancaster, Pa. (1830–40).

Schroeter, Charles, Baltimore, Md. (1817).

Schuyler, P. C., New York City (1802). "Begs leave to inform his friends and the public in general that he has again commenced business at 48 John street, one door west of William street. From the knowledge he has of the above business he flatters himself he will give general satisfaction."

Searson, John, New York City (1757).

Sedgwick & Bishop, Waterbury, Conn. (1820).

Sedgwick & Botsford, Watertown, Conn. Wood clocks.

Seymour, Robert, Waterbury, Conn. (1814).

Seymour, Williams & Porter, Unionville (on Roaring Brook), Conn. (about 1835). Began making clocks about 1835, but a destructive fire in 1836 or 1837 seriously interrupted. The clock business seems never to have flourished in Unionville after the fire, though it was carried on in the screw factory after the abandonment of the screw business by Pierpont & Co.

Shaw, Seth W., Providence, Rhode Island (1856).

Shearman, Robert, Wilmington, Del. (1760–70).

Shearman, Robert, Philadelphia, Pa. (1799).

Shepherd & Boyd, Albany, N. Y. (1813).

Sherman, Robert, Philadelphia, Pa. (1799).

Shermer, John, Philadelphia, Pa. (1813).

Shields, Thomas, Philadelphia, Pa.

Shipman, Nathaniel, Norwich, Conn. (1789). Apprentice of Thomas Harland. Worker in gold and silver, and offered for sale handsome assortments of jewelry and time-keepers.

Shipman & Son, N., Norwich, Conn. (1879). Clockmakers and silversmiths.

Sibley, Asa, Conn. (?)

Sibley, Gibbs, Canandaigua, N. Y. (1788).

Sibley, S., Great Barrington, Mass. (1790).

Simonton, Gilbert, New York City (1820).

Sinnett, John, New York City (1774). He advertised clocks of all kinds and "Watches neat and plain, gold, silver, shagreen and metal. Some engraved and enamelled with devices new and elegant; also the first in this country of the small new-fashioned watches the circumference of a British shilling."

Smith, Aaron, Ipswich, Mass. (1825). "Smith's Clock Establishment, corner of the Bowery and Division St."

Smith, Edmund, New Haven, Conn. (1817). He advertises that he always has cheap and handsome clock cases on sale.

Smith, Capt. Elisha, Sanbornton, N. H.

Smith & Goodrich, Bristol, Conn. (1827–49).

Smith, Henry, Plymouth Hollow (now Thomaston), Conn. (1840).

Smith, Henry C., Waterbury, Conn. (1814).

Smith, James, Philadelphia, Pa. (1846). "Wholesale clock establishment No. 82 North Third street where watchmakers and merchants will find the largest assortment ever offered at prices exceedingly low. Year, month, 8 day and 30 hour and alarm."

Smith, Jesse, Concord, Mass. (about 1800). Apprentice of Levi Hutchins.

Smith, Jesse, Jr., Salem, Mass. (1837).

Smith, Luther, Keene, N. H. (about 1785–1840). In 1794 he made town clock for Keene.

Smith & Sill, Waterbury, Conn. (1831).

Smith, Stephen.

Snelling, Henry, Philadelphia, Pa.

Souers, Christopher, Philadelphia, Pa. (1724–   ). A very gifted man. Was author, printer, paper-maker, doctor, and farmer. In these callings he spelled his name Sower, but on his clocks Souers.

Southworth, Elijah, New York City (1793–1810).

Souza, Samuel, Philadelphia, Pa. (1819).

Spalding & Co., Providence, R. I. Makers of hall clocks.

Sparck, Peter, Philadelphia, Pa. (1797).

Spaulding, Edward, Providence, R. I. (1789–97).

Spence, John, Boston, Mass. (1823).

Spencer, Wooster & Co., Salem Bridge (now Naugatuck), Conn. (1828–37).

Sperry, Anson, Waterbury, Conn. (about 1810).

Sperry & Shaw, New York City (1844). Sold clocks with spurious labels (Chauncey Jerome).

Sprogell, John, Philadelphia, Pa. (1791).

Spruck, Peter, Philadelphia, Pa.

Spurch, Peter, Philadelphia, Pa. (1795–99).

Squire & Bros., New York City (1847).

Stanton, Job, New York City (1810).

Stanton, Wm., Providence, R. I. (1816).

Stanton, W. P. & H., Rochester, N. Y. (1838).

Staples, John I., Jr., New York City (1793).

Starr, Frederick, Rochester, N. Y. (1834). "Cabinet and Clock Factory."

Stebbins & Howe, New York City (1832). "Store of Watches, Jewelry, Silver Ware and Fancy Goods."

Stebbins, Lewis, Waterbury, Conn. (1811). "A singing master." Chauncey Jerome worked for him, fall and winter of 1811, making dials for old-fashioned long clocks.

Stein, Abraham, Philadelphia, Pa. (1799).

Stein, Daniel H., Norristown, Pa. (1837).

Stevenson, Howard & Davis, Boston, Mass. (1845).

Stever & Bryant, Burlington (village of Whigville), Conn. (1830).

Stewart, Arthur, New York City (1832).

Stickney, Moses P., Boston, Mass. (1823).

Stillas, John, Philadelphia, Pa. (1785–93).

Stillman, William, Burlington, Conn. (1789–95).

Stillson, David, Rochester, N. Y. (1834).

Stoddard & Kennedy, New York City (1794).

Stokel, John, New York City (1820–43).

Stollenwerck, P. M., New York City (1820 and earlier). In 1816 he advertises: "P. M. Stollenwerck's Mechanical Panorama. This ingenious piece of mechanism . . . presents on a scale of 340 square feet a view of a commercial and manufacturing City. . . . Admission 50 cents; children half

price. To see the mechanism, 25 cents additional. Mr. Stollenwerck, inventor and proprietor of the Mechanical Panorama, continues his profession of *Clock* and *Watch-maker*, at No. 157 Broadway; and also repairs all kinds of Mechanical, Mathematical and Musical Instruments."

Stollenwerck, P. M., Philadelphia, Pa. (1813).

Stow, D. F., New York City (1832). "Dealer in Clocks, Watches, Jewelry, etc."

Stow, Solomon, Southington, Conn. (1828–37). Came to Southington 1823 and began cabinet-making. In 1828 began clockmaking. In 1834 built dam and shop near depot. In 1837 entered employ of Seth Peck & Co., tinner's machines. "Manufacturer of Eli Terry's Patent Clocks."

Stowell, Abel, Worcester, Mass. (1790–1800). Abel Stowell carried on a very extensive manufacture of tower and church clocks. The town clock in the Old South Meeting-House, Worcester, was made by Abel Stowell in 1800.

Stowell, Abel, Boston, Mass. (1823–56).

Stowell, John, Boston, Mass. (1825–36).

Stowell, John, Medford, Mass. (1815–25).

Stowell, John J., Charlestown, Mass. (1831).

Stratton, Charles, Worcester, Mass. (1820).

Strech, Peter, Philadelphia, Pa. (1750–80).

Studley, David, Hanover, Mass. (1806–35). He learned the trade of John Bailey.

Studley, David F., North Bridgewater (now Brockton), Mass. (1834). He came from Hanover, Mass., in Sept., 1834, and made watches and jewelry, also

repaired all kinds of clocks. Later
became associated with his brother
Luther in the business, and afterwards sold out to Luther.

Studley, Luther (brother of David F.),
North Bridgewater (now Brockton),
Mass. (18–).

Sutton, Robert, New Haven, Conn.
(1825).

Swan, Benjamin, Haverhill, Mass., and
Augusta, Me. (1810–40).

Syberberg, Christian, New York City
(1755–75).

Syderman, Philip, Philadelphia, Pa. (1785–
94).

Taber & Co., S., Providence, R. I. (1849).

Taber, Elnathan, Roxbury, Mass. (1784–
1854). Native of New Bedford, of
Quaker parentage, came to Roxbury at
age of 16 or 19, served as apprentice
to Simon Willard, and afterwards engaged in clockmaking on his own
account. When Simon Willard retired, Taber bought most of his
tools and the good will of the business, his clocks being as good as
Simon Willard's. He made clocks for
Simon Willard, Jr., & Son (1838–54).

Taber, H. (son of Elnathan), Boston,
Mass. (1852–57).

Taber, S. M., Providence, R. I. (1824).
Maker of hall clocks.

Taber, Thomas (son of Elnathan), Boston,
Mass. (1854). Continued his father's
business.

Taf, John James, Philadelphia, Pa.
(1794).

Tappan, William B., Philadelphia, Pa.
(1819).

Tarbox, H. & D., New York City (1832).
" Importers of Watches, Clocks, Watch
and Clock-Makers' Tools and

Materials, and keep constantly on hand
a general assortment of Goods suitable for Country Watch and Clock-
Makers. Also manufacturers of
Watch Cases and Jewelry."

Taylor, Samuel, Philadelphia, Pa. (1799).

Taylor, Samuel, Worcester, Mass, (1855).

Tenny, William, Nine Corners, Dutchess
Co., N. Y. (1790).

Terry & Andrews, Bristol, Conn. (1735–
40).

Terry & Barnum, East Bridgeport, Conn.
(1855). They made preparations for
manufacturing, but apparently never
made any clocks. Instead, merged
their company and the Jerome Co.,
into one, thus causing the failure of
the latter in fall of 1855.

Terry Clock Co., Pittsfield, Mass. (1880).
It was through efforts of Geo. H. Bliss
in 1880 that the Terry Clock Co.
was organized, and that the three
brothers Terry were persuaded to
come to Pittsfield from Connecticut.
In 1885 C. E. Terry (grandson of Eli)
was superintendent and manager. In
1888 the business was reorganized
under title The Russell & Jones Clock
Co., and soon afterwards it was dis-
continued.

Terry, Downs & Co., Bristol, Conn. (1851–
57).

Terry, Eli, Plymouth, Conn. (1793–).
Learned clock-making and engraving
of Daniel Burnap in Hartford; also
received instruction from Thomas
Harland. In 1792 he made his
first tall wooden clock, which is now
owned by his descendants and is
still going. In 1792 or '93 he went
to Northbury (then a part of Watertown, now Plymouth), Conn., and began making hang-up clocks. His

first clocks were made by hand, but soon he began using water power. By 1800 he had some help but was able to make and sell only a few each year, at about $25 apiece (for movement and dial alone). In 1807 he sold to Heman Clark, an apprentice, and bought an old mill, with water-power, in the southeast part of Plymouth, now called Greystone. Seth Thomas and Silas Hoadley joined him, forming the firm Terry, Thomas and Hoadley. In 1810 Terry sold out to his partners and removed to Plymouth Hollow. Before this, he had made several different forms of shelf clock. Finally, in 1814, he devised what he called his "perfected wood clock," with the "pillar scroll top case." In construction it was radically different from all previous clocks, and it became popular at once. Seth Thomas paid $1000 for the right to manufacture it, and he and Terry each made about six thousand the first year. That same year Terry began to teach two of his sons, Eli, Jr., and Henry, the clock business. Although his fame and fortune were made with the improved wood shelf clock, he also made fine clocks with brass works and some tower clocks. He died at Terryville, 1852.

Terry, Eli, Jr., Plymouth Hollow (now Thomaston), Conn. (1814–24), Terryville, Conn. (1824–41). In 1814 he began working with his father. When twenty-five years old he built a shop of his own on the Pequabuck, and the village where he lived was called Terryville in his honor.

Terry, Eli, 3rd, Plymouth, Conn. (1862).

Terry, Henry (son of Eli 1st), Plymouth

Hollow (now Thomaston), Conn. (1814–30). He continued the business in his father's factory, but finally gave up clockmaking for the woolen business.

Terry, L. B., Albany, N. Y. (1831).

Terry, Samuel (brother of Eli), Bristol, Conn. (1820–35). Came to Bristol about 1825 and began making Jeromes' "Bronze Looking-Glass Clock." "Manufacturer of Patent Thirty Hour Wood Clocks with various Patterns of Fancy Cases, and Eight Day Church Steeple Clocks, also Brass Founder."

Terry, Silas Burnham (son of Eli), Plymouth Hollow (now Thomaston), Conn. (1823–76). Had a shop at junction of Pequabuck and Poland brooks in 1831. After 1852 was in employ of Wm. L. Gilbert at Winsted, and of Waterbury Clock Co. Then he and his sons organized the Terry Clock Co., and he continued at head of this firm till his death.

Terry, Theodore, Ansonia, Conn. (1860).

Terry, T., Boston, Mass. (1810–23).

Terry, Thomas, Boston, Mass. (1823).

Terry (Eli), Thomas (Seth) & Hoadley (Silas), Greystone (town of Plymouth), Conn. (1809). This association lasted but a year, when Terry sold out his interest. Thomas and Hoadley continued at Greystone; Terry removed to Plymouth Hollow.

Thibault & Brother, Philadelphia, Pa. (1832). "Manufacturers and Importers of . . . Watches. . . ."

Thomas & Hoadley, Greystone (town of Plymouth), Conn. (1810). In 1810 Seth Thomas and Silas Hoadley bought out the Terry factory and continued the manufacture of works for tall cases,

Thomas, Joseph, Philadelphia, Pa. (1830).

Thomas, Seth, Plymouth Hollow (now Thomaston), Conn. (1809–50). Worked for Eli Terry as a joiner. In 1809 formed partnership with Eli Terry and Silas Hoadley at Greystone. In 1810, after buying out Terry's interest, Thomas & Hoadley continued the manufacture of tall clocks. In 1812, Thomas sold to Hoadley and went to Plymouth Hollow. Began clockmaking on his own account and was successful, though he was not inventive. In 1853 incorporated the Seth Thomas Clock Company, which is still in business. He died in 1859. Soon after, that part of Plymouth was named Thomaston in his honor.

Thomas Co. (Seth), Thomaston (formerly Plymouth Hollow), Conn. (1853 to present time).

Thompson, William, Baltimore, Md. (1799).

Thomson, James, Pittsburgh, Pa. (1815).

Thornton, Joseph, Philadelphia, Pa. (1819). Clock- and watchmaker.

Thownsend, Charles, Philadelphia, Pa. (1819).

Thownsend, John, Jr., Philadelphia, Pa. (1819).

Tiebout, Alexander, New York City (1798).

Tinges, Charles, Baltimore, Md. (1799).

Tobias & Co., S. & I., New York City (1829).

Todd, Richard J., New York City (1832).

Tolford, Joshua, Kennebunk (also Portland), Me. (1815, before and after). Watch- and Clockmaker, offers for sale "rich jewelry." He moved to Portland, whence he came, after remaining in this town about a year.

Tolles, Nathan, Plymouth, Conn. (prior to 1836). Made parts of clocks.

Tompkins, George S., Providence, R. I. (1824). Made clocks, watches and silverware.

Torrey, Benjamin B., Hanover, Mass.

Tower, Reuben, Plymouth, and Hingham, Mass. (1813–20).

Townsend, Charles, Philadelphia, Pa. (1799–1811).

Townsend, Christopher, Newport, R. I. (1773).

Townsend, David, Philadelphia, Pa. (1789).

Townsend, Isaac, Boston, Mass. (1790).

Townsend, John, Jr., Philadelphia, Pa. (1813).

Troth, James, Pittsburgh, Pa. (1815).

Trott, Andrew C., Boston, Mass. (1800–10).

Tuller, William, New York City (1831).

Turell, Samuel, Boston, Mass. (1789).

Tuthill, Daniel M., Saxton's River, Vt. (1842). Both brass and wooden clocks. Brass works were purchased in Connecticut, wooden works made by him. He made all the cases, and put the finished product on the market.

Twiss, B. & H. (Benjamin, Ira, and Hiram), Meriden, Conn. (1820–32). "Benjamin & Hiram Twiss began manufacture of clocks in 1828." "Manufacturers of the Improved Clocks." Ira removed to Montreal, Canada, about 1829.

Union Mfg. Co., Bristol, Conn. Made brass clocks.

Upjohn, James (came to America in 1802). Was a member of the London Clockmakers' Company.

Upson, Merrimans & Co., Bristol, Conn. (1830).

Urick, Valentine, Reading, Pa. (1760).

Van Vleit, B. C., Poughkeepsie, N. Y. (1832). Watch and clockmaker and silversmith. "Dealer in Watches, Clocks, . . .; Repairer of Clocks and Watches; Manufacturer of Silver Spoons, etc."

Van Wagenen, John, Oxford, N. Y. (1843). "Fine Pieces, Brass and Wood Clocks of the best kind warranted to keep correct time, for sale lower than ever offered before, at the cheap store."

Veazie, Joseph, Providence, R. I. (1805).

Vinton, David, Providence, R. I. (1792).

Vogt, John, New York City (1758).

Voight, Henry, Philadelphia, Pa. (1775–93).

Voight, Sebastian, Philadelphia, Pa. (1775–99).

Voight, Thomas (son of Henry), Philadelphia, Pa. (1811–35).

Vuille, Alexander, Baltimore, Md. (1766).

Wadsworths & Turners, Litchfield, Conn. (1832). "Terry's Patent."

Wadsworth, Lounsbury & Turner, Litchfield, Conn. (1830). Made Terry's Patent clocks.

Wadsworths & Turners, Litchfield, Conn. (1800).

Wady, James, Newport, Rhode Island (1750–55).

Wales, Samuel H., Providence, R. I. (1849–56).

Walker, A., Brockport, N. Y. (1832).

Wall & Almy, New Bedford, Mass. (1820–23).

Walsh, ——, Forestville (town of Bristol), Conn. (about 1825).

Ward, Anthony, New York City (1724–50).

Ward, Anthony, Philadelphia, Pa.

Ward & Govett, Philadelphia, Pa. (1813).

Ward, Isaac, Philadelphia, Pa. (1813).

Ward, John & William L., Philadelphia, Pa. (1832). "Watches, Jewelry and Silver Ware."

Ward, Joseph, New York City (1735–60).

Ward, Lauren, Salem Bridge (now Naugatuck), Conn. (1832–40).

Ward, Lewis, Salem Bridge (now Naugatuck), Conn. (1829–40).

Ward, Macock, New Haven, Conn. (1800).

Ward, Nathan, Fryeburg, Me. (1801).

Ward, Richard, Salem Bridge (now Naugatuck), Conn. (1832–40).

Ward, Thomas, Baltimore, Md. (1817).

Ward, William, Salem Bridge (now Naugatuck), Conn. (1832–40).

Warner, Cuthbert, Baltimore, Md. (1799).

Warner, George J., New York City (1795, and later).

Warner, John, New York City (1790–1802).

Warner (George J.) & Reed, New York City (1802).

Warner (George J.) & Schuyler, New York City (1798).

Warrington, John, Philadelphia, Pa. (1811).

Waterbury Clock Co. (successor to Benedict & Burnham Co.). Included: Deacon Aaron Benedict, Mr. Burnham of New York, Noble Jerome (making movements), Edward Church (making cases), Arad W. Welton (1855).

Watson, J., Chelsea, Mass. (1847).

Watson, Lumas, Cincinnati, O. Ephraim Downs made clocks for him, 1816–21.

Weatherly, David, Philadelphia, Pa. (1813).

Weaver, N., Utica, N. Y. (1844).

Welch, Elisha N., Bristol, Conn. (1855–). In 1855 he bought the property and business of J. C. Brown.

In 1864 he organized The E. N. Welch Manufacturing Company.

Welch Mfg. Co., The E. N., Bristol, Conn. (1864). Organized by Elisha N. Welch. This is now the Sessions Clock Company.

Weldon, Oliver, Bristol, Conn. (1820).

Weller, Francis, Philadelphia, Pa.

Welton, Hiram & Heman, Plymouth, Conn. (1841–44). They bought the "upper shop" of Eli Terry, Jr., in Terryville, and used it for many years. They underwrote for some firm that failed; this caused their failure also, in 1845.

West, James L., Philadelphia, Pa. (1832). "Fillagree Worker; orders for Jewelry, Watches, Plate and Fancy Articles promptly attended to."

West, Thomas G., Philadelphia, Pa. (1819).

Weston, J., Boston, Mass. (1849–56).

Wetherell, Nathan, Philadelphia, Pa. (1830–40).

Wheaton, Caleb, Providence, R. I. (1784–1827).

Wheaton, Caleb, & Son, Providence, R. I. (1824).

Wheaton, Calvin, Providence, R. I. (1790).

Wheaton, Godfrey, Providence, R. I. (1824).

Whipple, Arnold, Providence, R. I. (1810).

Whitaker, George, Providence, R. I. (1805).

Whitaker, Gen. Josiah, Providence, R. I. Partner of Nehemiah Dodge.

Whitaker (Josiah) & Co., Providence, R. I. (1824).

Whitaker, Thomas, Providence, R. I. He and George Dana bought out Nehemiah Dodge.

White, Peregrine, Woodstock, Conn. (1774–   ). Made "tall clocks, with full moons and elaborate appurtenances." David Goodell of Pomfret made cases for his clocks.

White, Sebastian, Philadelphia, Pa. (1795).

Whitehead, John, Philadelphia, Pa. (1831).

Whiting, Riley, Winsted (town of Winchester), Conn. (1807–35). In 1807, with Samuel and Luther Hoadley, he started making clocks at Winsted. When Luther died and Samuel retired, Mr. Whiting continued business. He died in 1835. (See Lucius Clark.) "The machinery (of these wood clocks) was carried by a tin wheel on an upright iron shaft. The cog-wheels were of cherry, the pinion was of ivy, or calmia (mountain laurel), and the face of white-wood — all home products. These, with a little wire, a very little, steel, brass, tin and cordage made up the staples of material of the old one-day shelf clocks which they produced and scattered all over the United States and Canada."

Whiting, Samuel, Concord, Mass. (1808–17). In partnership with Nathaniel Munroe, 1808–17; worked for himself, 1817.

Whitman, Ezra, Bridgewater, Mass. (1790–1840).

Whittaker, William, New York City (1731–55).

Whittemore, J., Boston, Mass. (1856).

Wiggin, Henry, Jr., Newfield, N. H. (19th century). He made cases for John Kennard's clocks.

Wiggins, Thomas, & Co., Philadelphia, Pa. (1832).

Wilbur, Job B., Newport, R. I. (1815–49).

Wilcox, A., New Haven, Conn. (1827).

Wilcox, Cyprian, New Haven, Conn. (1827). Clock and watchmaker and silversmith.

Wilder, Ezra (son of Joshua), Hingham, Mass. (1800–70).

Wilder, Joshua, Hingham, Mass. (1780–1800).

Willard, Aaron, Roxbury, Mass. (1780–90), Boston, Mass. (1790–1823). Son of Benjamin and Sarah Willard. Born in Grafton, Mass., 1757. Probably learned clockmaking from one of his brothers. In 1780 opened a shop near Simon's in Roxbury. Was a better business man than his brothers. About 1790 moved to Washington St., Boston, and established a factory connected with his house. Employed twenty or thirty workmen. A little colony of clockmakers and the allied trades grew up here. Retired, 1823. Died, 1844.

Willard, Aaron, Jr., Boston, Mass. (1806–50). Son of Aaron and Catherine Willard. Born, 1783. Learned trade in his father's factory. For short time was in partnership with Spencer Nolen, as clock and sign painters. In 1823 took over his father's business. The lyre clock was originated by him. He closed out business and removed to Newton, 1850.

Willard, Alexander T., Ashburnham, Mass. (1796–1800), and Ashby, Mass. (1800–40). Brother of Philander, and third cousin of Simon Willard. (See Philander.)

Willard, Benjamin, Grafton, Lexington, and Roxbury, Mass. (1764–1803). Son of Benjamin and Sarah Willard. Was the first of this family to engage in clockmaking. Probably started about 1764. Removed to Lexington about 1768, and to Roxbury, 1771. Advertised in the Boston Gazette Feb. 22, 1773, " Musical clocks playing different tunes, a new tune every day in the week, and on Sunday a Psalm tune. These tunes perform every hour." In 1790 he was living in Worcester. In 1803 he went to Baltimore, Md., where he died the same year. His clocks are marked Grafton, Lexington, or Roxbury.

Willard, Benjamin F., Roxbury, Mass. Son of Simon, and Mary Willard. Born, 1803. Was skilled mechanic and inventor. Learned clockmaking from his father. Did not engage in business for himself, but worked for others and at times for his father. In last year of his life conducted jewelry and silversmith business in Boston under name Rich & Willard. Died in 1847.

Willard, Ephraim, Medford, Mass. (1777), Roxbury, Mass. (1798), Boston, Mass. (1801), and New York City (1805). Son of Benjamin and Sarah Willard. Born in Grafton, 1755. Though he appears to have been in clockmaking business over twenty years, clocks made by him are rare.

Willard, Henry, Boston, Mass. Son of Aaron and Mary (2nd wife) Willard. Born in 1802. Was apprentice of William Fisk, a noted cabinet maker. Made clock-cases for his father, Aaron Willard, his brother, Aaron Willard, Jr., William Cummens, Elnathan Taber, Simon Willard, Jr., and Son, but not for Simon Willard. In 1847 removed to Canton, Mass. In 1887 returned to Boston and died there same year.

Willard & Nolen, Boston, Mass. (1806–12). Dial makers.

Willard, Philander J., Ashburnham, Mass. (?–1825), Ashby, Mass. (1825–40). Brother of Alexander, and third cousin of Simon Willard. Made clocks in Ashburnham till 1825; then moved to Ashby and was associated with his brother in clock-making business. Both were ingenious and skilful, and did a large business, mostly on orders. Philander made a gravity clock, very curious, still in existence.

Willard, Simon, Roxbury, Mass. (1770?–1839). Son of Benjamin and Sarah Willard. Born in Grafton, Mass., 1753. Was the most famous of this clockmaking family. Apprenticed to an English clockmaker named Morris, also helped by his brother Benjamin. At age of 13, he made without assistance a tall clock far superior to those of his master. Probably started in business for himself in Grafton, but moved to Roxbury, 1780, and set up his shop at 2196 Washington St., where he lived until his retirement, 1839. In 1802 he brought out his Patent Timepiece, an instant success, later called the banjo clock. No improvement has since been made on the original design. He also made regulator clocks, gallery clocks and tower clocks. Among them are two clocks which he presented to Harvard College, the large clock in the Capitol at Washington, made at the age of 82, and that on the old State House, Boston. Simon Willard died in Boston, 1848. (After he retired from business, 1839, Elnathan Taber, his best apprentice, bought most of his tools and the good will of the business, and received permission to put the name Simon Willard on his dials. Simon Willard, Jr., took these clocks and sold them at his store in Boston. All clocks sold from there had name "Simon Willard, Boston" or "Simon Willard & Son, Boston." As early as 1780, his reputation was so high that other clockmakers put the name Willard on their clock-dials.)

Willard, Simon, Jr., Boston, Mass. (1828–70). Son of Simon and Mary Willard. At West Point, 1813–15. Resigned from army in 1816. Crockery-ware business in Roxbury, 1817–24. In his father's clockmaking shop, 1824–26. In New York learned chronometer and watch business from D. Eggert in eighteen months. Set up in business for himself in 1828 at No. 9 Congress St., Boston, and remained till 1870. Made the astronomical clock now in observatory of Harvard University. His astronomical regulator was standard time for all railroads in New England.

Willard, Zabdiel A., Boston, Mass. (1841–70). Son of Simon, Jr., and Eliza Willard. Born in 1826. Apprentice in father's store, 1841. Admitted as partner, 1850.

Williams, David, Newport, R. I. (1825).

Williams, Orton, Prestons & Co., Farmington, Conn. (1820). "Improved Clocks with Brass Bushings."

Williams, Stephen, Providence, R. I. (1799). In 1799 associated with Nehemiah Dodge. In 1800 doing business by himself.

Wills, Joseph, Philadelphia, Pa.

Wilmurt, John J., New York City (1793–98).

Wilmurt, Stephen M., New York City (1802).

Wilson, Hosea, Baltimore, Md. (1817).

Wingate, Frederick B., Augusta, Me. (1800).

Wingate, Paine, Newburyport, Mass., (1803), in Boston directory (1789), in Augusta, Me. directory (1811).

Winship, David, Litchfield, Conn. (1832). "Clock Case Maker and Dealer in Clocks."

Winslow, Ezra, Westborough, Mass. (1860). A brass-worker, he made and repaired brass clocks.

Winston, A. L. & W., Bristol, Conn. (1849). Makers of brass clocks.

Winterbottom, T., Philadelphia, Pa.

Wood, David, Newburyport, Mass. (about 1790–1824). Had a shop in 1792 in Market Square. In 1824 he advertised "new and second-hand clocks for sale." Many of his clocks are still running (1906).

Wood, John, Philadelphia, Pa. (1770–93). "Clocks, watches, gold and silver work made, mended and sold at the sign of the Dial, the corner of Front and Chestnut streets."

Wood, Josiah, New Bedford, Mass. (1800–10).

Woolson, Thomas, Jr., Amherst, N. H. (1805).

Wriggins, Thos., & Co., Philadelphia, Pa. (1831). "Watch and Jewelry Store, Manufacturers of Silver Plate, Spoons, etc."

Wright, Charles Cushing, New York City. After 1812 settled in Utica.

Wright, John, New York City (1712–35).

Wright, Samuel, Lancaster, N. H. (1808–). Did well here for some years.

Yeomans, Elijah, Hadley, Mass. (1771–83). Goldsmith and clockmaker.

Young, David, Hopkinton, N. H.

Young, Francis, Philadelphia, Pa.

Young, Stephen, New York City (1810–16).

Youngs, Ebenezer, Hebron, Conn. (1778).

Zahm, G. M., Lancaster, Pa. (1843).

LIST OF FORMER FOREIGN CLOCKMAKERS

(*From* BRITTEN)

THROUGHOUT the list C.C. stands for Clockmakers' Company, B.M. for British Museum, S.K.M. for South Kensington Museum, and h.m. for Hall Mark. On some of the early clocks and watches the name inscribed was that of the owner; but in 1777 an Act of Parliament required the name and place of abode of the maker to be engraved.

Aaron, Benjamin (1840–42).

Abbis, J. (1807).

Abbott, Philip, C.C. (1703).

Abbott, Peter, C.C. (1719).

Abbott, John, C.C. (1788); charged with making an agreement to go to St. Petersburg to work at clockmaking, and convicted at Hicks' Hall of the offence (1787–1800).

Abbott, Thos. (1820–22).

Abbott, Francis, Manchester; wrote a book on the management of public clocks, about 1828.

Abdy, William (1768–1817).

Abeling, William (1835–42).

Abraham, John (1820–23).

Abrahams, H. (1800–20).

Abrahams, Godfrey (1835–42).

Abrahams, Samuel (1840–42).

Abrahams, A. (1840–42).

Abrahams, Elijah (1840–47).

Absolon, —, London; (about 1770).

Acklam, John Philip (1816–1840).

Acklam, T. (1825–33).

Acton, Thos., C.C. (1677).

Acton, Chris.; bracket clock (about 1725).

Acton, Abraham, C.C. (1790).

Adams, John (1770–72).

Adams, C. and J. (1788).

Adams, Stephen, and Son (1788).

Adams, John (1790–94).

Adams, Hy. (about 1800).

Adams, Francis Bryant, master C.C. (1848; 1815–48).

Adams, F. B., and Son (1830–42).

Adamson, Humfry; maker of a clock for Whitehall Chapel (1682).

Addis, William, master (1764).

Addis, George (1786–94).

Addis, George Curson (1780–98).

Addison, Josh., Lancaster (1817).

Adeane, Henry, C.C. (1675).

Adeane, Henry, C.C. (1705).

Agar, Jno., York (1740–1756).

Agar, Jno., son of the foregoing (1765–90).

Airy, George Biddell, Astronomer Royal (1853–81).

Aitken, John, received in 1824 a prize (1800–26).

Albert, Isaac, C.C. (1731).

Alcock, Thomas; petitioner for incorporation of C.C. (1630).

Alder, J., London (about 1700).

Alderhead, Jno. (1780–94).

Alderman, Edwin, C.C. (1822).

Aldred, Leonard, C.C. (1671).

Aldridge, John, C.C. (1726).

Aldridge, James (1816–30).

Aldworth, Samuel, C.C. (1697).

Alexander, Robt., Edinburgh (1709).

Alexander, W. (1830–40).

Alexander, A., and Co. (1840).

Aley, Thomas (1840–42).

Alkins (Atkins?), London (about 1730).

Allam, Andrew, C.C. (1664).

Allam, Michael, London (1723).

Allam, Robt., London (1765).

Allam, William, Fleet St. (1770–80).

Allam and Stacy (1783).

Allan and Clements (1785–94).

Allan, John (1798–1800).

Allan and Caithness (1800–4).

Allaway, John, C.C. (1695).

Allcock, Jno., B.M. (1787).

Allen, Elias, C.C. died 1654.

Allen, John, C.C. (1653).

Allen, John, C.C. (1720).

Allen, John (1772–75).

Allen, George, C.C. (1776).

Allen, George (1817–42).

Allet, George, C.C. (1691).

Alling, Richard, C.C. (1722).

Alling, James (1842).

Allman, W., B.M. (1798).

Allsop, Joshua, Northamptonshire, C.C. (1689).

Allvey, Hy. (about 1795).

Almond, Ralph (1646–79).

Almond, John, C.C. (1671).

Almond, William, C.C. (1633).

Ambrose, Edward (1634).

Ambrose, David, C.C. (1669).

Ames, Richard (1653–82).

Ames, William, C.C. (1682).

Amyot, Peter, Norwich (about 1660).

Amyot and Bennett; in 1793 they issued a little book by J. Bennett on the management of a watch.

Amyott, Thos., London; watches, h.m., 1751–71; one Nelthropp collection, about 1770.

Andrew, J., Ratcliff Cross (1820).

Anderson, Richard, Lancaster (1767).

Andrews, John (1688–1710).

Andrews, Thomas, C.C. (1705).

Andrews, Robert, C.C. (1709).

Andrews, James, C.C. (1719).

Andrews, William, C.C. (1719).

Andrews, Abraham (1759).

Andrews, Rich. (1775).

Andrews, Eliza (1790–1800).

Angel, Richard (1484).

Anness, William, C.C. (1802).

Annis, Jno. (1810–18).

Ansell, Hy. (1838).

Anthony, ——; clockmaker to Henry VIII (1529).

Antis, Jno. (1805).

Antram, Joshua (about 1700).

Antt, G. (1769–88).

Apelyne, Francis, C.C. (1687).

Appleby, Edward, C.C. (1677).

Appleby, Joshua (1719–46).

Applegarth, Thomas, C.C. (1674).

Appleton, Henry (1840–42).

Archambo, Jno. (1720–45).

Archer, Henry (1630–49).

Archer, John, C.C. (1660).

Archer, Edward, C.C. (1711).

Archer, Samuel.

Archer, Sam. Wm. (1805–12).

Archer, Thomas (1814–20).

Argand, L'Aîné, Geneva (about 1740).

Ariel, John (1822–39).

Aris, Jno., and Co. (1794).

Armitage and Co. (1798).

Armstrong, John, C.C. (1724).

Arnold, Thomas, C.C. (1703).

Arnold, Hy. (1769–88).

Arnold, John (1780).

Arnold and Son (1798).

Arnold, John Roger (1816–30).

Arnold, John R., and Dent (1830–40).

Arnold, John R. (1842).

Arnott, Richard (1810–25).

Arthanel, Aron Louis (about 1640).
Arthur, William, C.C. (1676).
Ascough, see Ayscough.
Ash, ——, subscribed £2 for incorporation of C.C. (1630).
Ash, Ralph, C.C. (1648).
Ashbourne, Leonard (1731).
Ashley, J. P. (1800).
Ashley and Mansell (1825–35).
Ashley, Edward (1842).
Ashurst, William, C.C. (1699).
Ashwell, Nicholas, C.C. (1649).
Aske, Henry (1676–96).
Askell, Elizabeth (1734).
Aspinwall, Josiah, C.C. (1675).
Asselin (about 1700).
Atchison, Robert, C.C. (1760).
Atkins, Francis, C.C. (1759).
Atkins, George, C.C. (1809).
Atkins, George, and Son (1840–42).
Atkins, Robert (1769).
Atkins, Robert (1770–88).
Atkins, Samuel (1753–56).
Atkins, Samuel Elliott, master in 1882 (1807–98).
Atkins, Samuel, and Son (1759–63).
Atkins, William (1835–42).
Atkins, W. (1835).
Atis, Leonard, London (about 1660).
Atkinson, James, C.C. 1667, assistant 1697.
Atkinson, Lancaster; Thos. (1767); Richard (1785); Wm. (1817).
Atkinson, Thos. (1814–17).
Attwell, Thos. (about 1750).
Attwell, Robt. (1810–18).
Attwell, Wm. (1815–25).
Atwood, George (1820).
Atwood, Richard (1800–10).
Auber, Daniel (1750).
Aubert and Klaftenberger (1835–42).
Auld, William, Edinburgh (1790–1818).
Ault, Thomas (1820–25).
Austen, John (1711–25).

Austin and Co. (1820).
Austin, John (1830–40).
Aveline, Daniel, died 1770, when warden C.C. (1760–70).
Avenall, a family well known as clockmakers in Hampshire (1640–1810).
Avenall, Ralph (about 1640).
Avenell, Thomas, C.C. (1705).
Avery, Amos (1774).
Avery, Philip (1790–94).
Ayeres, Richard, C.C. (1680).
Aylward, Jno. (about 1690).
Aynsworth, J., Westminster (1645–80).
Ayres, Thos. (1800–30).
Ayres and Bennett (1815–20).
Ayscough, Ralph (1766–75).

Bachoffner, Andrew (1775).
Backhouse, Jas., Lancaster, (1726).
Backquett, Davyd, C.C. (1632).
Bacon, John, C.C. (1639).
Bacon, Charles, C.C. (1719).
Bacott, Peter, London (1700).
Baddeley, Phineas, C.C. (1662).
Badger, John, C.C. (1720).
Badollet, J. J., Geneva, (1770).
Badollet, John (1842).
Baffert (about 1780).
Baggs, Samuel (1820–35).
Bagley, Thomas, C.C. (1664).
Bagnall, W. H. (1835–40).
Bagnell, William, C.C. (1719).
Bagot, Jno., Lancaster (1823).
Bagshaw, William, C.C. (1722).
Bagwell, Richard (1790–94).
Bailey, Jeffery, admitted C.C. (1648), master (1674).
Bailey, Jeremiah, C.C. (1724).
Bailey and Upjohn (1798).
Bailey, Chas., London (about 1805).
Bailey, W. (1835).
Bain, Alexander, Edinburgh; inventor of electric clocks (1838–58).

Baird, John (1770–83).

Baird, W. and J. (1810–30).

Baker, Richard, C.C. (1685).

Baker, Henry (about 1700).

Baker, Richard, C.C. (1726).

Baker, Francis (1738).

Baker, John, hon. freeman, C.C. (1781); (1770–84).

Baker, Hy., hon. freeman, C.C. (1781).

Baker, Thos. (1833).

Baker, W. (1835–42).

Baker, Edward (1840–42).

Baldwin, T. (1830–35).

Baldwin, Thomas (1840–42).

Baldwyn, Thomas, C.C. (1706).

Bale, Thomas, C.C. (1724).

Bale, Robert Brittel (1813).

Balestree, J. (1811).

Baley, Thos., C.C. (1786).

Ball, Edwd. (1794).

Ballantyne, Wm. (1820–42).

Balliston, Thos. (1842).

Baltazar, Chas., Paris (about 1710).

Banbury, John, C.C. (1685).

Banfield, Jno. (1814–17).

Banger, Edward (1695–1720).

Banks, William, C.C. (1698).

Banks, J. (1830–35).

Banister, Henry (1852).

Banister, Joseph (1836).

Bannister, Anthony, C.C. (1715).

Bannister, Thomas and James (1825).

Bannister, James (1810–42).

Banting, William, C.C. (1646).

Barachin, Stephen (French), C.C. (1687).

Barber, Jonas, C.C. (1682).

Barber, Wm. (1785–94).

Barber, Benjamin (1788–94).

Barber, Josh. (1795–1817).

Barber, Thos. (1810–17).

Barber, Abraham (1835–40).

Barbot, Paul (1768–69).

Barclay, Samuel (1722).

Barclay, Hugh, Edinburgh (1727).

Barclay, James (1820–42).

Barcole, John, C.C. (1648).

Bareham, Samuel (1842).

Baril, Lewis (1754–59).

Baril, Bercher (1763–72).

Barin, John, livery, C.C. (1776).

Barjon, John, C.C. (1685).

Barked, Edward (1820).

Barker, William, C.C. (1632).

Barker, Benj. (1788).

Barker, James (1840–42).

"Barkley and Colley, Graham's Successors" (about 1765).

Barlow, Steward, C.C. (1677).

Barlow (Booth), Edward (1636–1716).

Barlow, J. H. and Co. (1812–20).

Barnard, Thos. (1783–1823).

Barnard and Savory (1786–99).

Barnard and Kidder (1809–12).

Barnard, Jno. (1817).

Barnard, Franz (1840–42).

Barnes, Jno. (1794).

Barnett, John, C.C. (1682).

Barnett, John, Lothbury (1686–93).

Barnett, G. (1800).

Barnett, J. (about 1790).

Barnett, J. (1810–15).

Barnett, Montague (1842).

Barns and Co. (1800).

Barnsdale, John, a well known clockmaker (1840).

Barr, Thos., Lewes (about 1700.)

Barratt, P. (1812–30).

Barraud, Hy., C.C. (1636).

Barraud, Francis and Paul Jno. (1789–94).

Barraud, Paul Philip, master C.C. (1810, 1811); (1798–1813).

Barraud, Fredk. Joseph, C.C. (1813).

Barraud and Sons (1838).

Barraud and Lund (1838–42).

Barrett, Robert, C.C. (1687).

Barrett, Henry, C.C. (1692).

Barrett, Samuel, C.C. (1701).

Barrett, Thomas, C.C. (1702).

Barrett, Joseph, clock-watch (about 1760).

Barrett, William (1783).

Barrett, Henry William (1815–42).

Barrett, John (1820).

Barrister, Jas. (1815–17).

Barrow, John, C.C. (1681), master (1714).

Barrow, Samuel, C.C. (1696–1720).

Barrow, James, see Brown, Andrew.

Barrow, William, C.C. (1709).

Barrow, Wm., Lancashire; left London soon after 1746 (Ludlam).

Barry, Walter (1788–94).

Bartholomew, J., C.C. (1675).

Barton, Samuel, C.C. (1641).

Barton, Thomas (1750–78); Earnshaw challenged him to a contest of work in 1776.

Barton, John (1780–83).

Barton, James (1819–23).

Barton, Thos. (1799–1823); "eminently skilled."

Bartram, Simon, petitioner for incorporation of C.C., and one of the first assistants; master (1646).

Bartram, William, C.C. (1684).

Bartram and Austin, B.M. (1808).

Barugh, William, C.C. (1715).

Barwick, H. and B. (1794–96).

Barwick, A. (1788–93).

Barwise, John (1820–42).

Barwise and Sons (1819–23).

Baseley, Thomas, C.C. (1683).

Basil, John (1768).

Basire, John, livery C.C. (1760).

Bass, George, C.C. (1722).

Bassett, Chas. (1788–93).

Bateman, H., Dublin (1802–5).

Bateman, Hy. (1780–85).

Bateman, P. and A. (1798–1818).

Bateman, Andrew (1804–20).

Bateman, Teresa (1820–30).

Bateman, Wm. (1828–32).

Bates, Thomas, C.C. (1684).

Bates, Joseph, C.C. (1687).

Bates, Ed., London; a good workman (1780–90).

Bath, Thomas (1740).

Batten, John, C.C. (1668).

Batterson, Robert, C.C. (1693).

Batterson, Henry, C.C. (1701).

Battin, Thomas (1658).

Batty, Edwd., Lancaster (1826).

Baudit, Peter (1790–94).

Baufay, B., and Son (1790–94).

Baugham, John (about 1745).

Baumgart, Charles (1840–42).

Bawdyson, Allaine, clockmaker to Edward VI. (1550).

Baxter, Charles, C.C. (1680).

Baxter, Pointer, London (1772).

Baxter, Thos. (Grimshaw & Baxter), died 1897.

Bayes, Benjamin, C.C. (1675).

Bayford, George, Upper Shadwell.

Bayle, Richard, C.C. (1660).

Bayle, Thomas, C.C. (1653).

Bayley, William, C.C. (1653).

Bayley, John (1768–75).

Bayley, Thomas, livery C.C. (1786).

Bayley and Upjohn (1794).

Bayley, Barnard, and Son (1800–5).

Bayley, Richard (1807).

Bayly, John, C.C. (1700).

Bayre, James, C.C. (1692).

Bayse, Thomas, C.C. (1695).

Bazeley, Nathaniel, C.C. (1694).

Bazin, Paris (about 1700).

Beach, Thomas (1765–70).

Beal, Martin (1842).

Beale, Jas. (1820–25).

Beard, Wm. (1812–17).

Beasley, John, C.C. (1719).

Beaton, Andrew (1835).

Beaton and Campbell (1840).

Beauchamp, R. (1819–23).

Beaumont, —; said to have made a clock at Caen in 1314.

Beauvais, Simon, C.C. (1690); a celebrated maker (1690–1730).

Beavin, Hugh (1800–30).

Beck, Richard, C.C. (1653).

Beck, Nicholas, C.C. (1669).

Beck, Joseph, C.C. (1701).

Beck, Christopher, livery C.C. (1787); (1780–94).

Beck, James (1818–23).

Becke, John, C.C. (1681).

Beckett, Jno. (1796–1803).

Beckman, John, C.C. (1695).

Beckman, Daniel, C.C. (1726).

Beckwith, Wm. (1794).

Bedford, Helkiah, C.C. (1667); (1660–80).

Beeg, Christiana, C.C. (1698).

Bell, Joseph, C.C. (1691).

Bell, Benjamin, C.C. (1660), master (1682).

Bell, John, C.C. (1719).

Bell, Joseph (1759).

Bell, Wm. (1812–18).

Bell, John, musical clock maker (1835–40).

Bellamy, Adey (1779–85).

Bellard, John, C.C. (1674).

Bellefontaine, A. (1835).

Belliard, Chas. (1769–94).

Bellinger, John, C.C. (1725).

Bellinghurst, Henry, liveryman C.C. (1776); (1765–77).

Bellis, Jas. (1769–88).

Belsey, John (1835).

Benfey, B., and Son (1794).

Benford, John (1832–38).

Benjamin, A. (1835).

Benjamin, Joel (1820–35); J. Benjamin and Co. (1840).

Benjamin, M. (1840–42).

Benn, Anthony, died when master C.C. (1763).

Benn, Robert, C.C. (1716).

Bennett, Mansell, C.C. (1685–99); S.K.M. (about 1695).

Bennett, John, C.C. (1678).

Bennett, William, C.C. (1692).

Bennett, John, C.C. (1712).

Bennett, Richard, C.C. (1715).

Bennett, Samuel, C.C. (1716).

Bennett, Thomas, C.C. (1720).

Bennett, William, C.C. (1729).

Bennett, R. (1817).

Bennett, Joseph (1835–38).

Bennett, Wing, and Co. (1840).

Bennett, E. (1840).

Bennett, John (1804–95).

Benoit, A. H. (1804–95).

Benson, Robt., auditor Watch and Clockmaker's Pension Society (1820).

Bentley, John (1823).

Bentley and Beck (1815).

Beraud, Henry, Sedan (1565).

Beraud, Jas. (1632).

Berg, F. L., Augsburg (1719).

Bergstien, Lulam (1842).

Berguer, John (1810–20).

Berguer, Frederick (1818–20).

Berguer, Franz (1817).

Berguer, Charles (1825).

Berkenhead, John (1783–94).

Berman and Co. (1830–35).

Berman, J., and Co. (1830–35).

Berquez, Francis (1822).

Berrand. See Berraud.

Berridge, Jno.; clock with compensated pendulum in 1738.

Berridge, Wm. (1780–94).

Berridge, Robert (1790–95).

Berridge, William (1800–25).

Berrington, Uriah, C.C. (1684).

Berry, John, C.C. 1688; master 1723; 1688–1730.

Berry, Samuel, CC. (1705).

Berry, Francis, Hitchin (about 1700).

Berry, John, C.C. (1728).

Berry, Frederick (1842).

Bertram, William, died (1732) when master C.C.

Bertrand, Robert.

Besse, Jeremy (1840–42).

Best, Thos. (1770–1794).

Best, Robert, S.K.M., hallmark 1769; (1765–88).

Best, T., B.M. (1780).

Best, Robert (formerly foreman to Brockbank) (1790–1820). He attested the value of Earnshaw's improvements in 1804.

Best, Richard (1835–42).

Besturck, Henry, C.C. (1686).

Bezar, Stephen, C.C. (1648).

Bibley, Jno. (1790–94).

Bickerton, Benjamin (1795–1810).

Bickerton, T. W. (1816–20).

Bickley, Thomas (1790–94).

Bicknell, Francis, C.C. (1665).

Bicknell, Joseph, and Co. (1807–13).

Biddle, Joseph, C.C. (1684).

Bidlake, Jas. (1765–94).

Bidlake, James (1798–1804); livery C.C. (1816).

Bidlake, Thomas (1804–18); livery C.C. (1818).

Bidlake, James, and Son (1820–40).

Bidles, Thomas, London (about 1790).

Bidley, Wm. (1840–42).

Biggs, Roger (1800).

Bilbee, London (about 1710).

Bilbie, Edwd. (about 1700). The Bilbies were a well known Somerset family of clockmakers.

Bille, John, C.C. (1687).

Billing, H. C. (1835).

Billinghurst, Henry, livery C.C. (1766); (1760–71).

Billop, William, C.C. (1688).

Bindley, William (1842).

Bingham, William (1842).

Binley, J. W. (1790).

Binns, George (1832–38).

Birch, Thomas, C.C. (1682).

Birch, William (about 1840).

Birchall, Wm. (1834–42).

Bird, Michael, C.C. (1682).

Bird, Luke, C.C. (1683).

Bird, John (1765).

Bird and Branstor (1775).

Bird, Jacob (1783).

Bird, John, and Son (1822–25).

Bird, John (1840–42).

Birdwhistell, Francis, C.C. (1687).

Birdwhistell, Isaac, C.C. (1692); (1692–1705).

Birdwhistell, Thomas, C.C. (1693).

Birdwhistell, John, C.C. (1718).

Birkhead, Nicholas (1693).

Bishop, Samuel, hon. freeman of C.C. (1781).

Bishop, James Griffin (1816–24).

Bishop, William (1830).

Bishridger, William (1700).

Bisse. See Bysse.

Bissett, Jas. (1815–20).

Bittleston, John, hon. freeman C.C. (1781).

Bittner, William (1840–42).

Blackborow, James, died (1746), when warden C.C.; (1734–46).

Blackburn, William, livery C.C. (1786).

Blackburn, Robt., Lancaster (1817).

Blackie, George, died 1855.

Blackwell, J. (1820).

Blake, Wm. (1789–90).

Blake, Chas. (1813).

Blanchard, Robt. (1675).

Blanchard, Charles, London (about 1760).

Bland, Jas. (1816–23).

Blay, William (1825).

Bliss, Ambrose, C.C. (1653).

Blissett, Isaac (1823).

Blog, — (1825).

Bloud, Ch., à Dieppe (1660).

Blundell, Richard; threatened with prosecution by C.C. for exercising the art (1682).

Blundell, William, C.C. (1715).

Blundell, Henry.

Blundy, Joseph (1790).

Boak, Samuel (1692).

Bock, Johann, Frankfort; clock by him, Vienna treasury, about 1630.

Bockett, Richd., London (1712).

Bodenham, Edward, C.C. (1719).

Bodily, Elizabeth, C.C. (1692).

Bodily, N. (1823).

Bone, Wm., Essex (about 1790).

Boney, Caleb, a well-known Cornish clock-maker (1827).

Bonner, Charles, C.C. (1659).

Bonner, Charles, C.C. (1704).

Bonner, Thos. (1790–94).

Boone, Edward, C.C. (1691).

Boot, Jno. (about 1735).

Booth, Jas. (1788–92).

Booth, R. (1812–17).

Bor, J., Paris; maker of a fine clock (about 1590).

Bordier, Frères, Geneva (1820–30).

Borellas, J. (1840).

Borelli, J. (1790–95).

Borrel, A. P., Paris (1818–87).

Borrell, Henry (1798–1840).

Borrell, Maximilian, J. (1830–42).

Borret, P. (1805–16).

Borrett, M. M., London (about 1790).

Bosley, Chas. (1750–66); livery C.C.

Bosley, Charles, livery C.C. (1766).

Boucher, W. (1820).

Boucheret, Jacob, C.C. (1728).

Boudry, Gustavus (1826–42).

Boufler. See De Boufler.

Bouguet. See Bouquet.

Boult, Joseph, C.C. (1709).

Boult, Michael (1738).

Boulter, Samuel (1840–42).

Bouquet, Solomon, C.C. (1650); a celebrated maker (1650–70).

Bourchier, W. (1835).

Bourelier, John Francis (1769–83).

Bouillard, Paul (1775).

Bourne, Aaron (1769).

Boursault, Helie, Chatellerault (about 1680).

Bouteville and Norton (1810–19).

Bouteville, Wm. Hy. (1823).

Bouts, David, died 1883.

Bowen, Francis, C.C. (1654).

Bowen, John, C.C. (1709).

Bowen, Thomas, livery C.C. (1811).

Bowen, John (1812–42).

Bower, Jno., London (about 1690).

Bowley, Devereux, a well-known maker (1696–1773); master C.C. (1759).

Bownes, Geo., Lancaster (1820).

Bowrd (Bowra ?) John (1820–23).

Bowtell, Samuel, C.C. (1681).

Bowtell, William, C.C. (1703).

Bowyer, Wm., a good maker (1623–42).

Bowyer, Jno., possibly successor to Wm. See Bowen, F., and Bower.

Box, John (1775–83).

Box, William B., died (1892).

Boyce, Jas., London (1720).

Boyer, T., London (about 1690).

Boyle, William (1840–42).

Bracebridge and Pearce (1800).

Bracebridge, Edward (Bracebridge and Sons, 1816–18).

Bracebridge, J. and E. C. (1820–42).

Bracebridge, James, treasurer Watch and Clockmakers' Benevolent Institution; died (1892).

Brackenrig, Robert, Edinburgh (1770).
Brackley, George, C.C. (1677).
Bradford, Thomas, C.C. (1680).
Bradford, Thomas, C.C. (1692).
Bradford, Thomas, C.C. (1710).
Bradford, Hy. (1820).
Bradin, Caspar, C.C. (1715).
Bradl, Anthony, Augsburg (1680).
Bradley, Henry, C.C. (1681).
Bradley, Langley, C.C. (1694); master (1726).
Bradley, Benjamin, C.C. (1728).
Bradley, L. and B. (1734).
Bradley, John H. (1842).
Bradshaw, Richard, C.C. (1725).
Bradshaw, John, C.C. (1731).
Bradshaw and Ryley, Coventry (1760).
Brafield, William, C.C. (1678); fined 5s. by C.C. in 1688.
Braithwaite, Geo. (1738).
Braithwaite and Jones (about 1800).
Bramble, Joshua (1804–35).
Bramble, Wm. and Edwd. (1840).
Bramble, Eliza (1842).
Brambley, Joseph, in 1797 founder and citizen.
Brand, Alexander, Edinburgh (1727).
Brandon, Benjamin, C.C. (1689).
Brandreth, Joseph, C.C. (1718).
Branster and Bird (1775).
Brant, Richard, C.C. (1700).
Brasbridge, Joseph (1794).
Brasbridge and Son (1825).
Bray, Robert, C.C. (1728).
Bray, Thomas (1798–1825).
Bray, Wm. (1840).
Brayfield, William, C.C. (1712).
Brayfield, John, C.C. (1716).
Brayley, Joseph (about 1810).
Breakspear and Co. (1807).
Breese, Jas. (1842).
Brett, Jas. (about 1695).
Brett, Thos., London (about 1730).

Brewer, John, C.C. (1677).
Brewer, Richd., Lancaster (1783).
Brewer, J. (1810–15).
Brewer, W. (1825).
Breynton, Vaughan, C.C. (1693).
Brickle, William (1842).
Bridge, Thos., London (1720).
Bridgden, Henry, C.C. (1682).
Bridgeman, Edwd., C.C. (1662).
Bridger, Samuel, C.C. (1703).
Bridges, Henry (about 1740).
Bright, J. (1790–94).
Bright, Richard (1815–26).
Brimble and Rouckliffe, Bridgewater (1770).
Brind, Walter (1783–88).
Brinkman, George (1815–40).
Brinkman and Gollin (1842).
Briscoe, Stafford (1738–59).
Briscoe and Morrison (1768).
Bristow, Wm. G. (1820–35).
Brittayne, Stephen, C.C. (1692).
Britton, Stephen, C.C. (1728).
Britton, Sandys (1835).
Broad, Thomas, C.C. (1682).
Broad, R. (1820).
Broad, Wm. (1804–30).
Broadhead, Benjamin, C.C. (1709).
Broadley, Jas. (1772).
Broadwater, Hugh, C.C. (1692).
Brock, John, died 1893.
Brockbank, John, livery (1777).
Brockbank, John and Myles, C.C. (1776).
Brockbank and Grove (1812–15).
Brockbank and Atkins (1815–35).
Brockbank, Atkins, and Son (1840–42).
Brockhurst, Thos., Coventry (about 1720).
Brocot, Achille, Paris; a celebrated clock-maker (1817–1878).
Brogden, James, liveryman C.C. (1765–94).
Brogden and Marriott (1770–1804).

Brogden, James (1820-28).

Brogden and Garland (1830).

Bronson, Jno., London (1760-80).

Brook, Edmund, C.C. (1709).

Brook, Richard, and Son (1795-1810).

Brooke, John, C.C. (1632).

Brooke, George, C.C. (1681).

Brooke, William (1783-94).

Brooker, Richard, C.C. (1694).

Brookes, Edward, C.C. (1690).

Brooks, John, liveryman C.C. (1786-88).

Brooks, John (1794-1813).

Brooks, W. (1825).

Broome, Thomas, C.C. (1652).

Broomhall, Chas. (1794).

Bross, John (1820-35).

Brown, James (Croydon), C.C. (1687).

Brown, Jno., Edinburgh (1720).

Brown, Philip, C.C. (1688).

Brown, Thomas, C.C. (1703).

Brown, Jas., liveryman C.C.; master (1770).

Brown, Thos., Chester; Goldsmiths' Company (1773).

Brown, Nathaniel, liveryman C.C. (1776).

Brown, John (1775-83).

Brown, John (1769-83).

Brown, John Wm. (1769-83).

Brown, Thos., liveryman C.C. (1776).

Brown, John (1790-94).

Brown, —— B.M. (1798).

Brown, J. (1780-1810).

Brown, Thos. (1788-1800).

Brown, Wm. (1800-10).

Brown, John (1783-1810).

Brown, Geo. (1820).

Brown, James (1810-42).

Brown, James (1842).

Brown, Roger (1842).

Brown, Edwd.; an accomplished horologist, head of the house of Breguet, died at Paris, 1895; aged 66.

Browne, Matthew, C.C. (1633).

Browne, John, C.C. (1652); master (1681).

Browne, Richard, C.C. (1675).

Brownlie, Alexander, Edinburgh (1710-25).

Bruce, James, C.C. (1721).

Bruce, George, London (about 1740).

Brugercia, C. (1820).

Brugger, John (1830).

Brugger, Beck, and Co. (1840-42).

Brugger, L. A. (1840-42).

Brumwell (about 1760).

Brunette, Samuel (1825).

Brunion, Henry (1775).

Brunner, Gaspard, clock at Berne (1557).

Brunsley, William (about 1675).

Bryan, Richard, C.C. (1696).

Bryan, Henry (1768).

Bryan, Jno. (1790-94).

Bryan, Saml. (1790-94).

Bryant, and Son (1781).

Bryant, John, Hertford, maker of good clocks (1790-1829).

Bryer, John, died 1894.

Bryson, Alexander, Edinburgh (1830-60).

Bryson, Jno., Dalkeith (1842).

Buchan, H. (1840-42).

Buck, Edward, C.C. (1632).

Buckenhill, Edward, C.C. (1687).

Bucket (Bouquet?) subscribed to incorporation of C.C. (1630).

Buckingham, Joshua, Black-moor's Head and Dial, Minories (1690-1725).

Buckingham, Joseph, Junior (1740-60).

Bucklie, David (1780-94); livery C.C. (1787).

Buckman, John (German), C.C. (1692).

Bucknell, W. (1810).

Bucknell, Wm. (1816-23).

Buckner, Richard, C.C. (1701).

Bucknor, Philip, C.C. (1667).

Bucksher, J., 37 (1817).

Bucquet, Dan. (1812-20).

Bukenhill, John, C.C. (1672).

Bulet, D., Geneva (about 1750).

Bull, Rainulph, keeper of the " great clock in His Majesty's Palace of Westminster," (1617).

Bull, Edmd. (1610).

Bull, John, subscribed to incorporation of C.C. (1630).

Bull, John, C.C. (1637).

Bull, Jas. (1813–18).

Bullby, John, C.C. (1632).

Bullman, Thos. (about 1690).

Bullock, Jas. (1790–94).

Bullock, Widcombe, Bath; Zephaniah (about 1740); Thos., son of Z. (1765–95); Wm., son of Thos., died 1846, succeeded by his nephew Wm. Vokes, who died 1870.

Bult, James, and Co. (1815–25).

Bunce, Matthew, C.C. (1698).

Burchett, John, C.C. (1731).

Burckhardt, J. C. (1816).

Burdon, Francis (1816).

Burgar, John W. (1842).

Burges, Jno., London (about 1720).

Burgess, — (1774).

Burgi, J. (De Burgi or Burguis), Prague, born 1552, died 1632. In 1602 was appointed clockmaker to Rudolph II.

Burgis, Thomas (1654).

Burgis, John, London (1680).

Burgis, Elais, C.C. (1681).

Burgis, Charles Edward (1685).

Burgis, — (about 1720).

Burgis, George, London (1720–40).

Burleigh, Ninyan, C.C. (1692).

Burnct, Thomas (1700).

Burnett, Richard, C.C. (1705).

Burnett, Philip, C.C. (1715).

Burnett, Jno. (1822).

Burns, James (1804–42).

Burpull, John (1750).

Burrill, Boys Err (1805–20).

Burrows, James (1820–25).

Burrows, E. (1835–42).

Burton, John, livery C.C. (1776).

Burton, Jas. (1806–20).

Burwash, William (1790).

Burwash, Thomas (1825).

Buschman, Hans, Augsburg; astronomical clock by him about 1600.

Buschman, John Baptist, C.C. (1725).

Bush, James, admitted C.C. (1729).

Bush, James (1804–42).

Bush, James (1835).

Bushell, Edward, London (1694–1700).

Bushell, Samuel, London (1697–1710).

Bushman, John Baptist, livery C.C. (1786).

Bushnells, Thos. (1692).

Butler, John, C.C. (1724).

Butter, Joshua (1804–1807).

Butto, Daniel, C.C. (1653).

Button and Putley, B.M.

Bye, Henry (1413).

Byford, William (1820–35).

Byworth, Thos. (1804–42).

Cabrier, Charles (1707).

Cabrier, John, C.C. (1730).

Cabrier and Leeky (1781–1804).

Cabrier, Favey, and Exchequer (1794).

Cabrier, Favey, and Son (1798).

Cachard, Gaspar (1820).

Cade, Simon, C.C. (1688).

Cade and Robinson (1822–25).

Caesar, Daniel, C.C. (1703).

Caillate, A., Geneva (1725).

Caille,— , London (1770).

Calcot, Tobias, C.C. (1664).

Calderwood, Thomas, C.C. (1724).

Callam, Alexander, C.C. (1790–96).

Callam Brothers (1795–1725).

Calliber, John, C.C. (1703).

Calliber, Thomas, C.C. (1727).

Calson, John, C.C. (1647).

Calston, John, C.C. (1653).

Cam, William, C.C. (1686).
Cambridge, Samuel, C.C. (1697).
Camden, William (1708–30).
Camerer, Ropp, and Co. (1794).
Camerer, A., and Co. (1830–40).
Cammerer, M. (1840).
Campbell, John (1691–1701).
Campbell, Alex. (1800–05).
Campbell, W. F. (1825–35).
Camper, James (1800–40).
Cann, John, C.C. (1649).
Cannans, John, London (1790).
Cannon, Joseph, London (1790).
Capt, Henry (1840–42).
Card, Edmund, C.C. (1679).
Carduroy, Philip, C.C. (1679).
Carey, George, C.C. (1679).
Carey, Thomas, C.C. (1705).
Carey, George (1842).
Carfoot, Chas. (1814–25).
Carley, George (1842–1879).
Carncel, C., Strasburg, S.K.M. (1600).
Carolan, James (1816–25).
Caron, Peter, Paris (1720–60).
Carovagius, —, Paris (1550).
Carpenter, Thos., C.C. (1767).
Carpenter, William, C.C. (1770–1817).
Carpenter and Son (1785–90).
Carpenter, Thomas, livery C.C. (1786).
Carpenter, F. (1830).
Carpenter, William (1842).
Carr, Fred (1822–25).
Carrington, Robert, livery C.C. (1766).
Carrington, Thos., liveryman C.C.
Carrington, Geo., livery C.C. (1786).
Carrington and Son (1789–94).
Carruthers, Geo. (1789–94).
Carswell, Joseph (1760).
Carswell, Wm. (1822–25).
Carter, Thomas, C.C. (1699).
Carter, Leon Augustus, C.C. (1726).
Carter, John, C.C. (1728).
Carter, J. (1772).

Carter, William (1760–1794).
Carter, Wm., Junr. (1805–26).
Carter, J. (1804–20).
Carter, John (1817), master C.C. (1878).
Cartwright, George, C.C. (1706–12).
Cartwright, William, C.C. (1713).
Cartwright, Benj. (1769–72).
Cartwright, Ann (1783).
Carver, Isaac, C.C. (1667).
Casper, Ellis and Co. (1804–42).
Casper, Nathaniel (1804–42).
Castlefranc, Peter (1769–83).
Catchpool, Thos. (1823).
Catchpool, Wm. (1830–35).
Cater, — (1671).
Cater, J., London (1780).
Catherwood, Joseph (1775–1825).
Catherwood, Joseph and William (1804–42).
Catherwood, G. and R. (1809–30).
Catherwood, Robert (1835).
Catsworth, John, C.C. (1669).
Cattell, William, C.C. (1671); (1671–90).
Cattell, Thomas, C.C. (1688–1692).
Cattey Daniel, C.C. (1731).
Cattle, John (1633).
Cattlin, James (1804–42).
Cauch, James, C.C. (1692).
Caul and Dennis (1816).
Cauldroy, Julien (1529).
Cavendish, Richard, livery C.C. (1810).
Cawley, Sam (1842–8).
Cawson (1779–1817).
Cayne, Andrew (1696).
Cellier-Lyons (1580–90).
Cext, Catharine (1730).
Chaband, Hy. (1816–25).
Chadd and Ragsdale (1775).
Chadwick, John (1783–1817).
Chadwick, Joshua (1820–25).
Chadwick, James (1804–42).
Chalk, James (1798).
Challoner, William, C.C. (1776).

Chalmers, George (1783–88).

Chambers, James (1690).

Chambers (1823).

Champion, John, C.C. (1641).

Champion, John, C.C. (1651–76).

Champion, Charles, Paris (1770).

Chams, Chas. Sampson, C.C. (1692).

Chancellor, Jno. (1793).

Chancellor and Son, Dublin (1800–40).

Chandler, Robert (1793–1825).

Chapman, Simon, C.C. (1675).

Chapman, Thos., Bath (1760).

Chapman, William (1790–94).

Chappel, Robert, C.C. (1720).

Chappel, Thomas (1753–63).

Chappuis, Jubilé, Geneva (1800).

Charle, George (1804–42).

Charlestrom, William, livery C.C. (1800–38).

Charlton, John, master C.C. (1640).

Charlton, Matjonat (1728).

Charlton, Jas. (1842).

Charman, Peter (1816–25).

Charrington, S., master, C.C. (1768).

Chartier, Francis (1765–71).

Chassereau, Robt. (1804–8).

Chasseur, —, London (1690).

Chater, James, C.C. (1727).

Chater, James, and Son (1754–59).

Chater, Eliezer, livery C.C. (1776).

Chater and Livermore (1790–1800).

Chater, Richd. (1787–1812).

Chater, Wm. (1804–42).

Chatier, Isaac (1768–88).

Chaulter (1773).

Chawner, Thomas (1783–88).

Cheeseman, Daniel, C.C. (1699).

Cheltenham, Michael, C.C. (1712).

Cheneviere and Deonna, Geneva (1800).

Cheneviere, Urbain, Geneva (1760).

Cheney, Wither (Walter?), elected master C.C. (1695).

Cherril, Edwd. (1814); E. & Son (1825–30).

Chesson, Thos. (1754–59).

Chester, Wm. (1804–40).

Chettle, W. Lambeth (1830–38).

Chevalier and Cochet, Paris (1790–1805).

Chilcott, Richard, C.C. (1690).

Chilcott, John, C.C. (1721).

Child, Richard, C.C. (1632).

Child, Henry, C.C. (1642–1664).

Child, Ralph, C.C. (1662).

Chilton, Thos., London (1700).

Chismon, Timothy, livery C.C. (1786–1803).

Christie, Wm. (1804–42).

Christie, Hy. (1842).

Church, Jno. Thos. (1835).

Churchman, Michael, C.C. (1694).

Clampson, Richard, C.C. (1673).

Clare, Henry T. (1804–42).

Clark, Thomas, C.C. (1720).

Clark, Jas. (1750).

Clark, Anthony (1763).

Clark, Edw. 1768–75.

Clark, Wm. (1730–1775).

Clark, Edw., 75.

Clark, Cornelius (1733); Thos. (1767).

Clark, Francis (1789–94).

Clark, Wm. (1800).

Clark, Jno. (1794–1823).

Clark, Thos. (1830–40).

Clark, George (1842).

Clarke, George, Whitechapel, C.C. (1632–1690).

Clarke, William, C.C. (1654).

Clarke, Humphrey, C.C. (1668–1700).

Clarke, John, C.C. (1696).

Clarke, Thomas, C.C. (1709).

Clarke, Geo. (1736).

Clarke, Edward (1768).

Clarke, William (1769–72).

Clarke, John Basul, livery C.C. (1776).

Clarke, Jas. (1778–1840).

Clarke, Hy., C.C. (1822–26).

Clarke, Wm. (1804–20).

Clarke, William, and Sons (1830–42).

Clarke, William (1875).

Clarke, Abraham (1890).

Clarke, Daniel, master C.C. (1892–1897).

Clarke, Job Guy (1852–6).

Claxton, Thomas, C.C. (1646); master (1670).

Clay, William (1646–70).

Clay, Thomas, Chelmsford (1650).

Clayton, Thomas, C.C. (1646).

Cleeke, Henry, C.C. (1655).

Cleeve, William, C.C. (1654).

Cleghorn, Saml. (1790).

Clement, Edward, C.C. (1670).

Clement, William, C.C. (1677–1694).

Clements, Robert, C.C. (1686).

Clements, Thos., London (1760).

Clerke, Danl., Amsterdam (1720).

Clerke, George, livery C.C. (1820).

Clerke, Geo., livery C.C. (1810–42).

Clerke, F. W. (1885).

Clewes, James, C.C. (1670).

Clifton, Thomas, C.C. (1651).

Clifton, Thomas, C.C. (1687).

Cliverdon, Thomas, C.C. (1722).

Closon (or Closson) Peter, C.C. (1626–40).

Clowes, John, C.C. (1672).

Cluer, Obadiah, C.C. (1709).

Cluer, John, Clerkenwell (1835).

Cluter, William, C.C. (1709).

Clutton and Co. (1825).

Clyatt, Samuel, C.C. (1671).

Clyatt, Abraham, C.C. (1680).

Clyatt, John, C.C. (1708).

Clyatt, William, C.C. (1709).

Claytee, Samuel, C.C. (1711).

Cobb, John, C.C. (1703).

Cochard, Geo., Covent Garrden, (1822–25).

Cochran, Saml. (1780–94).

Cochran, W. (1825).

Cockerton, Jonas (1751–78).

Cockford, Matthew, C.C. (1693).

Coggs, John (1690–1700).

Cohen, Sam Jacob (1815).

Cohen, A. S. (1820).

Coker, Ebenezer (1754–69).

Colambell, Anthony, livery C.C. (1776).

Colbert, J. G. I. (1825).

Cole, Daniel, C.C. (1726).

Cole, Thos. (1754–63).

Cole, John, C.C. (1729–60).

Cole, I. B. (1785).

Cole, Wm. (1780–1805). B.M.

Cole, Thomas, Bloomsbury (1864).

Coleman, John, C.C. (1781–83).

Coleman, William (1790–99).

Coleman, Thomas (1810–42); livery C.C.

Coleman, Geo., London (1780).

Coles, M. A. (1790).

Collett, John (1780–99).

Colley, Robt. (1770–85).

Collier, John, Clerkenwell (1770–75).

Collier, Archibald (1790–1830).

Collingridge, Edmund, livery C.C. (1793–1830).

Collingridge, Thos. (1838–42).

Collingwood, Samuel James, livery C.C. (1766–94).

Collins, John, C.C. (1701).

Collins, Clement, C.C. (1705).

Collum, A. (1800).

Colson (Colston), Richard, C.C. (1682–1700).

Combs, Joseph, C.C. (1720).

Comfort, William, C.C. (1647–1756).

Compart, Ebenezer, C.C. (1728).

Compton, Walter (1692).

Compton, Adam, C. C. (1716).

Conden, Robert (1780–85).

Congreve, William, inventor of curious clocks.

Connelly, Wm. (1825).

Conrad and Reiger, S.K.M. (1590).

Constable, W. and G. (1804–1807).

Constantine, Pet., B.M. (1802).

Cony, John, C.C. (1641).

Conyers, Richard, C.C. (1716).

Cook, Edwd. (1763–72).

Cook, John (1768–75).

Cook, Joshua (1793).

Cooke, Lewis, C.C. (1630–32).

Cooke, John, C.C. (1649–56).

Cooke, John, C.C. (1662).

Cooke, Robert, C.C. (1667).

Cooke, William, C.C. (1681).

Cooke, Thomas, C.C. (1699).

Cooke, William, C.C. (1708).

Cooke, John, C.C. (1712).

Cooke, Joseph, C.C. (1715).

Cooke and Gurney (1754–59).

Cooke, John (1775).

Cooke, Robert (1804–10).

Cooke, G. E. (1822).

Cooley, Hy., London (1805).

Coombes, Fisher, C.C. (1728).

Coombes, Jas. (1815–1825).

Coope, James, C.C. (1654).

Cooper, Hugh, C.C. (1653).

Cooper, Thomas (1800).

Cooper, Wm. (1804).

Cooper, E. (1820).

Cooper, William (1816–42).

Cope, Peter, C.C. (1638).

Cope, Chas. Jno. (1800–30).

Copeland, Alexander (1800–15); livery C.C.

Copestake, Hy. (1793).

Corbett, J. (1825).

Corbett, T. (1835).

Corbit, — (1835).

Cording, Jno. (1812–30).

Cording, Chas. (1822–25).

Cording, Josh. (1817–25).

Cording, Thomas (1822–30).

Cordon, Richard, C.C. (1729).

Cordrey, Thomas, C.C. (1670).

Cordwell, Robt., C.C. (1646).

Corghey, John (1754–59).

Corker, D. (1820–42).

Corker, Nath. (1842).

Cornelius, Jacob, London (1620,.

Cornish, Michael, C.C. (1661)

Corp, Wm. (1835).

Corson, Thos. (1835–42).

Cosbey, Robert, C.C. (1653–79).

Cosson, S. (1835).

Coster, Robert, C.C. (1655).

Coster, William, C.C. (1660).

Cother, William, C.C. (1668).

Cotter, Ebenezer (1775).

Cotterel, William, C.C. (1694).

Cotterel, John, C.C. (1721).

Cotterell, Thos. (1830).

Cottle, John, a lantern clock inscribed, "John Cottle, fecit 1653."

Cotton, John, London, C.C. (1695–1710).

Cotton, John, C.C. (1718).

Cotton, Francis (1822).

Cottonbult, John, C.C. (1729).

Couche, Charles, C.C. (1727).

Coulon, Charles (1765–68).

Coulon, —, Geneva, (1780).

Coulson, Charles (1769).

Coulson, Robert (1800–38); livery C.C. (1810).

Coulson, Saml. (1825).

Cortauld, Samuel (1759–63).

Cortauld, P., and Cowles (1768–75).

Courvoisoir, à Paris (about 1780).

Cousens, Thos. (1793).

Cousens, R W. (1835).

Cousins, Wm. (1814–18).

Cousins and Whitside (1842).

Couta, G. (1822–25).

Coventry, R. (1830).

Coventry, J. (1835).

Coward, William, C.C. (1681).

Coward, Wm., Lancaster (1797–1830).

Coward, and Jefferys, 149, Fleet St. (1783).

Cowdery, Geo. (1817).

Cowell, John (1763–1800).

Cowen, H. (1800).

Cowie, Jno. (1814–18).

Cowles, Geo. and Co. (1780–90).

Cowley, Robt., Chester; Goldsmiths' Company (1773).

Cowpe, Edward, C.C. (1687).

Cowta, Geo. (1817).

Cox, Thomas, C.C. (1708).

Cox, Jason (1745–60).

Cox, Samuel (1770).

Cox, Wm. (1763–72).

Cox, James, opened at Spring Gardens a museum of quaint clocks (1765–88).

Cox, Jas., and Son (1789–1800).

Cox and Watson (1780–85).

Cox, Nathaniel (1835–42).

Coxeter, William, C.C. (1654).

Coxeter, John, master C.C. (1661–63)

Coxeter, Nicholas, C.C. (1648); master (1671–1677); a celebrated maker (1648–80).

Cozens, William (1804–20). A prominent man in the trade.

Cozens, William, and Son (1822–42).

Cozens, J. (1835–42).

Cradock, E. (1835).

Cragg, Jas., Lancaster (1779).

Cragg, John (1842).

Craggs, Richard, C.C. (1660).

Craigingle, John (1839–42).

Cranfield, Henry, C.C. (1706).

Cranze, F. and J. (1788).

Cratzer, Nicholas, clockmaker to Henry VIII. (1538).

Craven, Thomas, C.C. (1688).

Crawley, Thomas, C.C. (1660).

Crayle, Richard, petitioner for incorporation of C.C. (1610–55).

Creed, Thomas, C.C. (1668).

Creed, Thomas, C.C. (1674).

Creede, John, C.C. (1727).

Creeke, Henry (1654).

Cressener, A. M. (about 1735).

Cressner, Robert, London (1690–1730).

Creswell, Joseph (1775).

Cripple, Wm., C.C. (1702).

Cripps, John (1758–63).

Cripps, John and Francillon (1793).

Crisp, Nicholas (1754–59).

Crisp, John (1783).

Crisp, William Baker.

Croak, Sampson, C.C. (1668).

Crocker, James, C.C. (1716).

Crocker, Wm. (1842).

Croft, John, C.C. (1665).

Crooke, Benj. (1804–8).

Crooke, Peter, C.C. (1724).

Cross, James, liveryman C.C. (1776).

Cross, Edward (1780–94).

Cross, John (1823).

Cross, John Berryhill, livery C.C. (1834).

Crossley, James, London (about 1710).

Crossley, Jas. (1814–18).

Crossley, Richd. (1800–25).

Crosthwaite, Jno., Dublin; a good maker (1760–95).

Crouch, George, C.C. (1668).

Crouch, Edward, C.C. (1691); master (1719).

Crouch, Robert, C.C. (1722).

Crouch, John (1761).

Croucher, Joseph, livery C.C. (1828).

Croudhill, Thomas (1790–94).

Crucifex, Robert, C.C. (1689); long-case clock (about 1725).

Crucifex, John, C.C. (1712).

Cruickshanks, Robert (1772–75).

Crump, Henry, C.C. (1667).

Cruttenden, Thomas, C.C. (1677).

Cruze, Francis, and J. (1759–71).

Cryton, Wm. See Crayton.

Cubley, Thos. (1820–1830).
Cue, William, C.C. (1691).
Cuendel, Samuel (1815).
Cuff, James, C.C. (1699).
Cuff, John, C.C. (1718).
Cuff, Broadhurst (1823).
Cuff, Jno. (1823).
Cuff, Jas. (1823).
Cufford, Francis, C.C. (1718).
Culliford, J., Bristol (1680).
Cullum, A. (1789–94).
Cumming, Alexander (1732–1814); a celebrated clockmaker, who first suggested curved teeth for the cylinder escape wheel; author of an excellent treatise on clockwork, which was published in 1766.
Cumming, John. See Panchaud and Cumming.
Cuper, Josiah (French), C.C. (1627–1634).
Curson, George, livery C.C. (1756).
Curteen; see Monkhouse.
Curtis, John, C.C. (1671).
Cusin, Noel, Autun (about 1630).
Cuthbert, Amariah, C.C. (1694).
Cuthbert, J. (1790–94).
Cutlove, John (1760).
Cutting, Christopher, C.C. (1694).

Dalby, John (1783–1804).
Dalemaige, Jehan, Paris; clockmaker to the Duchess of Orleans (1401).
Dalton, Jno. (1816–22).
Dammant, Barn., Colchester (about 1735).
Dane, Thos. (1790–1823).
Dane, Robert (1807).
Danell, Joseph (1822–30).
Daniel, Isaac, C.C. (1648); warden (1674).
Daniel, Stephen, C.C. (1698).
Daniel, Robert, C.C. (1708).

Daniel, Thomas (1783).
Daniell, William, C.C. (1632).
Daniell, Edward, C.C. (1648).
Dannes, Robert, C.C. (1776); (1766–80).
Dapin, Paul, London.
Darby, John (1820–42).
Dare and Peacock (1770–72).
Dargent, James, C.C. (1700–05).
Darle, Thomas, London (about 1769).
Darling, Robert, Sheriff of London, knighted (1766), on the court of C.C. (1766).
Darrell, Joseph (1812–15).
Darvell, Edwd. (1775–94).
Dashper, Frederick.
Dasypodius, Conrad, maker of second Strasburg clock (1571).
Dauthiau, Paris (1735–56).
Davenport, Sam. (1788).
David, Louis (1550–60).
Davidson, J. (1814–17).
Davidson, Adam (1835–1842).
Davie, Joseph (1830–42).
Davies, Timothy (1783–1793).
Davies, Robert (1788–94).
Davies, John (1788).
Davies, T. and H. (1800).
Davies, Richard (1790–1800).
Davies, James Callard. In 1840 patented one-year clock.
Davis, Samuel, C.C. (1648–60).
Davis, Tobias, C.C. (1653).
Davis, John, C.C. (1653).
Davis, Thomas, C.C. (1674).
Davis, Benjamin, C.C. (1678).
Davis, Jeffry, C.C. (1690).
Davis, John, C.C. (1697).
Davis, William, C.C. (1699).
Davis, George, C.C. (1720).
Davis, Thomas, C.C. (1726).
Davis, John (1769).
Davis, Wm., Lancaster (1761).

Davis, Wm. (1810–23).

Davis, David (1830–42).

Davis and Plumley (1830).

Davis, A. and C. (1835).

Davison, William, C.C. (1686).

Daw, Josh (1822).

Dawes, Wm. (1835–42).

Dawkes, John, C.C. (1707).

Dawson, Thomas, petitioner for incorporation of C.C. (1630).

Dawson, Robert, C.C. (1678).

Dawson, John (1763).

Day, Isaac, C.C. (1678).

Day, Thomas, C.C. (1691).

Day, Edmund, C.C. (1692).

Day, Richd. (1780–94).

Deacon, Joseph (1814–18).

Deacon, F. (1835).

Deacon, J. C. (1835–42).

Dealtry, Thomas (1783).

Dean, Deodadus (1793–1804).

Dean, Thos. (1810–42).

Deane, George, C.C. (1671).

Deard, J. (1775).

Debaufre, Peter, Soho; C.C. (1689).

De Boufler, Andrew, London (1769).

De Charmes, Simon (French), C.C. (1691); (1688–1730).

Decka, John (1757–90).

Decka and Marsh (1790–1800).

De Cologny, Geneva (about 1770).

Dee, William, C.C. (1729).

De Féalins, Jehan, made a clock for Rouen (1389).

De Fontaine, L., Somers Town (1835).

De la Corbiere, à Nismes (1790).

De Crüe, Geneva (about 1775).

De la Fonds, John (1790–94).

De la Fons, James (1790–95).

Delafosse, Samuel (French), C.C. (1692).

De la Garde, Gustavus (1840–42).

De Jersey (about 1810).

Delacroix, —, Paris; died 1862.

Delander, Nathaniel, C.C. (1668); (1658–80).

Delander, John, C.C. (1705).

Delander, Nathaniel, C.C. (1721); (1721–59).

De Landre, Roger, C.C. (1641); (1635–50).

Delandre, James, C.C. (1668).

De la Salle, Thomas (1800–18).

De la Salle, Jas. Thos., (1810–42); livery C.C. (1826).

Delaunce, James, C.C. (1650).

De Laundre, Peter, C.C. (1640).

Delauney, Peter (1822–25).

Delaversperre, Wm., C.C. (1650).

Demaza, George (1825).

De Moylym, John, keeper of Dulwich College clock in 1553.

Demster, Roger, London (about 1790).

Denison, Edmund Beckett, born 1816; president British Horological Institute (1868); called to the House of Lords as Baron Grimthorpe (1886); designer Westminster clock.

Denman, Geo. (1820–1823).

Denman, John F. (1842).

Denne, John (1820–23).

Denning, J. (1840).

Dennis, Francis, C.C. (1673).

Dennis, Peter, C.C. (1712).

Dennis, D. (1816).

Dent, William, C.C. (1674).

Dent, Edward John (1790–1853). Accepted stipulation by Denison that the Westminster great clock should give exact time within a minute a week.

Dent (Rippon), Richard (1857).

Dent (Rippon), Frederick (1860).

Denton, Joseph, Hull.

Denton, Isaac, London (about 1790).

Denton, Wm., Poultry (1816–20).

Derham, William (1657–1735); Canon of

Windsor, author of "The Artificial Clockmaker," published in 1696.

Dermere, Abraham, C.C. (1703).

Desbois, Jacob, C.C. (1730).

Desbois, Daniel, died 1848.

Desbois, Daniel, died 1885.

Desborough, Christopher, C.C. (1666).

Desbrow, Robert, admitted C.C. (1704).

Des Granges, Peter (1816–42).

Deshais, Matthew, London (1690–1710).

Desmarais, Peter (1794).

Desmore, T. (1830).

Dethau, Matthew, London (about 1750).

Dettacher, John, C.C. (1660).

Deveer, Frederick (1769–75).

De Vick, Henry. About 1364 made for Charles V. of France the first turret clock of which we have reliable record.

Devis, William (1750–65).

Devis, John, hon. freeman C.C. (1764–83).

Dewey, William, Dutch (1835).

Dickens, John, C.C. (1688).

Dickerson, F. C. (1840).

Dickie, Andrew, London (about 1765).

Dickinson, Thos., Lancaster (1817).

Dike, Nathaniel, C.C. (1663).

Dingley, Robert (1738–40).

Dingwall and Bailliam (1813).

Dixon, Wm. (1835–42).

Dobb, William, C.C. (1646).

Dobell, Ebenezer, Hastings; electric clocks in 1853.

Dobree, John (1815–1823).

Dobson, William, C.C. (1670).

Dobson, Charles, livery C.C. (1776).

Dockwray and Norman (1815–19).

Dod, Richard, London (1695–1720).

Dodd, G. P., & Son (about 1855).

Dodsworth, John, C.C. (1648).

Dolley, Thos., master C.C. (1808).

Donaldson, Geo. (1842).

Dondé, John, maker of a clock with wheels and balance (1334).

Dondi, Joseph, son of the foregoing (1350–60).

Donisthorpe, Geo. (1770–1810). Ludlam speaks of him as "the best maker of church clocks I know."

Donne, Robert (1763–94).

Donne, Griffith, died 1884.

Door, George, C.C. (1671).

Dorigny, Robert, clockmaker to the Duke of Orleans (1397).

Dorer, Robt., Glaris (about 1760).

Dorrell, Francis, C.C. (1702).

Dorrell, Francis, C.C. (1755).

Dorrell, William, livery C.C. (1786).

Dossett, Gregory, C.C. (1662).

Doughty, Thomas, C.C. (1696).

Doughty, Thos., invented a compensation pendulum (1811).

Doughty, Wm. P. (1816–20).

Douglas, Walter (about 1790).

Douglas, Alex. (1810–18).

Douglas, Jno. (1816).

Dove, Henry, C.C. (1667).

Dovey, Richard (1765–70).

Dow, Roger (1780–85).

Dow, Robert (1790–1835).

Dow, Robert (1842).

Downes, Jno., C.C. (1725).

Downes, Robt. (1793).

Downes, Robt. (1798–1818).

Downinge, Humfrey (1637).

Dowsett, Jeremiah, C.C. (1708).

Dowson and Peene, Gray's Inn (1800).

Drabble, J., London; bracket clocks (1710–20).

Draper, John, C.C. (1703).

Draper, James, C.C. (1712).

Draycott, Francis, C.C. (1678).

Drew, John, C.C. (1684).

Drew, Edward, C.C. (1692).

Drills, Jno., London (1780).

Droeshout, John, C.C. (1632).

Droz, Pierre J. (1721–1790)

Drury, James, C.C. (1694), clerk (1731); died (1740).

Drury, John, C.C. (1720).

Drury, Dru. (1770–85).

Drury, Wm. (1800–25).

Drury, J. F. (1810).

Dryden, G. (1835).

Dubie, —, Paris, Court goldsmith (1640–50).

Dubois, Pierre, Paris; wrote "La Tribune Chronometrique" (1852).

Ducastel, Isaac, C.C. (1703).

Duchemin, Dr., horologer, Rouen (1570).

Duchesne, Claude, C.C. (1693). John Wesley's long-case clock by him in the Wesley Museum, City Rd. (1693–1720).

Duck, H., London (about 1720).

Ducker, H. (1835–42).

Duddell, Thos. (1817–23).

Dudds, Joseph, livery C.C. (1766); (1750–72).

Dudson, Simon, C.C. (1653).

Duduict, Jacques, Blois (1560–90),

Dufalga, —, Geneva (about 1760).

Duff, James (1840–42).

Dufour and Ceret, associated with Voltaire (1770).

Dugard, Thos. (1812–19).

Dugard and Simpson (1830).

Dugdale, Richd. (1817).

Du Hamel, Isaac (about 1790).

Duke, Joseph, C.C. (1682).

Duke, Joseph, C.C. (1728).

Duke, George (1835–42).

Dulin, W. T. (1816–30).

Duncan, Jas. (1804–30).

Duncombe, Richard, master C.C. (1798).

Dundas, Jas., Edinburgh (1710).

Dunkerley, Samuel (1770).

Dunkley, John (1835).

Dunkley, Thos. (1840–42).

Dunlop, Andrew, C.C. (1701); (1720–40).

Dunlop, Conyers, master C.C. (1758); (1747–94).

Dunn, Henry, C.C. (1677).

Dunn, Anthony, C.C. (1719).

Dunn, William (1835).

Duntnell, Danl. (1783).

Duplock, Chas. (1790–1815).

Duplock and Wiggins (1816–30).

Dupont, Chas. (1798–1800).

Duppa, James (1765–70).

Durant, James (1765–70).

Durant, Oswald, petitioner for incorporation of C.C.; warden in 1645.

Durdent, Andrew, C.C. (1662).

Durley, T. (1835).

Durrant, Richd. (1820–42).

Durrant, Thomas, Hammersmith (1840).

Durtnall, Daniel (1780–1805).

Duseigneur, Pierre, Geneva (about 1750).

Dutens, Peter (1759–65).

Dutertre, Jean Baptiste, Paris; inventor of escapement with two balances (1724).

Dutton, William, liveryman C.C. (1766); (1750–94).

Dutton, Matthew and Thomas, C.C. (1793); master (1800); (1798–1802). Matthew Dutton and Son (1810–18).

Dutton, Matthew (1819–42).

Dutton, Guy (about 1760).

Duval, John, C.C. (1677).

Duval, Francis and John (1755–65).

Dwerryhouse, John (1770–1805); hon. freeman C.C. (1781).

Dwerryhouse and Carter (1810–1823).

Dwerryhouse, Ogston, and Co. (1835–42).

Dwerryhouse and Bell (1840).

Dyde, Thomas, London (about 1670).

Dyer, Joseph (1735–40).

Dyer and Newman (1768–72).

Dyke, —, Exchange Alley (1685).

Dyson, John, C.C. (1694).

Eady, Wm. (1800–18).

Eagle, John, C.C. (1690).

Eames and Barnard (1816).

Earle, Thos., C.C. (1720).

Earles, — (or Eryles) subscribed to incorporation of C.C. (1630).

Earles, Jno., London (1700–15).

Earnshaw, Edwd., Stockport; an ingenious clock and watchmaker, his shop was a "regular Noah's Ark of mechanical nicknacs"; friend of Jas. Ferguson (1740–70).

Earnshaw, Thomas (1749–1829).

Earnshaw, Thomas, junior (1825–42).

East, Edward (1610–73).

East, Thomas, C.C. (1677).

East, Peter, C.C. (1692).

East, Edward, C.C. (1696).

East, Jordon, C.C. (1720).

Eastley, — (1810).

Eastwick, Adrian (1780–85).

Eave, John (1790).

Eayre, Thos. (1757).

Ebben, Wm. (1816–42).

Ebsworth, John, C.C. (1665–1697).

Ebsworth, Christopher, C.C. (1670).

Eden, William, C.C. (1726).

Edgecombe, Thos. (1780).

Edington, — (1815).

Edington, Jno. (1816); Edington and Son (1830).

Edkins, James (1835–42).

Edlin, John, C.C. (1687).

Edlin, George, livery C.C. (1800–13).

Edlyne, Edgar (1690–1710).

Edmonds and West (1797–1810).

Edmonds, Jno (1820–30).

Edwards, Isaac, C.C. (1719).

Edwards, Wm. Jno. (1783).

Edwards, William (1775–94).

Edwards, James (1790–94).

Edwards, Wm. (1800).

Edwards, Jas. (1820–25).

Edwards, Robt. (1820–25).

Edwards, Benj. (1830–42).

Edwards, Jas. (1814–35).

Edwards, W., and Son (1835–42).

Edwards, Jas. (1849).

Effington, John, C.C. (1702).

Egleton, Christopher (1683); C.C. (1696).

Eldridge, John, C.C. (1677).

Eley, Jas. (1780–85).

Elfin, Benjamin, C.C. (1674).

Eliason, Daniel (1785–90).

Elisha, Caleb (1820–1842).

Elkins, William, C.C. (1709).

Ellerton, Robt. (1721).

Elley, Jas. (1816).

Ellicott, John (1696–1733).

Ellicott, John (1706–1772).

Ellicott, John, and Sons (1769–88).

Ellicott, Edward, and Sons, C.C. (1783–1810).

Ellicott and Taylor (1811–30).

Ellicott and Smith (1830–42).

Elliott, Henry, C.C. (1688).

Elliott, Thos. (1740).

Elliott, Josh. (1750).

Elliott, Jas. (1780–1800).

Elliott and Son (1805).

Ellis, James, C.C. (1667).

Ellis, Thomas, C.C. (1682).

Ellis, Paul, C.C. (1682).

Ellis, John, C.C. (1726).

Ellis, Richard, Westminster (1790).

Ellis and Collins (1804).

Ellis, Henry, Exeter (1810).

Ellis, David, Oxford Rd. (1817).

Ellis, Michael (1842).

Elliston, Robert (1770–1820).

Ellwood, John, C.C. (1702–25).

Elmes, William, C.C. (1667).

Elson, David, C.C. (1646).

Elton, John, C.C. (1675).

Ely, James (1825).

Emanuel, Joel (1812–17).

Emanuel, Lewis, and Son (1820–42).
Emanuel Brothers (1830).
Enderlin, —, Bale (1720–40).
Engall, Abraham, C.C. (1648).
Ennis, Edward, C.C. (1658).
Enys, Edward, C.C. (1684).
Erbury, Henry, C.C. (1650–56).
Ericke, Robert, C.C. (1719).
Ericke, William, C.C. (1730).
Errington, F. (1835).
Essex, Robt. (1823).
Esterbrook, — (1730–80).
Eston, Edward, C.C. (1708).
Etty, Marmaduke, C.C. (1716).
Evans, Thomas, C.C. (1673).
Evans, Henry, C.C. (1682).
Evans, Thomas, C.C. (1718).
Evans, William (1775).
Evans, James, and Son (1770–1800).
Evans, David.
Eve, John (1842).
Evill (1750–1800).
Exchagnet, Louis (1790).
Exelby, James, C.C. (1718–30).
Eyre (Ewer), John, C.C. (1703–30).
Eyston, Edward, C.C. (1659).

Fage, Edward, C.C. (1667).
Faircloth, Thos., C.C. (1660).
Fairer, Joseph (1850).
Fairey, John (1810–42).
Fairey, Richard (1814–42).
Fairey, Richard, junior, Borough (1835).
Falkner, Edwd., London (1750).
Falkner, John (1824–28).
Falks, Robert, C.C. (1720–25).
Farewell, John, C.C. (1695–1700).
Farmer, Leonard (1617).
Farmer, Thomas, C.C. (1647).
Farmer, Thomas, C.C. (1658); (1653–60).
Farmer, Richard, C.C. (1684).
Farmer, Thomas, C.C. (1689).
Farmer, William (1800).

Farmer, G. W. (1822–30).
Farquhar, W. (1835–42).
Farquharson, Geo. (1775–1793).
Farrend, V. (1825).
Farrer, William (1730).
Farrett, Richard, C.C. (1670).
Fatton, Frederick Louis (1822).
Faulkner, Edward, C.C. (1710–35).
Faulkner, William (1770–88); livery C.C. (1787).
Faux, John (1780–85).
Favey, Francis (1785–90).
Favey and Son (1804).
Favre, Henrique, London (1730).
Favre, Henry (1800–18).
Fawcett, Jno., Yorkshire, died 1869, aged 88.
Fayrer, Thos., Lancaster (1744).
Fazakerley, Thos. (1780).
Fazy, John (1780–85).
Fearon, Daniel, livery C.C. (1776).
Feilder, Thomas, C.C. (1689–1716).
Fell, William, C.C. (1705).
Fell, John, C.C. (1727).
Fell, Jas. (1767).
Felter, Nicholas, C.C. (1632).
Felter Thomas, C.C. (1709).
Fenn, Robert, C.C. (1689).
Fenn, Daniel and Samuel, master C.C. (1760–1804).
Fenn, Samuel, and Sons, master C.C. (1793–1815).
Fenn, Joseph, master C.C. (1830–1868).
Fennel, Richard, Kensington, C.C. (1676–1700).
Fenton, John, C.C. (1662).
Fenton, Sam. (1840).
Ferron, Lewis, London (1720).
Fetters, Henry (1630); C.C. (1653).
Fidgett, William, C.C. (1789); (1780–1825).
Field, Thomas, C.C. (1676–1706).
Field, William, C.C. (1691–1720).

Field, Robert, C.C. (1691).
Field, Simon, C.C. (1706).
Field, Daniel (1798).
Fielder, Thomas, London (1715).
Filton, Charles, C.C. (1674).
Finchett, Arnold, Cheapside; a water clock by him in B.M. (1735).
Findley, J. (1820).
Findley, Geo. (1835–42).
Finé, Oronce, Paris; professor of mathematics and designer of clocks (1540–60).
Finer, John (1791–1800).
Finer, Thomas and Nowland (1800–23).
Finer, Horatio (1840–42).
Finlow, Zach, London (1780).
Finnie, Henry, C.C. (1728).
Fish, Henry (1730–75).
Fish, John, C.C. (1766).
Fish, C. H. (1830–35).
Fisher, Rebeckah (1715).
Fisher, Ebenezer, C.C. (1725).
Fisher, Joseph (1783–1815).
Fisher, Dan. (1769–72).
Fisher, Daniel, and Son, Finsbury (1790–1804).
Fisher, Isaac (1804–23).
Fisher, — (1810).
Fishwater, John, C.C. (1726).
Fitree, Samuel (1790).
Fitter, Thomazon (1759–83).
Flack, G. (1820).
Fladgate and Wilder (1765).
Fladgate, John, C.C. (1760–83).
Flaig, Robert, and Co. (1840).
Flashman, George (1790–1813).
Fleetwood, Robert, livery C.C. (1760–90).
Fleming, Andrew, C.C. (1725).
Fleming, David (1817).
Flemming, Wm. (1815–19).
Fletcher, Daniel, C.C. (1646).
Fletcher, Thomas, C.C. (1676–1682).
Fletcher, Edward, C.C. (1697).
Fletcher, Charles (1840–42).

Fletcher, M. (1835).
Fleurian, Esaye (1705).
Flockhart, Andrew, Covent Garden (1814–35).
Floden, William, Clerkenwell (1835).
Flood, Humphrey (1607–17).
Flook, J. (1750).
Fogg, Hugh, Strand (1765–70).
Foissey, Jules, Boulogne, died 1892, aged 57.
Fole, Robert, C.C. (1667).
Folkard, Jas. (1823).
Foote, William, C.C. (1726).
Forbes, John (1835–40).
Ford, William, C.C. (1770).
Ford, Thomas, C.C. (1724).
Ford, — (1820).
Ford and Simmons (1842).
Fordham, Thomas, C.C. (1689–1730).
Foreman, Francis (1629–49).
Foreman, Michael, livery C.C. (1810).
Forester, J. (1810).
Forgat, — (1680).
Forrest, Joseph, C.C. (1692).
Forrest, John, died (1871).
Forster, William, C.C. (1681).
Forster, Clement, C.C. (1682).
Forster, John, C.C. (1689).
Forster, John, C.C. (1726).
Forsyth, James (1790).
Forte, John, C.C. (1672).
Fortfart, Isaac (1585).
Foss (Fox?) Thomas (1780–95).
Foster, Joseph, C.C. (1691).
Foster, Isaac (1788).
Foster, J. Benj. (1817).
Foulcon, Benj., London (1780).
Fowde, John, C.C. (1653).
Fowkes, Gabriel (1750–1780).
Fowlds, Andrew (1790–94).
Fowll, Edward, C.C. (1670).
Fox, Charles, C.C. (1662).
Fox, Mordecai, C.C. (1689).
Fox, Isaac (1772–94).

Fox and Son (1788).

Fox, Thomas (1790).

Frail, Thos. (1814–18).

Framborough, Edward, C.C. (1689).

Francis, Bulmer, C.C. (1731).

Francis, William, livery C.C. (1805–40).

Franklin, William, C.C. (1712).

Franklin, William, C.C. (1731).

Frazer, — (1788).

Frearson, John, C.C. (1689).

Freeman, Stafford, C.C. (1664).

Freeman, John, C.C. (1646–1680).

Freeman, Thomas, C.C. (1698).

Freeman, James, C.C. (1719).

Freeman, Nathaniel (1840–42).

French, John (1783–1800).

French, James (1810).

French, James, Moore (1800–42); C.C. (1810).

Frencham, James, C.C. (1698).

Frippett, John, C.C. (1665–70).

Frisby, Jno. (1816–25).

Frisquet, Peter (1768–75).

Frodsham, John (1807–14).

Frodsham, William James, C.C. (1836–1850).

Frodsham and Baker, Bloomsbury (1810).

Frodsham, John, and Son (1825–42); livery C.C.

Fromanteel, Ahasuerus, C.C. (1630–50).

Fromanteel, Ahasuerus, C.C. (1655–70).

Fromanteel, Ahasuerus, C.C. (1663–75).

Fromanteel, John (1663–80).

Fromanteel, Abraham, C.C. (1680–90).

Fromanteel and Clarke, London (1680).

Fry, Edward (1835).

Fryer, William James (1842).

Fryett, S. (1823).

Fueter, Berne (1740).

Fulkener, Edward, C.C. (1702).

Fuller, William, C.C. (1675).

Fuller, Samuel (1814–40).

Fuller, Crispin (1817).

Furness, John (1830).

Furnesse, Thomas (1701).

Furnifull, Richard, C.C. (1722).

Furnis, Thomas (1840–42).

Fury, Flack, C.C. (1658).

Gadsdon, Wm. (1750).

Gagnebin, Dan. (1750).

Gale, James (1783–89).

Gale, John (1790–1842).

Gambell, Thomas, C.C. (1656).

Gammage, I. (1823–42).

Gamp, P. J. (1835).

Ganeral, Aug. (1835).

Ganter, J. (1835).

Ganthony, Richard (1803); C.C. (1828–29).

Ganthony, Richard Pinfold (son of the above), master C.C. (1845).

Gany, Thomas, C.C. (1699).

Garde, Jas., London (1700).

Garden, William, C.C. (1712).

Garden, Philip (1759).

Gardener, John, C.C. (1682).

Gardener, Joseph (1767).

Gardener, Henry (1794–1804).

Gardiner, John, Croydon, C.C. (1687).

Gardiner, Henry (1759–60).

Gardner, Thomas, C.C. (1689).

Gardner, William Obadiah, C.C. (1711).

Gardner, William (1760).

Gardner, Edward, Lancaster (1841).

Garfoot, William, C.C. (1680).

Garland, John, livery C.C. (1766–98).

Garle, Thomas, livery C.C. (1766); (1760–76).

Garnegy, Chas., Soho (1817).

Garnett, Wm., London (1680).

Garnham, Abel (1816).

Garnier, J. P., Paris (1801–1870).

Garrard, Robt. (1815–18).

Garrard, R. J. and S. (1822–42).

Garrett, Charles, C.C. (1690).

Garrett, Charles, C.C. (1720).
Garrett, William (1804–15).
Garron, Peter, C.C. (1694–1706).
Garth, John, Clerkenwell (1750–55).
Gartly, Jno., Aberdeen (1810).
Gass, David, and Co. (1810–23).
Gathercole, John, London (1780).
Gaudron, à Paris (1710–30).
Gaudy, J. A., Geneva (1780).
Gaunt, John (1840–42).
Gavelle, James, C.C. (1683–1700).
Gaze, James, Bishopsgate (1782).
Gaze, Samuel B. (1814–59).
Gaze, Peter, died 1892, aged 73.
Gefael, U. (1835–42).
Gegenreiner, F. Z. (1720).
Gells, Thomas, C.C. (1720).
George, Richard, C.C. (1681).
Gernon, Bernard, C.C. (1659).
Gerrard, John, London (1740).
Gibbard, Thomas (1780–85).
Gibbons, Richard, C.C. (1730).
Gibbons, Benjamin, C.C. (1750–69).
Gibbons, Joshua (1810–18).
Gibbons, John (1810–1842); livery C.C. (1811).
Gibbs, Walter, C.C. (1648).
Gibbs, Thomas, C.C. (1681); master (1711).
Gibbs, Jno. (1815–19).
Gibbs, Thomas (1825).
Gibbs, Geo. (1835–42).
Gibson, James, C.C. (1669).
Gibson, Mary, at the Dial and Crown.
Gibson, Jno.; made a curious geographical clock (1761).
Gibson, Jno., C.C. (1800–10).
Gibson and Faust (1800).
Gibson, Edward, livery C.C. (1780–1803).
Gibson, John, Lothbury (1761–1813).
Gibson, C. (1830).
Gideon, Robert, C.C. (1691).
Giffin, Thos., London (1820).

Gifford, Thomas, C.C. (1693).
Gilbert, Faustin, C.C. (1661).
Gilbert, William, C.C. (1695).
Gilbert, Charles, C.C. (1700).
Gilbert, Phinlip (1807–30).
Gildchrist (or Gilchrist), Archibald, C.C. (1729).
Gildchrist, Sterling (1755–65).
Gilkes, Richard, C.C. (1686).
Gill, John, C.C. (1707).
Gill, John (1753–65).
Gimblet, Jno., junr., and Vale, Birmingham (1770).
Gingner, Anthony (French), C.C. (1687).
Ginn, William, C.C. (1699).
Girardier l'Aine, Geneva (1805).
Giraud, Christophe, Geneva (1814).
Girod, James (French), C.C. (1693).
Giroust, Alexander (1760).
Gladstone, Thomas, C.C. (1703).
Glanville, Richard (1775).
Glass, Alexander (1783).
Glazier, William, C.C. (1666).
Glenny, Joseph, livery C.C. (1810).
Glover, Samuel, C.C. (1694).
Glover, Daniel, C.C. (1699).
Glover, John, C.C. (1700).
Glover, Richard, C.C. (1703).
Glover, Boyer, C.C. (1740–68).
Glover, J. (1835).
Glynn, Richard, C.C. (1705).
Gobert, Peter (French), C.C. (1687).
Godbere, Saml.
Goddard, John, Hounsditch (from Paris), worked for Isaac Sunes (1615–18).
Goddard, Benjamin, C.C. (1701).
Goddard, Nicholas, Newark (1700–20).
Goddard, Benjamin, C.C. (1727).
Goddard, Francis (1792); (1794–1825).
Goddard, T. (1814–35).
Godfrey, George (1835).
Godwin, John.
Godwin, Jas. (1801–42).

Goff, Thos. (1793).

Gold, John (1806–19).

Golding, J. (1775).

Goldney, Thos. (1815–25).

Goldsmith, John, C.C. (1681).

Goldsmith, William, C.C. (1719).

Goldsmith, John, C.C. (1720).

Golledge, Richard, Stratford (1835).

Gooch and Harper, Clerkenwell (1810–13).

Gooch, Jno. (1814–18).

Gooch, Albert (1816–25).

Gooch, Wm. (1825).

Gooch, H. (1830).

Good, John, author of "The Art of Shadows"; C.C. (1678–1711).

Good, John (1780–94).

Goodall, Chas., Covent Garden (1793–1818).

Goodchild, John, C.C. (1726).

Goode, Charles, C.C. (1686).

Goodfellow, Wm. (1793).

Goodhugh, R. and B. (1825–35).

Goodhugh, William (1825).

Goodhugh, Richard (1840–42).

Goodlad, Richard, C.C. (1689).

Goodman, Geo., London (1771).

Goodman, J., and Son, Kentish Town (1840–42).

Goodrich, Simon (1799), improved escapement.

Goodwin, Wm., Stowmarket (1700–20).

Goodwin, John (1770–1800).

Goodyear, John, C.C. (1722).

Goodyear, Joseph, C.C. (1732).

Gordon, John, C.C. (1698–1712).

Gordon, Robert, Edinburgh (1703–30).

Gordon, Patrick, Edinburgh (1705–15).

Gordon, William, Islington (1794–1805).

Gordon, Alex. (1815–19).

Gordon, Theodore, died 1870, aged 81.

Gorham, James, Kensington (1815–42).

Gosler, Thos. (1815–19).

Gosling, Richard, and Son (1765–75).

Gosling, Joseph (1780–85).

Gosling, Robert (1770–85).

Goss, Jeremiah, C.C. (1667).

Goubert, James, C.C. (1890).

Gougy, Pierre Frederick, Westminster (1730–39).

Goujon, Samuel, master C.C. (1752–94).

Gould, Chester, Clerkenwell, patented a nautical time glass (1780–1803).

Gout, David Ralph (1830–42).

Gowerth, John, Oxford (1701).

Gowland, Jas. (1835–80).

Gowland, Thos. (1834–42).

Grafton, John (alias Solomons); (1831).

Grafton, J. and E. (1834–42).

Grafton, Henry (1840).

Graham, George, C.C. (1695–1751).

Graham, James (1800–5).

Graham, Jas., London (1825).

Grand, John (1780–1800).

Grandin, Jno. (1815–19).

Granger, Richard, C.C. (1695).

Grangier (French) (1650).

Grant, John, C.C. (1781–1810).

Grant, John, C.C. (1817–82).

Grant, Jesse (1830).

Grant and Terry (1840).

Grant, Henry (1835).

Grant, William (1835).

Grantham, J., London (1750–70).

Grave, Geo. (1815–42).

Gravell and Tolkein (1790–1820).

Graves, Hy. (1835).

Graves, Benjamin, C.C. (1676–1731).

Gray, Timothy, C.C. (1633).

Gray, Benjamin.

Gray and Vulliamy (1746–60).

Gray, Thomas (1780–93).

Gray, Adam (1788).

Gray, T. J. and G. (1800–5).

Gray, Robert and William (1800–28).

Gray, Jno. (1817).

Gray, G. and W. (1830).

Graye, —, C.C. (1630).

Grayhurst, P. and M. (1785–1800).

Grayhurst and Harvey (1810–30).

Grayhurst, Harvey, Denton, and Co.
(1835–40).

Greatrex, Ralph, C.C. (1653).

Greaves, Samuel, London (1720).

Greaves, Thos. (1770).

Greblin, — (1630).

Green, James, C.C. (1664).

Green, Joseph, C.C. (1723).

Green, Margaret (1765–71).

Green and Aldridge (1765–85).

Green, Jno. (1750–70).

Green, Richd., Yorkshire (1760).

Green, Robt., Lancaster (1767).

Green and Bentley, complicated musical
astronomical clock (1790).

Green, James, Ludlam (1755), C.C.
(1794).

Green, Samuel (1788–1800).

Green and Ward (1793).

Green, Ward, and Green (1800–38).

Green, J., and Son (1830).

Green, Henry (1835–42).

Green, Robt. (1842).

Green, Thomas (1835–42).

Greenaway, Richard, C.C. (1718).

Greenaway, John, St. Luke's (1842).

Greenaway, John, St. John's Square
(1842).

Greene, James, C.C. (1685).

Greene, John, C.C. (1711).

Greensill, Joseph (1775–1800).

Greensill, Edwd. (1793).

Greenwood, G. (1817).

Gregory, Jeremie, C.C. (1652–1685).

Gregory, Thomas, C.C. (1671).

Gregory, Robert, C.C. (1678).

Gregory, Jeremiah, C.C. (1694).

Gregson and Jefferson (1800–5).

Grennell, Richard (1750).

Gretton, William (1665).

Gretton, Charles, C.C. (1662–1701).

Grey, John (1823–30).

Grice, Thomas, C.C. (1675).

Grice, Job, Lancaster (1797–1830).

Griffin, John, C.C. (1720).

Griffin and Adams (1800–23).

Griffin, G. (1835).

Griffin, F. (1835).

Griffith, Jas., C.C. (1667).

Griffith, George, C.C. (1720).

Griffith, Richard (1790).

Griffith, J. W. (1840–42).

Griffiths, Edward, livery C.C. (1810).

Griffiths and Son (1835).

Grignion and Son (1775).

Grignion, Thos. (1800–25).

Grimalde and Johnson (1815–25).

Grimes, Thomas, C.C. (1671).

Grimes, William, C.C. (1682).

Grimley, William, C.C. (1694).

Grimshaw, William, senior (1851).

Grimshaw, James, died 1846, aged 43.

Grimshaw, William (1853).

Grimshaw, Frederick (1893).

Grimstead, Thomas (1753–63).

Grindley, William (1820).

Grinkin, Robert, C.C. (1632–1660).

Grinkin, Edwd.; C.C. (1656).

Gritting, Jno. (1750).

Grizell, John, C.C. (1687).

Grohe, James (1834–42).

Grollier de Serviere, Nicholas, maker of
many curious clocks and automata.
(1593–1686).

Grose, Richard, C.C. (1632).

Grosrey, Calestin (1840–42).

Grossmann, Moritz, Glashütte, Saxony
(1826–1885).

Grosvenor and Jones (1815).

Grounds, Jonathan (1710).

Grout, William, C.C. (1660).

Grove, Thomas, C.C. (1715).

Grove, George, C.C. (1715).

Grove, Richard, livery C.C. (1770–1817).

Grove, W. R., C.C. (1811–15).

Grover and Co. (1817).

Groves, George (1790–95).

Gruet, —, a Swiss (1664).

Gudin, —, Paris (1760).

Guest, Jno. (1816).

Guibet, L'Aîné, à Paris; S.K.M. (1790).

Guillaume, George (1842).

Gullock, Philip (1790–95).

Gunter, R. (1790–95).

Gurden, Benjamin, and Son (1775–1794).

Gutch, John, C.C. (1673).

Gutheridge, William, C.C. (1728).

Gutteridge, John (1835).

Guy, Henry, C.C. (1702).

Guy, Charles, C.C. (1714).

Guy, Samuel, London (1730).

Guy, Edward (1835–42).

Gwillim, Eli, C.C. (1648).

Gwinnell, J. (1812–15).

Habart, James, C.C. (1682).

Habrecht, Isaac, Strasburg clock (1570–89).

Hackings, John (1753).

Hackney, Thos., London (1740).

Haden, Thos. (1720).

Hadley, Humfrey (1708).

Hagger, James (1700).

Haines, Francis, C.C. (1706),

Haines, Hy. (1753).

Haines, Jno., Clerkenwell (1835–42).

Hair, George B., Borough (1835–42).

Hair, Wm., Birmingham, S.K.M. (1809).

Hairl, Jno. (1817).

Hale and Broadhurst (1800–5).

Haley, Thos., London (1781).

Haley, Charles (1770–1800).

Haley and Milner (1800–15).

Haley and Son (1832). (See Grohe.)

Halford, Robt., St. Luke's (1823).

Halked, Thomas, C.C. (1702).

Halksworth, William (1840–42).

Hall, Ralph, C.C. (1638).

Hall, Peter, C.C. (1648).

Hall, Edward, C.C. (1710).

Hall, Wm. (1720).

Hall, John (1760).

Hall, Wm. (1814–19).

Hall, Wm. (1815–19).

Hall, Charles (1817–20).

Hall, Chas. (1840).

Hallam, E. (1835).

Hallier, London (1800).

Hallifax, John.

Hally, Thos., London (1660–75).

Halsey, George, C.C. (1687).

Halstead, Richard, C.C. (1669).

Halstead, Charles, C.C. (1677).

Halstead, John, C.C. (1698).

Halstead, William, C.C. (1715).

Ham, John (1820–42), livery C.C. (1821).

Hambleton, George, C.C. (1669).

Hames, Jno. (1835).

Hamilton, Richard, C.C. (1712).

Hamley, J. O. (1800–40).

Hamley, junr., Strand (1810).

Hamley, J. O., and Son (1815).

Hamley, O. Jas. (1815–18).

Hammon, J. (1840–60).

Hammond, John, C.C. (1680).

Hammond and Co. (1768).

Hampton, W., and Sons (1842).

Hancock, Thomas (1830–35).

Hancorne, Thomas, C.C. (1658–83).

Hancorne, William, C.C. (1676).

Handcock, Edward (1842).

Handiside, Geo., London (1720).

Handley and Moore (1798–1824).

Hanet, John and George (1768).

Hannet, Samuel Stephen, London (1780).

Hanslapp, Robert, C.C. (1653).

Hanslapp, William, C.C. (1603).

Hanson, Charles, Huddersfield (1839–45).

Hanush, —, maker of a clock for Prague Town Hall (1497).

Hanwell, Zachariah, C.C. (1694).

Harbert, William, C.C. (1670).

Harbottle, Cornelius, C.C. (1667).

Harcourte, —, maker or repairer of clocks, near Westminster Abbey (1469).

Harden, Chas. (1816–25).

Harding, John, C.C. (1685).

Harding, Francis, C.C. (1687).

Harding, John, C.C. (1721).

Harding, Robert (1753).

Harding, Thomas, and Co. (1760–1800).

Harding, Sam. (1816–23).

Harding and Co. (1817).

Harding, Henry (1840).

Hardwidge, Wm. (1823).

Hardy, John (1760–90); livery C.C.

Hardy, Joseph (1800).

Hardy, William, Clerkenwell (1800–30).

Harker, George, master C.C. (1852).

Harlock, James, Westminster (1842).

Harlow, Samuel, Derby (1789–1813).

Harman, George, High Wycomb, chimes Cripplegate Church (1792).

Harmer, Jasper, cited by C.C. (1685).

Harns, Geo. (1808–10).

Harold, Richard, C.C. (1690).

Harper, Thomas, C.C. (1750–61).

Harper, John (1810–25).

Harper, Thos. (1800–30).

Harrache, Thos., Pall Mall (1765–75).

Harris, John, C.C. (1631); master (1641).

Harris, John, C.C. (1659).

Harris, Richard, maker of a pendulum clock for St. Paul's Church, Covent Garden (1641).

Harris, Thomas, in yᵉ Strand (1680).

Harris, John, C.C. (1677); master (1688).

Harris, Anthony, C.C. (1670–90).

Harris, John, C.C. (1690).

Harris, Francis Wm., C.C. (1702).

Harris, Samuel, C.C. (1708).

Harris, Christopher, C.C. (1695); (1695–1720).

Harris, Geo., Fritwell (1730).

Harris, William, Temple Bar, livery C.C. (1776).

Harris, Thos., St. Sepulchre's (1770).

Harris, William, master C.C. (1790–1833).

Harris, Richard (1790–1810).

Harris, John (1800–8).

Harris, L., Spitalfields (1810).

Harris, Jas. (1820).

Harris, H. (1815–25).

Harris, John, Clerkenwell (1835).

Harris, Clement (1822–42); livery C.C. (1825).

Harris, John James (1840–42).

Harrison, George, C.C. (1698).

Harrison, William, C.C. (1699).

Harrison, John (1693–1776).

Harrison, James (1720–50).

Harrison, Wm. (1780–94).

Harrison, Thos. (1795–1804).

Harrison, James, Barton-on-Humber (1810–30).

Harrison, Francis, Ratcliff (1835–41).

Harrocks, Lancaster; Josh. (1748); Jno. (1783).

Harrys (Harris), Thomas, clock with figures on the front of Old St. Dunstan's Church, Fleet St. (1671).

Harshell, D. (1830).

Hart, Noe, C.C. (1695).

Hart, John, C.C. (1720).

Hart, Henry, C.C. (1720).

Hart, S. and M. (1804–18).

Hart and Harvey, Finsbury (1825).

Hart, Napthali, and Son (1835–42).

Hart, Maurice (1842).

Hartley, —, cited by C.C. (1680).

Hartley, Jer., Norwich (1705).

Hartley, Jno. (1790–94).

Hartnup, John (1840–80).

Hartung, Chas. (1840).

Harvey, Samuel, C.C. (1696).

Harvey, Alexander, C.C. (1726).

Harvey, John (1798–1818).

Harvey and Co., Finsbury (1830).

Harvey, George (1830–42).

Harward, Robert, C.C. (1730).

Harwood, Laurence (1716).

Haskins, William (1830).

Hasleden, Charles (1840).

Haslewood, Roger (1772).

Hassell, Joshua (1746).

Hassenius, James, C.C. (1682).

Haswell, Alex. (1780–94).

Haswell, Archibald (1835–42).

Haswell, Robert (1842–74).

Hatch, John, C.C. (1693).

Hatchman, James, C.C. (1680).

Hathornthwaite, Lancaster; Peter (1703), Jno. (1744).

Hatton, James, C.C. livery (1799–1812).

Hatton and Harris (1816–20).

Hatton, Wm., London (1830).

Hatton, Geo. C., Lancaster (1826).

Hatton, J. (1835).

Hautefeuille John (1647–1724).

Havelland and Stephens (1794).

Hawes, John (1775).

Hawkesbee, Benjamin, C.C. (1709).

Hawkesworth, John, C.C. (1709).

Hawkins, James, C.C. (1730).

Hawkins, Thomas, C.C., Cornhill (1777–1816).

Hawley, Thos. and Co., Strand (1795–1828).

Hawley, — (1830).

Hawley, — (1860–62).

Hawley, John, Soho (1842).

Hay, Alexander, Edinburgh (1718).

Hay, Peter (1805–40).

Hayden, William, C.C. (1717).

Hayden, John, Deptford (1710).

Haydon, William, C.C. (1687).

Hayes, Walter, C.C. (1654); master (1680).

Hayes, Edmond, C.C. (1682).

Hayford, Henry (1842).

Hayley, William (1788–93).

Haynes, John, C.C. (1676).

Haynes and Kentish (1804–18).

Hayward, William, C.C. (1720).

Hayward, John (1820).

Hayward, Robert, Bermondsey (1815–35).

Hayward, J. (1835–42).

Haywood, Peter, Devon (1766).

Head, Thomas Cartwright (1693).

Headworth, P. (1815–42).

Heady, George, C.C. (1682).

Heap, Richard (1800–25).

Heathcock, Timothy, C.C. (1698).

Hebert, Anthony, London (1660–90).

Hebert, J. (1716).

Hebting, F., Soho (1835).

Heckel, Francesco (1730).

Heckstetter, Joseph, C.C. (1694).

Hedge, Nathaniel, Colchester (1740–80).

Hedge and Banister, Colchester (1800–08).

Hedger, George (1822–42).

Hedges, John, Clerkenwell (1800).

Heeley and Burt, Deptford (1780).

Heerman, John (Dutch), C.C. (1691).

Heffer, W. (1835).

Heitzman, F., and Co. (1840).

Heizman, Matthew (1840).

Helden, Onesiphorus, C.C. (1632–48).

Hele, Peter, Nuremberg, invented the mainspring (1500–40).

Hellam, James, C.C. (1689).

Heming, Thomas, Piccadilly (1763–75).

Heming, Artis, Shadwell, livery C.C. (1776).

Heming and Crawner (1780–90).

Heming, Geo. (1793).

Henche, Uldrich (1605).

Henderson, John (1775–1800).

Henderson, Robert (1772–1805).

Hendricks, Aaron (1760–68).

Hennett and Son (1772).

Hennon, William, C.C. (1674).

Henry, W. and S., Islington (1804).

Henry, S. (1810).

Henry, S. (1830).

Henry, Stephen (1835–40).

Henshaw, Walter, C.C. (1667–95).

Henshaw, John, C.C. (1696).

Herbert, Edward, C.C. (1664).

Herbert, Thomas, Whitehall, C.C. (1676).

Herbert, Evan, C.C. (1691).

Herbert, Cornelius, London Bridge (1670–96).

Herbert, Cornelius, London Bridge (1690); C.C. (1699); master (1727).

Herbert, Edward, C.C. (1710).

Herbert, Henry, C.C. (1713).

Herman, Ignaz (1840).

Herring (Herren), Joshua (1753–75).

Herring, John (1770).

Hertford, John, C.C. (1632).

Hesk, William (1835).

Hester, Henry, C.C. (1670).

Hewitt, Benjamin, C.C. (1724).

Hewitt, Sam. (1836).

Hewitt, Thomas (1799–1867).

Hewkley, John, C.C. (1732).

Heywood, William (1807–42).

Heyworth, John (1823).

Hibbert, John, Aldgate (1840).

Hickling, John (1835–42).

Hickman, Joseph (1779).

Hickman, Wm. (1816–25).

Hicks, Thomas, C.C. (1666).

Hicks, John, C.C. (1694).

Hicks, Samuel, London (1780).

Hicks, Jas. (1804–15).

Hicks, Chas. (1810–15).

Hickson, Thomas, C.C. (1690).

Higgins, Banger, C.C. (1724).

Higginson, Henry, C.C. (1662).

Higginson, John (1790–1815).

Higgs, John, C.C. (1661).

Higgs, Thomas, C.C. (1716).

Higgs, Robert and Peter (1750–1767).

Highfield, Josiah (1790–94).

Highmare, Edward, C.C. (1687).

Highmore, Jacob (1790–94).

Hill, John, C.C. (1630).

Hill, Francis, C.C. (1679).

Hill, Thomas (1689). There was also on the clock the further inscription, "The gift of John Woolfe, member of the Company." "Thos. Hill, over against Chancery Lane, Fleet St."

Hill, Edward, C.C. (1698).

Hill, John, C.C. (1705).

Hill, John, C.C. (1731–60).

Hill, Chas. (1793–95).

Hill, Jas. (1793–1810).

Hill, Sampson C. (1815).

Hill, John (1820).

Hill, Leonard (1817–23).

Hill, Sam. (1842).

Hillcoat, William (1790–94).

Hilliard, G. (1820).

Hills, — (1774).

Hillyard, William, C.C. (1679).

Hilton, John, C.C. (1698).

Hinde, Benjamin; musical clockmaker (1835–40).

Hindley, John (1730–65).

Hindley, Henry, York (1722–74).

Hine, Thos. (1760–74).

Hine, John (1790–94).

Hinton, J. (1815–35).

Hiorne, John, C.C. (1707–45).

Hiscocks, T. (1835).

Hiscocks, Zachariah (1840–42).

Hislop, Richard (1775–1803).

Hislop, Richard (1840–42).

Hislop, William (1820–1876).

Hitchins, Joseph (1779–94).

Hobbs, James, Lambeth (1830).

Hobbs, Jas. (1830).

Hobler, Paul, C.C. (1781); (1770–90).

Hobler, Fras. (1793).

Hobson, John, C.C. (1630).

Hobson, James, Oxford St. (1835).

Hochicorn, Isaac, C.C. (1728).

Hock, C., Hatton Garden (1840).

Hocker, John (1688); C.C. (1729).

Hocker, Jos., 30-hour clock (1740).

Hoddle, John, Reading, (1688); C.C. (1705).

Hodges, Nathaniel, C.C. (1680–1700).

Hodges, William, C.C. (1719).

Hodges, — (1780).

Hodges, J. (1835).

Hodgkin, Sarah, C.C. (1699).

Hodgkin, Robert (1705).

Hodgson, Lancaster; Hy. (1816); Wm. (1820).

Hodsoll, William, Bishopsgate (1800–8).

Hodsoll, William (1842).

Hohwii, Amsterdam; died (1889).

Holdway, George (1779).

Hole, Henry (1810–23).

Hole, F. W. (1852).

Holeyard, Samuel, C.C. (1735).

Holland, George, C.C. (1630–55).

Holland, Thomas, C.C. (1632); master (1656).

Holland, Thomas, C.C. (1658).

Holland, Lewis, C.C. (1699).

Holland, John (1765–75).

Holland, Thos. (1815–18).

Hollidaie, Edwd. (1656).

Hollier, Jonathan, livery C.C. (1776).

Holloway, Robert, C.C. (1632).

Holloway, Edward, C.C. (1650).

Holloway, William, C.C. (1697).

Holm, Jno., Lancaster (1783).

Holmden, John (1806–40). Livery C.C.

Holmes, John, C.C. (1697).

Holmes, John (1763–1810).

Holmes, Edward (1783–94).

Holmes, Wm. (1783).

Holmes, Wm. (1810–12).

Holmes, Matthew Steel (1822–42); livery C.C.

Holt, Lancaster; Thos. (1747); Wm. (1767).

Honeybone, Thomas, Old Brentford (1830–40).

Honison, J., Islington (1835).

Hooke, Robert (1635–1703); invented the anchor escapement for clocks.

Hooke, John, C.C. (1698).

Hooker, Jas., B.M. (1791).

Hope, Edward (1775–85).

Hope, Chas., London (1820).

Hopgood, T. B. (1823).

Hopkins, John, C.C. (1641),

Hopkins, John (1753–56).

Hopkins, A. B. (1823).

Hopkins, Edwd., Soho (1817).

Hornblower, William, C.C. (1713–40).

Hornblower, William H., C.C. (1779).

Hornblower, Wm. (1842).

Horne, Samuel, C.C. (1654–73).

Horne, George Henry, C.C. (1718).

Horne, Henry, master C.C. (1750–68).

Horne, William (1835–42).

Horseman, Stephen (1702), C.C. (1709); (1724–40).

Horstmann, Gustave, inventor of perpetual clock; died 1893.

Hoskins and Bird, Clerkenwell (1822–30).

Hoskins, Jonah (1840).

Hoskins, George (1842).

Houghman, Charles, C.C. (1680).

Houghton, Richard, C.C. (1690).

Houghton, James (1790–94).

Houghton, John Handsworth, Birmingham (1798–1842).

Houghton, Wm., died 1890, aged 75.

Houriet, Frederick (1810–25).

House, Robert (1790).

Houseman, Jacob, Lancaster (1732).
How, Benjamin, C.C. (1691).
How, William, C.C. (1697).
How and Masterman (1750–60).
Howard, John, C.C. (1694).
Howard, Richard, C.C. (1718).
Howard Wm. (1760).
Howard, John Jarvis (1790–94).
Howard, Edwd. (1775–1804).
Howe, Samuel, C.C. (1712).
Howe, Ephraim, C.C. (1729).
Howe, Samuel (1840).
Howell, Benjamin, C.C. (1699).
Howell, Joseph, C.C. (1721).
Howell, John, C.C. (1724–30).
Howells, William, Kennington (1780–1810).
Howes, Jno., C.C. (1672).
Howse, John, Croydon, C.C. (1687).
Howse, Joseph (1698).
Howse, John, C.C. (1706).
Howse, William, C.C. (1731–80).
Howse, Charles, master C.C. (1768–94).
Howson, John, C.C. (1699).
Hubbard, John, C.C. (1722).
Hubbard, E., musical clockmaker (1840).
Hubert, James (1725–1730).
Huchason, Richard, C.C. (1702).
Hudson, John (1780–85).
Hudson, William (1835).
Hues, Pierry (Peter), C.C. (1632–60).
Huges, Jno. (1710).
Hughes, John, C.C. (1703).
Hughes, Thomas, C.C. (1712).
Hughes, S. (1774).
Hughes, Thomas, master C.C. (1750–83).
Hughes, John (1800).
Hughes, David (1835–42).
Huguenin, A. (1830–42).
Hulbert, William (1708).
Hulme, Jas. (1817).
Hulst, Jacob, C.C. (1646).
Hulton, John, C.C. (1724).

Humber, Thos., London (1790).
Humphrey, W. H. (1830–35).
Humphreys, Samuel, C.C. (1728).
Humphries, J., London (1750).
Humphrys, William, C.C. (1699).
Hunot, Sam. (1842).
Hunt, John, C.C. (1671).
Hunt, — (1700).
Hunt, James, C.C. (1708).
Hunt, William (1753–56).
Hunt, Jas. (1772).
Hunt, Thos. (1835).
Hunt, Wm. (1835).
Hunt, Saml., Hoxton (1842).
Hunter, Thomas (1754–94).
Hunter, Thomas, Junior (1781–1800).
Hunter, William (1766–94).
Hunter, Thomas (1788–94).
Hunter, Wm. (1804).
Hunter and Son (1810–17).
Hunter and Edwards (1840–42).
Hurland, Henry, C.C. (1654).
Hurley, Isaac, Clerkenwell (1790).
Hurst, Isaac, C.C. (1677).
Hurst, W. (1835–42).
Hurt, Henry (1750–56).
Hussey, Joseph, C.C. (1685).
Hutchin, Joseph, C.C. (1697).
Hutchin, Joseph, C.C. (1703).
Hutchin, John, C.C. (1703).
Hutchinson, Richard, C.C. (1702–36).
Hutton, Patrick (1790).
Hutton, Thos., London (1776).
Hux, John (1840–42).
Hux, R. R., Clerkenwell, died (1869).
Hyams, Joshua (1840–42).
Hyde, Thomas (1783–94).
Hyde, James (1783).
Hynam, — (1750).
Hynam, Robert, livery C.C. (1769–80).

Imhof, N. (1842).
Inglish, Jas. (1790).

Ingram, Thomas, C.C. (1695).

Ingram, William, C.C. (1730).

Ingram, William (1842).

Inkpen, John, Horsham (1770).

Innocent, Robt. (1835).

Ireland, Henry, Lothbury; C.C.; maker of lantern clocks (1650–75).

Ireland, Francis, C.C. (1668).

Ireland, John (1779).

Ironside and Belchier (1737–40).

Irvin, Jean (1825).

Irving, Alexander, C.C. (1695).

Isaac, Daniel, C.C. (1660–70).

Isaacs, Levy (1769–83).

Isaacs, Lewis (1830–42).

Israel, John (1783).

Ive, G. H. (1825–42).

Ivery, John, repairer of the clock of St. Margaret's, Westminster (1548).

Ives, Francis, C.C. (1790).

Izod, William, C.C. (1649).

Jaccard, J. (1820–22).

Jaccard, David (1840–42).

Jackson, Richard, C.C. (1632).

Jackson, Joseph, C.C. (1648).

Jackson, Edward, C.C. (1669).

Jackson, Edward (1677); C.C. (1680).

Jackson, John, C.C. (1682).

Jackson, Thomas, C.C. (1688).

Jackson, James, C.C. (1689).

Jackson, Matthew, C.C. (1730).

Jackson, Martin, C.C. (1697), master (1721).

Jackson, John (1759–74).

Jackson, William, livery C.C. (1740–76).

Jackson, Randal (1780).

Jackson, John, livery C.C. (1776), master (1796); (1769–1800).

Jackson, John, Junior, master C.C. (1800–30).

Jackson, Henry (1790–94).

Jackson, Thomas (1790–1810).

Jackson, Lancaster; Wm. (1801); Wm. W. (1817).

Jackson, Isaac (1804).

Jackson, W. (1820).

Jackson, Geo. (1815–25).

Jackson, William, Brompton (1835–42).

Jackson, Henry, and Son, Clerkenwell (1835–42).

Jackson, William (1835).

Jackson, John (1842).

Jacob, Benjamin, C.C. (1706).

Jacob, Benjamin, C.C. (1718).

Jacob, Dennis (1775–1800).

Jacob, Dan. (1817).

Jacobs, Judah (1769–71).

Jacobs, E. (1820–35).

Jacobs, Edward (1835).

Jaggar, Edward, C.C. (1702).

James, John, C.C. (1662).

James, Joseph, C.C. (1689).

James, Robert (1835).

Jammett, —, C.C. (1704).

Janaway, Jno. (1815).

Janvier, Antide (1751–1835).

Jaques, William, C.C. (1687); master (1716).

Jaques, William, C.C. (1724).

Jaques, Aug. (1842).

Jarman, John, C.C. (1728).

Jarman, John B. (1815–23).

Jarman and Co. (1825).

Jarrett, Barnard, livery C.C. (1786).

Jarrett, John W., livery C.C. (1786).

Jarvis, George, C.C. (1728).

Jarvis, John (1775–94).

Jayne, John, C.C. (1687).

Jeanin, A. (1842).

Jefferies, John, C.C. (1639).

Jefferson, Samuel (1805–42).

Jefferson and Son (1815).

Jefferson, Reed and Walton (1820–25).

Jefferson, Matthew (1835–42).

Jeffery, William Knight, C.C. (1712).
Jeffery, Thomas, and Jones (1769–94).
Jefferys, Nathaniel (1771).
Jefferys, Nathaniel, junior (1780–94).
Jefferys, Henry (1793–1804).
Jefferys, G. (1800).
Jefferys and Gilbert (1800).
Jefferys, Nathaniel (1768–1804).
Jefferys and Ham (1810–1825).
Jeffreys, John, C.C. (1726–35).
Jeffs, John, C.C. (1697).
Jeffs, Benjamin, C.C. (1702).
Jelf, William, C.C. (1717).
Jenkins, Thomas, C.C. (1678).
Jenkins, Cornelius, C.C. (1678).
Jenkins, James, C.C. (1692); month clock, arch dial (about 1700).
Jenkins, —, Cheapside (1774).
Jenkins, Henry (1756–83).
Jenkins, F. (1835).
Jennings, Robert, C.C. (1703).
Jennings, Thomas, C.C. (1721).
Jennings, Charles, C.C. (1725).
Jernegan, Edward (1737–59).
Jersey, Francis (1760).
Jessop, Josias, Covent Garden (1781–90).
Jevon, May, C.C. (1706).
Job, Robert (1835–42).
Job, Fredk. (1835–42).
Jodin, Jean, Paris (1766).
Johann, A., born (1822).
Johnson, Roger, C.C. (1630).
Johnson, George, C.C. (1649).
Johnson, John, C.C. (1678).
Johnson, John, C.C. (1680).
Johnson, John (1701).
Johnson, Jeremiah, C.C. (1668–90).
Johnson, Cornelius, C.C. (1694).
Johnson, Robert, Edinburgh (1696).
Johnson, Thomas, C.C. (1700).
Johnson, John, C.C. (1701).
Johnson, James, C.C. (1706).
Johnson, Thomas, C.C. (1713).

Johnson, Isaac, C.C. (1723).
Johnson, William, C.C. (1702–25).
Johnson, Thomas (1730).
Johnson, James (1790–94).
Johnson, John (1770–99).
Johnson, John (1790–1820).
Johnson, C. (1820–23).
Johnson, Richd. (1815–20).
Johnson, Leond. (1825).
Johnson, J. and W. (1825).
Johnson, James (1835–42).
Johnson, William (1825–42).
Johnston, G. (1835).
Johnston, J. (1835).
Jolly, Joseph (1790–94).
Jon, J., London (1730).
Jones, Evans, C.C. (1648–71).
Jones, William, C.C. (1663).
Jones, Jonathan, C.C. (1687).
Jones, David, C.C. (1687).
Jones, Henry, C.C. (1697).
Jones, Valentine, C.C. (1704).
Jones, John, C.C. (1716).
Jones, Henry, master C.C. (1663–93).
Jones, John, master C.C. (1748–63).
Jones, Jenkin (1775–83).
Jones, Owen, livery C.C. (1786); (1780–94).
Jones, William, livery C.C. (1778–86).
Jones, William, livery C.C. (1780–1810).
Jones, Robert (1800).
Jones, James (1795–1810).
Jones, Wm. (1810–15).
Jones, John (1821–85).
Jones and Grant (1815–18).
Jones, F. (1825).
Jones, Sam. (1820–25).
Jones, W. (1825).
Jones, John and Timothy, Clerkenwell (1825–30).
Jones, Timothy (1826–40).
Jordan, Timothy (1769–80).

Jourdain, A. (1790–94).

Jourdain, William, London (1680–1710).

Jourdan, R. (1835).

Joyce, George, C.C. (1692).

Joyce, Stephen, Soho (1769).

Joyce, Samuel, and Co. (1790–1842).

Joyce, James, died 1883, aged 62.

Julian, Gregory, C.C. (1664).

Jullion, John, Brentford (1730).

Jullion and Son, New Brentford (1771).

Just, Leonard (1830–42).

Justin and Comp (1769).

Kaiser, Kleyser and Co. (1840).

Kaltenback and Fuller (1834–42).

Kammerer, Joseph (1840).

Kangiesser, S., Strand (1816–25).

Kanns, John, C.C. (1712).

Kater, Captain Henry, F.R.S. (1817).

Kay, Jno., London (1750).

Keandler, Chas. (1793).

Keat (Kent?), Joseph, Ratcliff (1810).

Keat, Edward (1830–40).

Keat, Mrs. Mary Anne (1840).

Keat, Sophia, (1842).

Keates, Wm. (1783–1800).

Keating, A. (1796–1815).

Keddon, Daniel, C.C. (1717).

Keef, Thomas (1835).

Keeling, George (1840).

Kefford, Thomas, Royston (1700–20).

Kelly, Richard, Strand (1790).

Kelme, —, London, maker of a small timepiece on a horse (1670).

Kelton, Simon, C.C. (1723).

Kemble, J. T. (1817).

Kemp, Charles, C.C. (1688–1694).

Kemp, Richard, C.C. (1701).

Kemp, William, livery C.C. (1786).

Kemp, Joseph (1790).

Kemps, Matthew, C.C. (1670).

Kendrick, John, C.C. (1719).

Kendrick, John, C.C. (1726).

Kendrick, Wm. (1772).

Keney, Vincent (1530).

Kenney, William, threatened with prosecution by C.C. for exercising the art, not being admitted (1682).

Kenning, Wm., C.C. (1684).

Kenning, Edwin, London (1705).

Kent, Henry, C.C. (1650).

Kent, Joseph (1806–17).

Kent, John (1817–35).

Kentish, John (1758–61).

Kentish, John, and Haynes (1769–88).

Kenton, Joseph, C.C. (1686).

Kerby, Thomas F., London (1760).

Kershaw, George (1790–94).

Kersill, William (1775).

Keyzor, Louis (1835–40).

Kidd, Gilbert (1760–80).

Kidder, John (1816–23).

Killingworth, Jno., Spitalfields (1815–18).

Kilminster, Henry, C.C. (1677).

Kimbell, Thomas (1842).

Kinable, —.

King, Jonathan, C.C. (1689).

King, Thomas, C.C. (1669); (1669–90).

King, Nehimiah (1693).

King, John, C.C. (1715).

King, John, C.C. (1729).

King, Isaac (1730).

King, John (1758–61).

King, Thomas (1773).

King, Thomas and Benjamin (1804–25).

King, W. (1822–30).

King, Thomas (1835–42).

Kingman, James (1783).

Kingsmill, George, C.C. (1667).

Kinnear, Charles (1830).

Kipling, William (1730–50).

Kirby, Robert, C.C. (1722).

Kirk, John, C.C. (1677).

Kirnier and Kleyser (1791).

Kissor, Samuel, C.C. (1712).

Kitchen, B. (1842).

Kitching, Joshua (1816–23).
Kleyser, Jno. (1790–94).
Kleyser, George, and Co. (1790–94).
Kleyser and Fritschler (1835–42).
Kleyser, T. and J. (1810–30).
Knibb, Samuel, C.C. (1663).
Knibb, Joseph, C.C. (1670).
Knibb, Peter, C.C. (1677).
Knifeton, Thomas, Lothebury (1690–1700).
Knight, Michael, C.C. (1677).
Knight, Richard, C.C. (1682).
Knight, Charles, C.C. (1685–97).
Knight, Henry, C.C. (1723).
Knight, John (1768).
Knight, Benjamin (1790).
Knowles, James, Chelsea (1835–40).
Krenckel, Peter, Eüchstet (or Füchstet); alarum table clock (1700).
Kullberg, Victor, Sweden (1824–1890).
Kyezor, Louis (1842).
Kynvyn, Jonas (1593).

Lacey, Chas. (1783).
Lacour, Daniel (1825).
Ladd, Ladd, C.C. (1709).
Ladd, J. (1823).
Lafosse, Wm. (1738–94).
Laidlau, Thomas (1770–94); C.C.
Lainy, John, C.C. (1720).
Laisne, Sibelin, Neuchatel (1750).
Lake, Bryan, C.C. (1674).
Lamb, Thos. (1790).
Lamb, Benj. (1769–79).
Lamb and Webb (1780–95).
Lamb, Sarah, Pentonville (1842).
Lambe, Thomas, C.C. (1632).
Lambe, Edmund, C.C. (1675).
Lambe, John (1800).
Lambert, Nicholas, London (1750–70).
Lambert, John (1775–1810).
Lambert, Francis (1800).
Lambert, Henry (1840).
Lambert, Henry (1842).

Lampe, John, C.C. (1713); (1713–65).
Lancaster, Francis, London (1790–1800).
Landlen, Thomas (1794).
Lane, Geo. (1893).
Langcroft, Richard, C.C. (1718).
L'Ange, A. (1835).
Langford, Goring, C.C. (1652).
Langford, Thos., C.C. (1781).
Langhorne, Thomas, livery C.C. (1776).
Langley, Thomas, C.C. (1664).
Langley, Cornelius, C.C. (1706).
Larard, Jas. (1842).
Larcay, — (1725).
Large, Augustus (1840).
Large, Jonathan, London (1790).
Laroch, John (1815–25).
Lasarus, Abraham (1760–65).
Lashbrook, Henry, C.C. (1715).
Lasoffe, William (1765–70).
Lasseter, William, Arundel (1770).
Latour, Réné, C.C. (1730).
Lauriere, J. (1822–30).
Laver, Benjamin (1790–1800).
Law, Thomas (1790–94).
Law, Anthony (1840–42).
Lawe, —; forbidden to work by C.C. (1632).
Lawell, Paul, C.C. (1653).
Lawley, Bernhard (1840–42).
Lawrence, —, Lancaster; Jno. (1761); Wm. (1785).
Lawrence, — (1763).
Lawrence, James (1835).
Lawrence, G. (1835–42).
Lawrence and Son (1835).
Lawriere, Jno., Pall Mall (1815–19).
Lawson, John Edwd. (1800–25); livery C.C.
Laxton, Thomas, C.C. (1642).
Laxton, Thomas, C.C. (1653).
Layfield, Robt., Lancaster (1785).
Layton, John, C.C. (1653).
Layton, Francis, C.C. (1726).

Layton, Thomas, livery C.C. (1776–1823).

Lazare, —, a Servian; made a clock for Moscow (1404).

Lazarus, H. (1815).

Lazarus, J. (1825–30).

Lazarus, J., Lambeth (1825).

Lazarus, H. L. (1835).

Larazus, E., and Son (1840–42).

Lazenby, R. (1770).

Lazenby, Wm. (1784).

Lea, Thomas, livery C.C. (1760–83).

Leach, Thos. (1753–60).

Leadbetter, William (1785–94).

Leah, Samuel Henry (1823–42).

Leah, Sam. Hy., jun. (1835–42).

Leake, Faith, C.C. (1685).

Leake, George, C.C. (1693).

Leaver, Wm. (1822–30).

Le Bon, Alex., Paris (1727–70).

Lecomte, James, C.C. (1687).

Lecomte, J. R. (1763–83).

Lecount, Peter, livery C.C. (1810–23).

Ledeur, —, London (about 1600).

Ledieu, Jas., Soho (1817).

Ledru, Wm., London (1795).

Lee, Cuthbert, C.C. (1676).

Lee, Samuel, C.C. (1694).

Lee, Ezekiel, London.

Lee, John, C.C. (1719).

Lee, George (1737–40).

Lee, John (1800–4).

Lee, Isaac (1840–42).

Leeds, W. H. (1817).

Leekey, Gabriel (1755–78).

Leekey, Gabriel, C.C. (1778–1815).

Leeming, Edwd., livery C.C. (1787).

Leeson, William, Birmingham, died 1886, aged 77.

Le Febuce, Charles (French), C.C. (1687).

Leffin, Thomas, C.C. (1720).

Lefosse, Wm. (1769–72).

Leg, Jno., London (1780).

Legg, John, C.C. (1724).

Le Grand, James, C.C. (1641).

Le Grand, Francis, C.C. (1647).

Legrand, James, junior, C.C. (1664).

Le Gros, P. J., Westminster (1800).

Le Guay (about 1750).

Leguesse, L. J.

Leicester, Jas. (about 1710).

Leigh, Thomas, C.C. (1730).

Leigh and Phillips (1840).

Leignes, Charles Peter, Strand (1790–94).

Lello, James, C.C. (1656).

Lemmon, Hy. (1835–42).

Le Noir, Etienne, Paris.

Lens, William, C.C. (1711).

Leon, George Isaac (1842).

Lepaute, J. A. (1709–89).

Lepine, — (1820).

Leplastrier, John (1790–1815).

Leplastrier, Louis, Shadwell (1804–15).

Leplastrier and Son, Shadwell (1820–28).

Leplastrier, Isaac, Strand (1828–42); C.C. (1829).

Leplastrier, Louis (1842).

Leplastrier and Son (1835).

Leptrope, —, London (1740).

Leroux, Alexander, C.C. (1706).

Le Roy, Pierre (1717–85).

Lesage, Augustine (1775–88).

Leslie, Robert, Clerkenwell (1793).

Lester, Thomas, C.C. (1697).

Lester, — (1774).

Lestourgen, David, C.C. (1721–51).

Lestourgeon, Thomas (1760–75).

L'Estrange, David, C.C. (1697).

Leutier, Pierre, Paris (1750).

Letwitch, William (1769–72).

Levens, John (1790–94).

Levin, Moses (1790–94).

Levin, Lewis (1804–30).

Levitt, partner Tobias.

Levy, Joseph (1780–85).

Levy, Lyon (1780–85).

Levy, Hyam (1775–85).

Levy, M. and C. (1790).
Levy, Philip (1798–1803).
Levy, Jonas (1800–20).
Levy, J. (1815).
Levy, B. (1820).
Levy, J., and Son (1820).
Levy and Co. (1825).
Levy, A. (1825–35).
Levy, S. (1830).
Levy, A. (1835).
Levy, Jonas, C.C. (1820–42).
Levy, Abraham (1840–42).
Levy and Moss (1842).
Levyson, Montague (1840).
Lewin, William, C.C. (1731).
Lewis, John, C.C. (1705).
Lewis, Ambrose, C.C. (1725).
Lewis, Joseph (1783).
Lewis and Alston (1815–25).
Ley, William, C.C. (1711).
Leyden.
L'Hospital, J. (1842).
Liddiard, Thomas (1775–83).
Lietuyt, John (1368).
Light, John, C.C. (1648).
Lightfoot, Peter (1335).
Like, George (1785–94).
Lily, — (1775).
Limmard, — (1796).
Limoniere, Stephen, C.C. (1712).
Lindd, Hy. (1700).
Lindesey, George (1770).
Lindley, — (1810).
Lindsey, John (1825).
Linnet, John (1815–25).
Lipp, Nicholas, Basle (1598).
Lipscomb, Benj., London (1760).
Lipsy, Dan (1817).
Lister, Thos., Halifax (1760–1802).
Litherland, Peter, Liverpool (1791).
Little, Joseph (1800).
Littlemore, Whitestone, C.C. (1698).
Littlewort, Geo. (1834).

Livermore, Edward (1798–1810).
Lloyd, William, C.C. (1668).
Lloyd, William, C.C. (1670).
Lloyd, Joseph, C.C. (1673).
Lloyd, David, C.C. (1677).
Lloyd, Richard, C.C. (1681).
Lloyd, Charles, C.C. (1691).
Lloyd, James, C.C. (1700).
Lloyd, James, Smithfield, C.C. (1722).
Lloyd, —, B.M. (1785).
Lloyd, —, B.M. (1790).
Lloyd, John (1790–94).
Lloyd, Wm., Hoxton (1842).
Lockwood, Benj., Norfolk (1740).
Loddington, Isaac (1719–34).
Lodowick, Peter, C.C. (1689).
Long, Thomas, C.C. (1653).
Long, John, C.C. (1677).
Long, John, C.C. (1698).
Long, Henry (1770–80).
Longford, Ellis, C.C. (1672).
Longford, Thomas, C.C. (1760–81).
Longland, John, C.C. (1677).
Loomes, Thomas, C.C. (1630–74).
Lord, Richard, C.C. (1632).
Lorimer, David (1805–18).
Lorimer and Edwards (1810–25).
Lorimer, William (1835–40).
Lormier, Isaac, London (1740).
Loseby, Edward Thomas (1846–90).
Louarth, Jasper, C.C. (1641).
Loudan, Wm. (1822–40).
Loughton, William, C.C. (1683).
Lounde (Lowndes), Jonathan, C.C. (1680–1700).
Loundes, Isaac, C.C. (1682).
Loundes, Charles (1700–26).
Love, Jas. (1780–90).
Love, Christopher (1816–25).
Lovelace, Jacob, Exeter.
Loveles, W., Hoxton (1796).
Lovell, Paul, C.C. (1630).
Lovett, William, C.C. (1702).

Lowe, Jno. (1802–18).

Lowry, Morgan, Holborn, (1700).

Lozans, Thos., London (1700–15).

Lucas, William, C.C. (1669).

Lucas, Edward, C.C. (1727).

Lucas, Henry, C.C. (1731).

Lucas, John (1800–10).

Lucie, John, C.C. (1663).

Ludlow, Samuel, C.C. (1706).

Lum, Joseph, Spitalfields (1700).

Lumb, John (1790–94).

Lumpkin, Thomas, C.C. (1694–1715).

Lund, John Richard (1868).

Lupton and Gillam (1825).

Lushbrook, —, C.C. (1701).

Luttman, William, C.C. (1720).

Lutwiche, — (1775).

Lutwyche, Thos. Wm., B.M. (1794).

Lynaker, Samuel, C.C. (1630–49).

Lynam and Bull (1785).

Lynam and Warwick (1793).

Lynch, Robert, C.C. (1670).

Lyndon, G., Soho (1825–30).

Lyne, William, C.C. (1703).

Lyon, Thos. Geo. (1793).

Lyon, Lewis (1840).

Lysney, Sebastian (1548).

Maberley, John, master C.C. (1718–39).

McCabe (1778); C.C. livery (1786); warden (1811).

McCarthy, Jas. (1793).

Mac-Dowall, Joseph Eden (1838).

McDowall, Charles (1836–72).

McDuff, Jas. (1835).

Mace, Lawrence, London (1749).

Macgregor, J. (1830).

Macham, Samuel (1750).

Mackarsie, G. (1820).

Mackarthy, James, (1790).

Mackdonald, Peter (1790–94).

MacKenny, G. (1840–42).

Mackie, James (1810–35).

Mackie, Geo., and Son (1822–25).

Mackie, James and George (1835–42).

Mackie, James (1830–42).

McLachlan, Hugh (1810–42).

Maclennan, Kenneth (1778–1825).

Maclennan, R. and W. (1815–25).

McMaster, Wm. Jno. (1814–19).

McNab, —, Perth (about 1816).

McPhail, C. (1830).

Macpherson, Normand, London; musical clock (about 1790).

Macure, Thomas, musical clock (1788).

Macy, Benjamin, C.C. (1712).

Madell, Charles (1835).

Maggs, William, claimed to be successor to D. Quare (1724–30).

Maginie, Samuel (1835).

Magniac, Francis, " Colonel," complicated clocks and automata (1770–94).

Magnus, N. (1823).

Maillett, Hy. (1790–94).

Maisonneuve, Benjamin (1769–72).

Makepiece, Robt. (1775–88).

Malden, Samuel, Rainham (about 1725).

Malleson, Thos. (1769–83).

Mallingley, Robt. (1790–93).

Malpas, J. (1753–75).

Manaviere, —, Smithfield (1774).

Manchester, John, C.C. (1700).

Maniglier, John, Soho (1840–42).

Mann, Jno., Kentish Town (about 1770).

Mann, Percivall (1790–94).

Mann and Muddell (1830).

Mansfield, Jno., London (1750).

Mantir, G. (1830).

Manwaring, Thomas, C.C. (1694).

Marchand, —, Geneva (about 1725).

Marchant, Samuel, C.C. (1700), warden (1704).

Marchant, —.

Marchant, William (1775–83).

Marchant, M. (1823).

Marchant, R. (1823).

Marchet, Richard (1790–94).

Marder, Henry and William (1842).

Marduit, Isaac, C.C. (1724).

Margan and Sherban (1793).

Margary, Thos. (1790).

Margetts, George, celebrated maker, livery C.C. (1799–1810),

Margot-Green (1700).

Margot-Green, D. (1835).

Marie, David (1762).

Marinot. (See Martinot.)

Markham, Robert (1736–40).

Markham, Markwick (1720–60).

Marks, L. (1830–35).

Marks, Lewis (1840–42).

Markwick, James, C.C. (1666).

Markwick, James, C.C. (1692); master (1720).

Marquet, Jacob, Augsburg (1567).

Marquet, — (Markwick?) (1674).

Marriott, John, C.C. (1715).

Marriott, W. (about 1760).

Marriott, John; musical clock maker (1780); master C.C. (1799).

Marriott, J. (1806–10).

Marriott, Wm. and J (1823–30).

Marsden, John, C.C. (1698); master (1731).

Marsden, Samuel (1820).

Marsden, Samuel (1835–42).

Marsh, Anthony, C.C. (1724).

Marsh, Jacob (1754–68).

Marsh, Sam. (1793–1818).

Marsh, James and Samuel (1790–1810).

Marsh, Thos.

Marsh, Wm. B., London (about 1800).

Marsh, Edward and John (1840).

Marsh, H. (1840–42).

Marshall, Benjamin, C.C. (1680).

Marshall, John, C.C. (1689).

Marshall, Samuel, C.C. (1689).

Marshall, Samuel, C.C. (1718).

Marshall, John, Newark (about 1730).

Marshall, Hy. (1817).

Marshall, E. (1825–30).

Marshall, Wm. (1816–35).

Marster, W. J. (1825).

Marston, Jno., his movement seized by C.C. (1661).

Marston, William, C.C. (1669).

Marston, John (1842).

Marten, Hy. and Wm. (1840).

Martin, John, C.C. (1679).

Martin, Jeremiah, C.C. (1687).

Martin, Richard, Northampton (about 1695).

Martin, Thomas, C.C. (1699).

Martin, William, Bristol (about 1700).

Martin, William, C.C. (1709).

Martin, John (1763–69).

Martin, Benjamin, maker of a curious table clock (1704–1782).

Martin, Thos., a good maker (1778–94).

Martin, Edmund (1790–94).

Martin, J. F. (1810).

Martin, G. (1835).

Martin, H. (1835).

Martin, James (1835).

Martin, M. (1835).

Martin, William (1810–40).

Martin and Saul (1817).

Martin and Mosse (1835).

Martineau, Joseph (1750–70).

Martineau, Joseph (1790–94).

Martinot, Barnaby (1618).

Martinot, Balthazar, Paris; horologer to Louis XIII. (1637).

Martinot, B., Rouen; specimen at B.M. (about 1680).

Martinot, Jerome, Paris; S.K.M. (about 1750).

Martinot, Baltazar, Paris (1725).

Masey, Thomas, mended St. Mary's Clock, Oxon. (1550).

Mason, Richard, C.C. (1632).

Mason, William, C.C. (1688).

Mason, Jno., Bristol (1673).

Mason, Samuel, C.C. (1712).

Mason, John, C.C. (1712); (1712–20).

Mason, Henry, C.C. (1715).

Mason, John, C.C. (1718); (1718–30).

Mason, William (1760–83).

Mason and Hudson (1772).

Mason, Robert (1790).

Mason, John (1840).

Masquerier, Lewis (1780–85).

Masquerier, Wm. (1790–94).

Masquerier and Perigal (1775).

Masse, James (1753–60).

Massey, Edmund, C.C. (1682).

Massey, John (1810–35).

Massey, Benj. (1810–26).

Massey, C. (1823–35).

Massey, Francis J. (1840–42).

Massey, Thomas (1835–42).

Massey and Windham (1830–35).

Masson, Denis, Paris; S.K.M. (about 1760).

Massy, Nicholas, a French refugee, C.C. (1682).

Massy, Jacob (1715–25).

Master, W. J. (1823).

Masterman, J. (1769–93).

Masters, William, C.C. (1701).

Masters, James, B.M (1803); livery C.C. (1810).

Matchett, John, C.C. (1648).

Matham, Robt. (1783).

Mather, Samuel, C.C. (1691).

Mathew, Francis, C.C. (1656).

Mathews, William, C.C. (1731); assistant and livery (1766).

Mathews, W. and C. S. (1817).

Mathews and Thorpe (1840–42).

Matthew, John, C.C. (1731); (1731 40).

Matthews, John, (1840).

Mattison, Thos. (1793).

Mattocks, John, livery C.C. (1786).

Maude, Benjamin (1780–94).

Maude, Edward (1793–98).

Mawley, Robt., London (about 1725).

May, William, C.C. (1679).

Mayes, John (1842).

Mayland, Thomas, C.C. (1698).

Maynard, Christopher, C.C. (1667).

Mayo, Joseph (1769–72).

Mayo, —, Coventry (about 1780–90).

Maysmore, Wm., Wrexham (1720).

Mayson, John, C.C. (1704).

Mead, Wm. (1835).

Meade, Garrett, C.C. (1703).

Meades, Thomas, C.C. (1687).

Meak, John (1825).

Measure, A. (1815–20).

Medhurst, Richard, Croydon, C.C. (1687).

Meek, Jno. (1812–18).

Meigh, Moses, C.C. (1712).

Melchior. (See Adam.)

Melville, John, hon. freeman C.C. (1781).

Melville and Stoddart (1804–10).

Melville, Robert (1835).

Menessie, Elisha (1790–95).

Meniall, James (French) (1682).

Menzies, John (1840–42).

Mercer, John (about 1720).

Mercer Brothers, Coventry (about 1770–90).

Merchant, Samuel, C.C. (1677); assistant (1698).

Mercier, Louis, Geneva (about 1690).

Meredith, Lancelot, signed petition against tyranny of C.C. (1656).

Meredith, John, C.C. (1664).

Merigeot, John, livery C.C. (1766).

Meriton, Samuel (1793–1800).

Merlin, John Joseph; mechanical genius; born 1735 at Huys. Arrived in England in 1760. He constructed a curious dial which never required winding up, as that was done by the room door opening.

Merny, Charles, liveryman. C.C. (1776).

Merrick, Joseph (1835–42).

Merrill, Charles, livery C.C. (1810).

Merrill, H. (1840).

Merriman, Benjamin, C.C. (1682).

Merrin, Henry (1840–42).

Merry, Charles, livery C.C. (1766); master (1768); (1755–69).

Merryman, Henry, C.C. (1674).

Mesniel, James (French), C.C. (1682).

Mestager, Henry, C.C. (1712).

Mesure, Anthony (1814–23).

Metcalf, George Marmaduke, C.C. (1781); livery (1786); (1794–1825).

Metcalf, Josh. (1816–30).

Metcalfe, Mark, Asknigg; died 1776.

Methem, Robt. (1775).

Micabius, John, C.C. ordered him to be sued (1632).

Michand, P., Paris (about 1755).

Michant, Daniel (1794).

Michell, Jo. (about 1700).

Michells (1830).

Micklewright, Erasmus, C.C. (1673).

Micklewright, —, C.C. (1708).

Middleditch, John (1835–42).

Middleton, William T. (1835–42).

Milborne, John, C.C. (1698).

Miles and Morgan (1790–94).

Miles, Septimus, livery C.C. (1810–42).

Miles, G. (1830).

Mill, David, C.C. (1655).

Millenet, Daniel; clock-watch with alarum; (about 1630).

Miller, John, C.C. (1674).

Miller, Peter, C.C. (1681).

Miller, Ralph, C.C. (1697).

Miller, Joseph, C.C. (1728).

Miller, —, Lurgan, Ireland; maker of a clock in which the hour was uttered by a human figure in a clear articulate voice (1762).

Miller, Fred (1797).

Miller, Chas. (1816–25).

Miller, Robt. (1820–42).

Miller, F., and Co. (1835–40).

Miller, Jas. (1842).

Millet, William, C.C. (1714).

Millett, Edward, C.C. (1680).

Millington, Thomas (1760–69).

Millington, Thomas (1790).

Million, William, C.C. (1671).

Millot. "Horologer du Roy, Paris"; (about 1680).

Mills, Thomas, C.C. (1652); (1648–60).

Mills, Ralph, C.C. (1697).

Mills, Richard, Edinburgh (1678–1705).

Mills, Robert (1790–94). Wm. Mills (1809–18).

Mills, Thomas, and Son (1812–23).

Mills, George (1825).

Milner, Thomas, London (about 1780).

Milner, Henry (1815).

Milton, —, B.M. (1802).

Milward, Geo. (1806–15).

Mimess, R. (1816).

Minchener, Saml., London (about 1810).

Minchinale, William, C.C. (1701).

Misplace, R. (1775–88).

Mitchell, Myles, C.C. (1640).

Mitchell, John, C.C. (1712).

Mitchell, Robert, livery C.C. (1766).

Mitchell and Viet (1768).

Mitchell, Jno. (1817).

Mitchell and French (1825).

Mitchelson, Jas. (1753–56).

Mitchelson, Alexander (1769–72).

Mitchelson, Walter (1780–1800).

Mitford, John (1714).

Mitford, Robert, liveryman C.C. (1776).

Mitten, Francis, Chichester (about 1750).

Moginie, Samuel (1822–42).

Moinet, Louis, author of "Nouveau Traité Général Astronomique et Civil d'Horlogerie Théorique et Pratique"; Paris (1848).

Molee, P. (1835).

Molens, Charles, C.C. (1709).

Molleson, Thos. (1788–1810).

Molyneux, R., and Sons (1835–42).

Moncas, John, Spa-fields (1835).

Monday, Joseph, C.C. (1654).

Monk, Edwd. (1793).

Monkhouse, Thomas (1759).

Monnier, John (1812–28).

Monro, Benjamin (1830–42).

Moodie, David, C.C. (1649).

Moody, Charles (1815–25).

Moon and Co. (1790).

Moon, William (1815–42); livery C.C. (1820).

Moor, William, C.C. (1701).

Mooran, Andrew, London (about 1760).

Moore, Joseph, C.C. (1690).

Moore, Daniel, C.C. (1697).

Moore, Thos., Ipswich (1729).

Moore, F. (1770–75).

Moore, John (1769–75).

Moore, Wm. (1793).

Moore and Gearing (1783).

Moore and Edwards (1793).

Moore and Starkey (1823).

Moore, Patrick (1806–10).

Moore, E. T. (1823–35).

Moore, George, died 1894.

Moore, Jno. (1824–42).

Moraley, Wm., London (1828).

Moran, Andrew (1740).

More, Charles (1840–42).

Morgan, Richard, petitioner to Charles I. for incorporation of C.C.

Morgan, Robert, C.C. (1639).

Morgan, Jude, C.C. (1654).

Morgan, Thomas, C.C. (1658).

Morgan, William (1696).

Morgan, John, C.C. (1703).

Morgan and Miles (1790).

Moriffet, R. and C. (1783).

Morland, Wm. (1780–85).

Morland, — (1790–94).

Morris, Edwd., assistant C.C. (1677).

Morris, Henry (1753–75).

Morris, John, C.C. (1799).

Morris, T. (1794).

Morriset and Lukin (1793).

Morrison, Richd. (1769–83).

Morrison, William N. (1840).

Morrison, John, a well-known clockmaker; died 1893.

Morritt and Lee (1816).

Morse, Richard (1835–42).

Morson and Stephenson (1760–72).

Morson, Richard (1775).

Morton, Samuel (1775).

Morton and Milroy (1800).

Mosbrucker, à Saverne (about 1750).

Moseley, William, C.C. (1680).

Mosely, Elinor, C.C. (1726–34).

Mosely, Martin (1804–35).

Mosely, Ephraim (1840–42).

Mosely, Moses (1830–42).

Mosely, Robert, and Son (1822–42).

Moses, Ephraim (1790).

Moses, Selegman, London (about 1775).

Moss, Thos. (about 1740).

Moss, Thomas (1775); livery C.C. (1786).

Moss, John (1825).

Moss, B. (1835).

Motley, Richard, C.C. (1682).

Mott and Bellin (1815).

Mott, William (1830–35).

Motteux, Samuel, C.C. (1697).

Mottram, John (1790–94).

Mottu, Brothers (1840–42).

Moule, Jas., London (about 1785).

Mouline, A., and Co. (1842).

Moulton, Henry. C.C. (1685).

Moulton, Saml. (1788–1800).

Mount, William, C.C. (1692).

Mountford, Zachariah, admitted C.C. (1684).

Mowlton, Conan, C.C. (1700).

Mowlton, Henry, C.C. (1715).

Moze, Henry (about 1740).

Muckarsie, George James (1794); livery C.C. (1824).

Mudge, Thomas, a celebrated maker (1715–94).

Mudge and Dutton (1766–90).

Mudge, Jno., London (1830).

Mulford, John, warden C.C. (1748); (1730–48).

Muller, Andreas (about 1570).

Muller, Johan Conrad; curious clock (about 1705).

Muller and Thum (1842).

Muncaster, Lancaster; Thos. (1797–1830); Wm. (1806); Jno. (1806).

Munden, Francis, C.C. (1653).

Murray, Wm., Edinburgh (1712).

Murray and Strahan (1816–25).

Murray, James (1814–42); livery C.C. (1817).

Musson, —, Paris (1780).

Muston, Geo. (1835–42).

Myddleton, Timothy, C.C. (1687).

Myers, John (1790).

Myers, John (1783–1804).

Myers, Hy. (1804).

Myers, Moses (1830).

Myers, Abraham (1840–42).

Myline, Humphrey, Edinburgh; died about 1690.

Mynuel, —, Paris; S.K.M. (1700).

Myson, Jeremiah, C.C. (1698).

Nadauld, Wm. (1804–20).

Nadauld, W. R. (1819–33).

Naizon, Francis (1780–85).

Nash, Thomas, C.C. (1717).

Nash, Samuel (1790–94).

Nathan, Henry, C.C. (1673); (1673–1700).

Nathan, Phineas (1840–42).

Nau, Richard, C.C. (1661).

Nau, George, C.C. (1675).

Naudey, Francis (1842).

Naylor, Jos., Nantwich; made an astronomical clock (about 1750).

Neale, John (1753–59).

Neat, J. (1817).

Neate, Wm. (1817).

Needham, Benjamin, C.C. (1709).

Needham, Robt. (1793).

Needham, Charles (1825).

Neighbour, William, C.C. (1685).

Neild, James (1755–94).

Neild, J. (1788).

Nelmes, Robert, C.C. (1717).

Nelmes, Robert (1842).

Nelson, Robert, C.C. (1697).

Nelson, John (1842).

Nemes, John, C.C. (1724).

Neuens, Peter (1840–42).

Neuwers, Michael (1599).

Newbrough, Jeremiah (1700–10).

Newby, John (1825).

Newcomb, Joseph, livery C.C. (1810).

Newell, William, livery C.C. (1810).

Newman, Joseph (1790).

Newman, John (1775–83).

Newman, John (1804–25); livery C.C. (1810).

Newman, Robert, livery C.C. (1810).

Newman, Wm. (1840–42).

Newnham, Nathaniel, C.C. (1703).

Newsam, Bartholomew (1572), clockmaker to Queen Elizabeth, in succession to Nicholas Urseau (1570–93).

Newsam, Jno., York (1586).

Newsham, Wm. (1765–93).

Newton, George, London (about 1680).

Newton, William, C.C. (1685).

Newton, Thomas (1753–56).

Newton, John (1788–1810).

Newton, Jno. (1788–1815).

Newton, Alexander, Levi, and Co. (1839–42).

Nicasius, John, C.C. (1632).

Nichol, Isaac, C.C. (1681).

Nicholas, W. (1825).

Nicholas, Samuel, and Son (1835–40).

Nicholls, Roger, C.C. (1667).

Nicholls, Thomas, C.C. (1707).

Nichols, Thomas, C.C. (1720).

Nicholson, John (1816–30).

Nickisson, S. (1815–42).

Nicole, John, keeper of the great clock within the palace of Westminster in 1731.

Nicoll, Wm. (1790–1835).

Nicoll, John (1814–42).

Nightingale, Wm., liveryman C.C. (1776–94).

Niloe, Hans (Dutch); musical clock for James I.

Noades, J. (1775).

Noakes and Nylder (1790–94).

Noakes, Jas. (1800–18).

Noble, Jas., Lancaster (1733).

Noble, Wm., London Bridge (about 1760).

Noble, Wm. (1804).

Noble and Harrison (1816–25).

Noble, C. (1830).

Nobson, John, C.C. (1697).

Nodes, John (1770–75).

Nodes, William (1783–94).

Nollorth, Chas., Yarmouth (1775).

Noon, — (1731).

Norcott, John, C.C. (1681).

Norgate, John, C.C. (1712).

Norman, Samuel (1825).

Norris, Joseph, C.C. (1670).

Norris, Edward, C.C. (1658); master (1686).

Norris, Dav., London (about 1750).

Norris, Charles, C.C. (1687).

Norris, Junr. (1795).

Norris, Chas. (1763–94).

North, John, C.C. (1650).

North, John, C.C. (1720).

North, Wm. (1790).

North, Richd. (1772–1800).

North, Fredk. (1816–20).

Northam, J. (1817).

Northam, G. (1825).

Northam and Son (1825).

Northcote, Samuel (about 1780).

Northey, John (1790–94).

Norton, Thomas, C.C. (1720).

Norton, Samuel, liveryman C.C. (1776); (1770–80).

Norton, — , Yarmouth (1788).

Norton, Eardley (1771).

Norton, Graham (about 1790).

Nourisson, Guillaume; reconstructed the Lyons clock in 1660.

Nourse, Thomas, livery C.C. (1766); (1756–94).

Nurse, John, C.C. (1718).

Oakes, John (1775–80).

Oakley, Wm. (1804–20).

Ogden, Thomas, C.C. (1659).

Ogden, Jno. (1681).

Okeham, Thomas, C.C. (1632).

Oliver, Thomas (1780–1800).

Olley and Clark (1817).

Orford, Robt. (1795–1810).

Orme, Jno., Lancaster (1712).

Orpwood, Richard, Finsbury (1800).

Orpwood, Geo. (1810–40).

Orr, Peter (1840).

Orton, Edward, C.C. (1687).

Orton, William F. (1835).

Osborn, William, C.C. (1700).

Osborne, Birmingham (1800–42).

Osmont, Jean B. (1840–42).

Otley, Thomas (1823).

Oughtred, Benjamin, C.C. author of several books on mathematics (1639–80).

Overbury, Thomas, C.C. (1688).

Overzee, Gerard, Isleworth, C.C. (1670–90).
Owen, Ben, London (1694–1740).
Owen, William, Cheapside (1737–40).
Owen, Joseph (1800–10).
Oyens, Peter, London (1730).

Pace, Thomas (1630–60).
Pace, Jno., Ratcliffe (1790–94).
Pace, Thomas (1788–1840).
Pace, John (1833).
Pace, Edmund (1840–42).
Pace, Chas. (1842).
Pace, Henry (1842–58).
Pacificus, Archdeacon, Verona; one of those to whom invention of wheel and weight clocks is ascribed (1850).
Pack, Richard, C.C. (1712).
Packer, Wm. (1840).
Pagars, Dan (1793).
Page, Joseph, C.C. (1683).
Page, Henry, C.C. (1713).
Page, John (1775–94).
Page, Wm. (1815–18).
Paget, Ambrose, C.C. (1728).
Pagnes, William, East Smithfield (1690).
Pain, William, C.C. (1729).
Pain, Thomas (1780).
Paine and Balleston (1840).
Paine, John P., St. Giles's; received 1826 a silver medal from the Society of Arts for a method of illuminating dials (1826–40).
Palfrey, John, C.C. (1654).
Palmer, Robert, livery C.C. (1776).
Palmer, Thomas, livery C.C. (1776).
Palmer, William, livery C.C. (1776).
Palmer, Thomas (1783–1810).
Palmer, Joseph (1814–18).
Palmer, B. (1830).
Palmer, John (1825–35).
Palmer, Robert, Kennington (1832–42).
Palmer, Hy. (1842).

Pamphillon, William, C.C. (1725).
Panchard, Abel (1765–80).
Panchaud, David (1790–1825); livery C.C.
Panchaud and Cumming (1806–10).
Panier, Jossué, Paris; S.K.M. (1725).
Pantin, Lewis (1770–1800).
Papanoine, Isaac (French), C.C. (1680–1710).
Papworth, John, C.C. (1688).
Paradise, John, C.C. (1716).
Paradise, John (1823).
Pare, Thos., London (1700).
Parish, Simon, C.C. (1723).
Park, Nicholas, C.C. (1641).
Parker, Thomas, C.C. (1669).
Parker, John, C.C. (1674–1677).
Parker, John, C.C. (1678).
Parker, Robert, C.C. (1698).
Parker, John, C.C. (1706).
Parker, Thos., Dublin (1750).
Parker and Wakeling (1760–75).
Parker, John (1769–75).
Parker, Thos. (1788).
Parker and Birketts (1804).
Parker, John (1793–1804).
Parker, James (1835).
Parkes, Jno. (1800).
Parkhouse, Roger, Yorks (1730).
Parkinson, Lancaster; Wm. (1708); Robt. (1732); Wm. (1789).
Parkinson, Wm., and Frodsham (1806–42).
Parkinson, James (1820).
Parkinson, Henry (1835–1842).
Parkinson, James (1842).
Parkinson and Bouts (1860).
Parkwick, Jas., C.C. (1698).
Parnell, Thomas (1815–42).
Parr, Thos. (1735–75).
Parr, Edward (1824).
Parsons, Richard (1690–1720).
Parsons, John (1696).
Parsons, John (1775).
Parsons and Horne (1825).

Parten, William, C.C. (1720).

Parter, William, C.C. (1692).

Parter, Francis, C.C. (1730).

Partington, J. (1790).

Partington, C. F. (1826).

Partington, William (1815–42).

Partridge, Wm., C.C. (1652).

Partridge, Joseph (1760–63).

Partridge, C. (1840–42).

Pashler, Edwd. (1774).

Passanine, Isaac (1770).

Passement, Admiral, designer of equation and astronomical clocks (1750).

Passevant, Wm. (1793).

Pasteur, Jacques, Geneva (1780).

Patching, Elisha, C.C. (1728).

Patmore, Peter, C.C. (1813).

Patrick, Edwd., London (1690).

Patrick, John, C.C. (1712).

Pattee, Thomas, livery C.C. (1810).

Patterson, Robert, C.C. (1668).

Patterson, George (1835).

Paul, Nowell, alien, threatened with prosecution for working as clockmaker within liberties of C.C. (1668).

Paul, Thomas, C.C. (1670).

Paule, Philip (1810–23).

Paule, George (1830–35).

Paulin, Lewis (1772).

Payn, John, Southwold (1451).

Payne, Nicholas, C.C. (1671).

Payne, H. and John (1753–75).

Payne, Southern, livery C.C. (1766), master (1778).

Payne, J. (1794–1825).

Payne, Wm. (1816–50).

Peachey, Newman, livery C.C. (1760–78).

Peachy, William, C.C. (1727).

Peacock, George (1769–75).

Peacock, Geo. (1778–81).

Peacock, Samuel (1793).

Pearce, Adam, C.C. (1664).

Pearce, Jno. (1753–63).

Pearce, William, livery C.C. (1787), master (1804).

Pearce, John (1835–40).

Pearkes, F. (1823).

Pearne, Wm. (1793).

Pearse, John (1753–60).

Pearson, Mary (1772–75).

Pearson and Price (1830).

Peatting, Thomas, C.C. (1682).

Peck, George, C.C. (1725).

Peckett, John, C.C. (1691).

Peckover, Richard, Cornhill (1737–56).

Peere, —, C.C. (1654).

Peers, Chester. A noted family of clockmakers (1745–1840).

Peirson, Worthy (1840).

Pelleter, Solomon (1775).

Penfold, Joshua, C.C. (1695).

Penfold, Miles (1769–75).

Penkethman, Thomas, C.C. (1692).

Pennington, Robert, and Son (1832–42).

Pennock, John, C.C. (1638), master (1660).

Penton, Charles (1760–75).

Pepper, Thomas, livery C.C. (1776–94).

Peppin, Sam. (1517).

Pepys, Richard, C.C. (1674–1707).

Pepys, John, junior, C.C. (1715), master (1739).

Pepys, William, C.C. (1723).

Perchard, Matthew (1753–59).

Perchard, Peter (1760–72).

Percival, N. (1798–1800).

Percival, Thos. (1804).

Percival, M. (1817).

Peres, Mark, C.C. (1680–1700).

Perigal, Francis, C.C. (1740–80).

Perigal, Francis, junior (1778); livery C.C. (1787).

Perigal, Francis, and Son (Francis S. Perigal, junior, master C.C., 1806), (1790–1808).

Perigal, John, C.C. (1770–1800).

Perigal and Browne (1794–1800).

Perigal, Jno., Soho (1810).

Perinot, Abraham (1780).

Perin, Chas. Henry (1842).

Perins, John (1750–94).

Perkin, R. (1790).

Perkins, Eysum, threatened with prosecution by C.C. for exercising the art (1682).

Perkins, James, C.C. (1730).

Perkins and Spencer (1765–74).

Perkins, Vineyard (1793).

Pernell, —, London (1730).

Perrenoud, F. (1810).

Perring, H. (1830).

Perringham, Francis (1790).

Perron, Richd. (1790–94).

Perry, Henry, C.C. (1691).

Perry, John (1835–42).

Peterkin, John (1810–40).

Petit, Guillaume, C.C. (1630–56).

Petit, William, C.C. (1632).

Peto, —, prohibited from working by C.C. (1632).

Peto, —, London (1780–1800).

Petter, Christopher, C.C. (1730).

Pettit, — (1835).

Pettit, Isaac, Whitechapel (1835).

Pettit, Eliza, Whitechapel (1840–42).

Pettit, William (1840).

Petty, William, C.C. (1646).

Pewtress, Thomas (1753–56).

Pfaff, Jeremas, Augsburg (1700).

Philcox, George (1835–78). He spent his life in endeavouring to improve timekeepers.

Philip, Robert, musical clockmaker (1779–88).

Phillipe, Adrien, died 1894.

Phillips, Philip (1790–1800).

Phillips, Joel (1820).

Phillips, P., Finsbury (1830).

Phillips, Abraham (1835).

Phillips, John (1817–35).

Phillips, Joseph (1835).

Phillips Brothers (1839–42).

Phillips, James and Charles, Clerkenwell (1835–40).

Phillips P. (1840–42).

Phipps, James (1783).

Pickett, William (1768–72).

Pickett and Rundell (1775–83).

Pickman, Wm., Soho (1816–1835).

Pierce, Thomas, died 1665, aged 77.

Pierre, Le Queux (1396).

Pierre, Pasquier, C.C. (1648).

Pigott, Henry, C.C. (1687).

Pike and Green (1806–30).

Pilkington, J., Woolwich (1815).

Pilkington, R. J., London (1760).

Pinard, Paul (1775).

Pinchbeck, Christopher (1690–1732).

Pinchbeck, Edward, son and successor of the above (1732–66).

Pinchbeck, Christopher, son of the above-named Christopher, died (1783).

Pine, Philip (1779–82); B.M.

Pinhorne, —, Portsea (1800).

Pinkerton and Miller (1842).

Pinson, Jno., London (1677).

Piolaine and Co. (1815–25).

Pipes, John, London (1750).

Pistor, Edward (1764–90).

Pistor, Edwd. and Jno. (1793–98).

Pitcher, John, C.C. (1689).

Pitman, John, C.C. (1714).

Piton, James, C.C. (1710).

Pitt, Thyar, livery C.C.; maker of a musical clock (1770–94).

Pitt, William, livery C.C. (1787).

Pitt, Caleb (1790–1830).

Pitt, Chas. (1835–40).

Pitt, John, Finsbury (1830–42).

Pitt, W. G. (1840–42).

Pitt, J. (1842).

Pittit, Jno. (1817).

Pittney, Thos. (1769–72).

Planck, Anthony (1760–72).

Plankh, Nicholas, Augsburg (1580).

Planner, Thomas, C.C. (1701–30).

Planner, Thomas, C.C. (1730).

Plant, Edward, C.C. (1664).

Plaskett, Reuben, died (1845), aged 80.

Plaskett, Jas. (1860).

Plate, Richard (1835).

Platt, Edward (1835).

Player, Robert, C.C. (1700); (1700–40).

Player, H. J. (1820–40).

Pleverie, Isaac, C.C. (1652).

Pleydell, Jno., London (1720).

Pluett, Anthony, C.C. (1697).

Plumbly, Jas. (1820–42).

Plumley, William, C.C. (1756–79).

Plumley, Wm., son of the preceding; C.C. (1780); livery (1797); master (1801); (1780–1825).

Plumley, Chas. (1835–42).

Plummer, Wm. (1793).

Plunkeld, Richard, Whitechapel (1820).

Pohlmann, Peter (1760–75).

Poidevin, F. (1830).

Poisson, Henry, London; S.K.M. (1695–1720).

Poncy, J. P. I. (1840).

Poney, Abraham (1840–42).

Pool, J. C. (1654).

Poole, Jno., London (1712).

Poole, Robert, livery C.C. (1766); master (1781); (1760–81).

Poole and Bickerlo (1769–75).

Poole, George (1783–85).

Poole, John (1822–40).

Pools, Edmonde, C.C. (1722).

Pope, Thos. (1793).

Portal and Coyle (1760–63).

Portal, Abraham, and Gearing (1769–75.)

Porter, Chas. (1835–40).

Porthouse, Thomas (1815–60).

Potter, James, livery C.C. (1810).

Pottinger, Jno. (1793).

Pouchoulin, J. L., Geneva (1750).

Poulton, R., Kennington (1840–42).

Powell, Bartholomew, C.C. (1668).

Powell, Robert, C.C. (1710).

Powell, H. (1793).

Powell, James (1828–35).

Powis, Robt. (1806–23).

Poy, Godfrie (1718–30).

Poy, Godfrey (1785–95).

Pratt, Smith, and Hardy (1793).

Pratt, Chas., Islington (1830–35).

Preddy, Wm., Taunton (1849).

Preist, Wm. (1763).

Prentis, Daniel (1788–96).

Prentis and Son (1804–7). John Prentis (1817).

Prerie, Humphrey, C.C. (1653).

Presbury and Son (1804).

Presciot, Peter (1790–94).

Prest, — (1774).

Prestbury, Chas. (1793).

Prestige, Bartholomew, C.C. (1703).

Preston, Edward, C.C. (1721).

Prestwood, Joseph, C.C. (1703–20).

Prevost, Adolphe (1840–42).

Price, George (1788–1806).

Price, W. (1825).

Priddith, John, C.C. (1639).

Prideaux, Edmund (1780–94).

Pridham, William (1760–63).

Priest, Thomas, C.C. (1729).

Priest, W., and James (1768–72).

Priest, — (1774).

Priestman, M. (1817).

Prigg, John, Bethlehem, livery C.C. (1776); (1766–77).

Priggin, Wm., Hull (1770).

Prime, Andrew, C.C. (1672); S.K.M.

Prince, Richard, C.C. (1680).

Pringle, Thos., Dalkeith (1810–30).

Print, Richard, C.C. (1698).

Prior, George (1765–94).
Prior, George (1798–1810).
Prior, John, Nessfield (1798–1820).
Prior, George (1809–22).
Prior, Edward.
Prior, I. W., Newington Causeway (1830).
Procter, Wm., livery C.C. (1810).
Prosser, William, Strand (1769–72).
Prosser, John (1822–30).
Pryme, Andrew, C.C. (1647).
Pryor, Robert (1835–40).
Puckridge, J. (1716–40).
Puckridge, Charles (1788–94).
Puckridge, John (1790–1818), livery C.C.
Puckridge, Alfred, Bloomsbury (1840–42).
Pugh, Ellis (1775–94).
Puller, Jonathan, C.C. (1683–1705).
Purnell, J. (1842).
Purrier, Richard, C.C. (1705).
Purse, William (1804).
Purse, George (1804–25).
Purse and Catchpole (1835).
Purton, Francis (1793).
Purvis, Alexander (1825–42).
Putland, G. and J. (1793).
Putley, Francis (1806–42), livery C.C.
Puzzy, Isaac, London (1625).
Pybus, William (1789–94).
Pyne, Nathaniel, C.C. (1677).

Quare and Horseman, Exchange Alley (1700–30).
Quari (or Quarie), London (1700). S.K.M.
Quelch, John, C.C. (1646); (1646–66).
Quin, T. D. (1840).
Quinton, Stephen, London (1750).

Radford, Henry, C.C. (1721).
Radford, Jas. (1793).
Ragsdale, George (1769–83).
Raiment, Thomas, C.C. (1719).
Rainaldi, Giovannia P., Venice (1495).
Rainaldi, Carl, son of the foregoing.

Raines (Raynes), William, East Smith-field; C.C. (1660).
Raingo, —, Paris (1780).
Rainier, John, livery C.C. (1787).
Rainsford, Francis, C.C. (1689).
Rainsford, Jno., London (1720).
Raitt, Alexander, London (1690–1720).
Raker, P. (1775).
Rambley, Wm. (1775–94).
Ramsay, —, Islington (1800–8).
Ramsden, Thomas, C.C. (1648).
Ranceford, Bernard, C.C. (1677).
Randall, John (1790–94).
Ransom, George, Soho (1825).
Rant, John, C.C. (1687).
Rant, Jonathan, C.C. (1687).
Rapson, Thos. (1814–18).
Ratcliffe, J. (1835).
Ratherain, C. (1825).
Raven, Crispin, London (1780).
Rawford, James (1770–90); livery C.C.
Rawlings, Charles, C.C. (1818), livery (1826); died 1864.
Rawlings, George (1790).
Rawlins, Henry, C.C. (1706).
Rawlins, James, livery C.C. (1787).
Rawlins, Geo. (1793).
Ray and Montague, Soho (1804–19).
Ray, Samuel (1820–30).
Ray, Henry (1835–40).
Raymond, Jno. (1774).
Raynesford, Benjamin, C.C. (1709).
Read, George (1820).
Read, Wm., Clerkenwell (1820).
Read, Geo. (1815–25).
Read, William (1825).
Reader, J., London (1825).
Redier, Antoine, Paris (1717–92).
Reed, Thos., C.C. (1632).
Reeve, Thomas, C.C. (1648–55).
Reeve, Henry, C.C. (1682).
Reeve, John, C.C. (1712).
Reeve, Jarvis, C.C. (1731).

Reeve, Wm. (1830–35).

Reeves, Wm. (1825–42).

Reeves, Richard, Shoreditch (1820–42).

Regard, Reymond, C.C. (1677–91).

Regnauld, —, Chalons, France (1833).

Regnier, "Maitre," Paris (1605).

Rehle, —, Freiburg; table clock (about 1690).

Reid and Auld, Edinburgh (1790–1820).

Reid, Wm. (1800–20).

Reid, Adam, Clerkenwell and Woolwich (1779–1835).

Reid, Thomas (1750–1834).

Reilly, J. C. (1815–25).

Reith, James, C.C. (1705).

Relph, E. (1835).

Rener, Michael E., Kronstat (1590).

Renshaw, Thomas (1825).

Rentzsch, Sigismund (1813—42).

Restell, Thos., Tooting (1848–52).

Rewalling, Thomas, C.C. (1715).

Rex, Thomas (1842).

Reyner, Stephen, C.C. (1691).

Reyner, Thos. (1740).

Reynolds, Joseph, C.C. (1691).

Reynolds, Thomas, C.C. (1705–40).

Reynolds, Jno., blacksmith, Hagbourn, Berks.; made a clock and chimes for Brampton Church (1732).

Reynolds, Francis, Kensington (1776).

Reynolds, Thos., and Son (1783–94).

Reynolds, G. (1830).

Reynolds, T., Clerkenwell (1835).

Rice, Stephen (1793).

Richard, Peter, C.C. (1679).

Richards, Luke, C.C. (1648).

Richards, Hugh, master C.C. (1735).

Richards, Thomas (1770–72).

Richards, William, Clerkenwell; livery C.C. (1776).

Richards, William (1794–1817).

Richards, Thomas (1804–30).

Richards, W. (1830).

Richardson, Richard, C.C. (1675).

Richardson, James, master C.C. (1788).

Richardson, John (1798–1811); livery C.C.

Richmond, Robt., Lancaster (1817).

Rickman, W. (1820).

Ricord, Richard, C.C. (1649).

Riddlesdon, Samuel, C.C. (1766).

Rider, John (1835).

Ridley, Josiah, C.C. (1685).

Ridley, Thos. (1830–42).

Riesle, E. (1840).

Rigby, E., and Son, Clerkenwell (1795–1800).

Rigby, James, Clerkenwell (1804).

Rigby, Thos. (1816–18).

Rigby, Joshua (1820).

Rigby, James (1806–30).

Rimbault, Stephen (1760–81).

Rimbault, Paul (1779–85).

Ring, Joseph, C.C. (1693).

Rippin, William, Holbeach, Lincolnshire; worked at his trade thirty years after he lost his sight, died 1857.

Risbridger, William, Dorking (1700).

Ritchie, David, Clerkenwell (1812).

Ritherdon, Geo., Aldgate (1753–83).

Ritherdon, Robert (1758–1800).

Rivers, David, livery C.C. (1760–83).

Rivers, David (1753–75).

Rivers, Jno. (1783).

Rivers and Son (1790–1812); Wm. Rivers, master C.C. (1794).

Rivers, William (1818–20).

Riviere, Samuel Newton (1790–1804).

Robbin, Fabian, London (1690–1700).

Robbins, J. (1842).

Roberts, Josiah (1793).

Roberts, Jno. (1790).

Roberts, Wm. (1806–30).

Roberts, George (1820).

Roberts, Jas. (1842).

Robertson, Benj. (1783).

Robin, R., Paris (1742–99); S.K.M.

Robins, John (1783–94).

Robins, Wm. (1783); master C.C (1813).

Robins, John (1800–17).

Robins, John (1823–30).

Robinson, Robert, C.C. (1652).

Robinson, William, C.C. (1667).

Robinson, Thomas, C.C. (1703).

Robinson, Ruhamer, C.C. (1713).

Robinson, William, C.C. (1720).

Robinson, Philip (1737–40).

Robinson, James (1730–70).

Robinson, Jno., Lancaster (1783).

Robinson and Cave (1770).

Robinson, Anthony (1783).

Robotham, Fras., Hampstead (1836–40).

Robson, Wm. (1780–94).

Robson, William, musical clockmaker (1797–1810); master C.C.

Roby, James (1793–1800).

Rochat, Jules, Soho (1840–42).

Rochford, M. F. (1804–30).

Roger, — (1424).

Rogers, William, C.C. (1641–53).

Rogers, John, C.C. (1731).

Rogers, William, livery C.C. (1776).

Rogers (1774).

Rogers, Isaac, C.C. (1776); master (1824–39).

Rogers, Thomas, livery C.C. (1810); Wm. Rogers (1817).

Rogers, C. (1820).

Rogerson, William, livery C.C. (1766); master (1774); (1760–75).

Rogerson, Henry, London (1800).

Rolf, Joseph, and Son (1769–88).

Rolfe, Robert (1835–50).

Roll, George, Augsburg. In 1588 made a clockwork globe. S.K.M.

Rombach, J. (1835).

Rome, Wm. (1842).

Romer, Flack, C.C. (1661).

Romer, Thos. (1817).

Romeux, Lewis de, C.C. (1706).

Romilly, Peter (1769–94).

Romley, Chris., and Romley, Rob. (1760).

Romney, Joseph, C.C. (1664).

Ronnizen, Adam, C.C. (1687).

Roof, Daniel, C.C. (1676).

Rooke, John (1765–94); C.C. (1781).

Rookes, Barlow, C.C. (1667).

Rose, Michael, C.C. (1676).

Rose, Joseph, and Son (1765–68).

Rose, —, jun. (1774).

Rose, Joseph, Son, and Payne (1771–94).

Rose, John (1830).

Roskell, Robert (1805–30).

Ross and Peckham (1310).

Rosse, Samuel, C.C. (1679).

Rossi, W. (1830).

Roheram, Thomas, C.C. (1662).

Rotheram, R. H., died 1864, aged 74.

Rothwood, Robert, C.C. (1632).

Rothwood, Robert, C.C. (1648).

Rouckleiffe, Jno., Bridgewater (1770).

Roumieu, Adam, C.C. (1695).

Roumieu, John, C.C. (1720).

Roumieu, Adam, C.C. (1726).

Roumyen, James, C.C. (1692).

Routh, Sam., London (1780).

Routledge, Geo., Lydford, Devon, died 1801.

Roux, Bordier and Roman, Geneva (1810).

Rowe, Thomas, C.C. (1699).

Rowe, Benjamin, C.C. (1708).

Rowe, John, livery C.C. (1770–80).

Rowland and Co. (1825).

Rowlands, William, and Son (1823).

Rowlands, Christopher (1815–40).

Rowning (1758).

Roy, David, C.C. (1682).

Roy, William (1804).

Roycroft, Thomas, C.C. (1699).

Royer, William (1820).

Roze, A. C. (1862).

Rudkin, Thomas, C.C. (1683).

Rudrupp, Jno., Amersham (1710).

Ruegger, — , Geneva (1800).

Rugendas, Nicholas, Augsburg (1605–30).

Rugless, Sam. (1815–25).

Rugless, T. (1842).

Rundell, Edwd. (1710).

Rush, Samuel, Leicester Fields (1759–90).

Russel, Charles (1790).

Russell, Nicholas (1653–1700).

Russell, Thomas, livery C.C. (1776).

Russell, Thos. (1797–1832).

Russell, Charles and Thomas (1787–1815).

Russell, T. (1842).

Rutland, Jonathan (1793–1804).

Rutland, James (1822–30).

Rutter, Jno. (1793).

Ruttiven, William (1630).

Ryder, Thomas, C.C. (1698).

Ryder, Thomas, C.C. (1712).

Ryler, William, C.C. (1712).

Ryley, Thomas, C.C. (1704).

Rymer, Hy., Adelphi (1817).

Saber, Edwd. (1783).

Sacheverell, Benassir, C.C. (1687).

Sadlier, Samuel, C.C. (1723); (1720–23).

Sadler, Stephen (1830).

Saer, Joseph, C.C. (1686–1700).

Saffory, John (1760–75).

Sagar, — , Middleham (1750).

Sainsbury, Richard, Clerkenwell (1840–42).

Salmon, Henry (1769–82).

Salmon, Robert (1790–94).

Salmon, C. E. (1823).

Salter, Edward (1788–94).

Salter, John (1825–30).

Saltmarsh, Samuel, Clerkenwell (1840).

Sambrook, John, C.C. (1680).

Samley, — (1775).

Samon, John, C.C. (1654).

Sampson, Robert, Westminster (1786–88).

Sampson, Wm., London (1800).

Samson and Grandin, Soho (1810).

Samuel, Humphrey.

Samuel and Hill (1793).

Samuel, Abraham (1820–25).

Samuel, J., Shadwell (1835).

Samuel, Abraham, and Son (1840–42).

Sanders, Daniel, C.C. (1632).

Sanders, George (1790–94).

Sanders, Jas. (1790–94).

Sanders, John (1810–15).

Sanders, George (1820).

Sanderson, Robert, C.C. (1703–50).

Sanderson, Jno. (1715).

Sanderson, Hy. (1778–81).

Sanderson, Thos. (1815).

Sanderson, Samuel (1840).

Sandford, William (1800–25).

Sandoz, J. G., Paris (1836–91).

Sands, Jno. (1790).

Sandys, Jas. (1800).

Saplin, P. (1835–42).

Saplin, T. (1842).

Sarbitt, John (1804).

Sargeant, B. (1835).

Sargeant, H. (1835).

Sargent, Robert, C.C. (1720).

Sargent, Benjamin (1769–88).

Sargent, Josh. (1794–1818).

Sarl, J. (1842).

Satchabell, Thomas (1804).

Sather, Thos., London (1730).

Saunders, John, C.C. (1721).

Saunders, John, C.C. (1730).

Saunders, Joshua (1765–70).

Saunders, Thos. (1817).

Saunders, D. (1820–40).

Saunier, Claudius, France (1816–96).

Savage and Vincent (1800–15); livery C.C. (1804).

Savage, Thos. (1816–40).

Savage, W. (1820–25).

Savage, Samuel (1825).

Savage, D. (1835).

Savage, Thomas (1842).

Saville, John, C.C. (1678–85).
Savory, Andrew, C.C. (1676–1700).
Savory, Joseph (1788).
Savory, Farrand and Co. (1793–1800).
Savory, Joseph and Co. (1820).
Savory, A. (1825).
Savory, Thos. Cox (1834–64).
Savory, Adey B., and Son (1865–93).
Sawyer, Paul, C.C. (1718).
Sawyer, John (1804).
Say, Nehemiah, C.C. (1654).
Scafe, William, C.C. (1720); master (1749).
Scale, G. (1840).
Scales, Edwd. (1775–80).
Scantlebury, W. (1780–92).
Scherer, George F. (1835–40).
Scheirer, Johan (1620).
Schilsky, Joseph (1840–45).
Schlott, Hanns (1578–81).
Schmidt, J., Hamburg; table clock (1710).
Schmidt, John (1800–10).
Schofield, Jno. (1793).
Schofield, W., Chelsea (1815–25).
Schofield, William (1830–35).
Scholefield, James, London (1800).
Schretger, Augsburg (1660).
Schuler, M. and J. (1835–42).
Schutt, Jasper, C.C. (1648).
Schwilgue, Jean B. (1776–1856).
Science, John, C.C. (1724).
Scolding, John (1794–1810).
Scott, Daniel, C.C. (1697).
Scott, — (1770–75).
Scott, James (1752); C.C. (1766).
Scott, John, C.C. (1770–94).
Scott, Wm. (1790–94).
Scott, Thos. (1810–20).
Scott, A., and Co. (1828–32).
Scott, Wm. (1830–42).
Scott, Jesse (1835–42).
Scott, Robert (1815–40).
Scott, Wing and Co. (1840–42).

Sea, Frederick (1820–30).
Seaborne, James, C.C. (1648–50).
Seagrave, Matthew, C.C. (1730).
Seagrave, Robert (1790).
Searle, George (1830–40).
Seatoun, G. (1795).
Seddon, James, C.C. (1662).
Seddon, Humphrey, Southwark (1730).
Sedwell, Edward, C.C. (1664).
Seignior, Robert (1670–82).
Sellars, John, C.C. (1685–96).
Sellers, William (1740).
Selwood, William, Lothbury, C.C. (1620–36).
Selwood, John, C.C. (1641).
Sens, William, C.C. (1711).
Sergeant, Nathaniel, master C.C. (1769–84).
Sergeant, Benjamin (1754–68).
Sermand, F. (1650).
Servant, H. (1775).
Seur, Chas., London (1695).
Sewell, Geo. (1790–94).
Sexty, R. (1830–40).
Seymore, John, C.C. (1710).
Seymour, Jno. (1712).
Seymour, William (1780).
Shalcross, Josiah (1800–66).
Sharp and Williams (1790).
Sharp, J. (1794–1808).
Sharp, John (1806–25).
Sharp, T. (1816); George Sharp (1822–25).
Sharpe, William, C.C. (1681).
Sharpe, Wm. (1793).
Sharpnell, James (1775).
Shaw, John, C.C. (1682–1714).
Shaw, Lancaster; Thos. (1726); Robt. (1789).
Shaw, Anna Maria (1733).
Shaw, William (1760–72).
Shayler, Richard (1753–56).
Shayler, William (1755–75).

Shearer, James (1825–42).

Shedel, Jos., London (1750).

Sheldrick, Edward (1798–1803).

Shelley, Jno. (1636).

Shelly, Joseph, C.C. (1717).

Shelly and King (1772–75).

Shelly, Samuel (1775).

Shelton, Samson, C.C. (1623–49).

Shelton, John, C.C. (1720); livery (1766).

Shepherd, Henry (1760–75).

Shepherd, Wm. (1815–25).

Sheppard, Samuel (1830).

Shepperd, Sarah (1830).

Shepperd, Charles (1840–42).

Sheraton, Thomas (1803).

Sherbird, J. (1820).

Sherborne, Thomas (1793–1800).

Shere, Henry, and Arnold (1753–68).

Sherwood, William, C.C. (1695–1721).

Sherwood, William, C.C. (1720); master in 1740.

Shick, William (1820).

Shields, John (1835).

Shields, John (1840–42).

Shindler, Thomas, Canterbury (1720).

Shirley, John, C. C. (1720–24).

Shirt, Wm. (1815–35).

Shole, Sim., Deptford (1825).

Short, Joshua, C.C. (1665).

Short, James (1740–70).

Shorter, E., Southwark (1830).

Shrapnell, James (1761–94).

Shuckburg, Charles, C.C. (1719).

Shuttleworth, Henry, C.C. (1669).

Shuttleworth, Francis (1806–10).

Sibbald, William (1815–35).

Sidley, John, C.C. (1701).

Sidley, Benjamin, C.C. (1710).

Silke, Jno., Elmsted (1670).

Silver, Fredk., livery C.C. (1810).

Silver, Joseph (1793).

Silver, J. and J. (1825–30).

Simcox, William, C.C. (1682).

Simcox, Samuel, C.C. (1708).

Simkin, Ben. (1788–93).

Simmons, John (1753–56).

Simmons, Ebenezer, Moorfields (1816–76).

Simmons, George (1840–42).

Simmons, Morrice (1842).

Simonds, Thomas, C.C. (1661–70).

Simonds, J. L. (1820–30).

Simons, G. (1840–42).

Simpkin, Benj. (1800).

Simpkins, Thomas, C.C. (1710).

Simpkins, Benjamin (1800).

Simpkinson, Roger (1758–75).

Simpson, John, C.C. (1700–10).

Simpson, John, C.C. (1723).

Simpson and Ward (1737–40).

Simpson, William Ellison, C.C. (1781).

Simpson, Archibald (1790–94).

Simpson, Hector (1785–94).

Simpson, R. (1795–1815).

Simpson, John (1815–40).

Simpson, Robert (1835–42).

Simpson, Robert, junior (1840).

Simpson, Thos. (1835–42).

Sims, Geo. (1738).

Sims, John (1773–78).

Sims, Henry (1780).

Sinclair, Chas., 69, Old St. (1835–42).

Sinderby, Francis H. (1790); livery C.C. (1810–40).

Sindry, Lawrence, C.C. (1661).

Singleton, Jno. (1806).

Skeggs, Wm., London (1760).

Skeggs, L. (1788–1810).

Skeggs, Wm. (1816–40).

Skerrow, Jas., Lancaster (1783).

Skerry, W., Westminster (1835–42).

Skinner, Matthew, master C.C. (1730–47).

Skinner, Chas. (1840).

Slack, Joseph, C.C. (1723).

Slater, W. (1835).

Sloagh, William, C.C. (1687).

Sloper, Jeremiah, C.C. (1726).

Sly, Robert, C.C. (1720).
Smalle, Lewis (1585–1605).
Smalley, Thomas, C.C. (1687–1700).
Smalley, Jno., Lancaster (1721).
Smart, John, C.C. (1682).
Smart, Orpheus (1750).
Smart, Benjamin (1800–18).
Smart, Thomas (1816–30).
Smart, Saml. (1835).
Smart, Alex. (1835–40).
Smeed, George (1835–42).
Smith, John, C.C. (1630–49).
Smith, George, C.C. (1632).
Smith, Walter, C.C. (1641).
Smith, Robert, C.C. (1648–50).
Smith, John, C.C. (1654).
Smith, John, C.C. (1656–57).
Smith, David, C.C. (1662).
Smith, Robert, C.C. (1680–1700).
Smith, John, C.C. (1674–1708).
Smith, Thomas, C.C. (1700).
Smith, Morris, C.C. (1702).
Smith, Henry, C.C. (1703).
Smith, John, C.C. (1703–40).
Smith, Tudor, C.C. (1717).
Smith, Thomas, C.C. (1718).
Smith, Obadiah, C.C. (1725).
Smith, Joseph, Chester (1740).
Smith, Maurice (1728–32).
Smith, Edward, Bury (1730).
Smith, John, Pittenweem; maker of an 8-day musical clock.
Smith, Susanna (1747).
Smith, Wm., Lancaster (1767).
Smith, Gabriel, Chester (1773).
Smith, Jas. (1758–60).
Smith, Jas. (1776–90).
Smith, Geo. (1770–76).
Smith, James (1760–80).
Smith, William (1759–80).
Smith and Sharp (1780–85).
Smith, Richd. (1780–85).
Smith, Joseph (1783–90).

Smith, Geo. (1783–90).
Smith, Jas. and Son (1769–94).
Smith and Wareham (1790).
Smith, Jabez (1790).
Smith, Walter (1795).
Smith, Chas. (1790–1823).
Smith, James (1776–94); C.C.
Smith, John, livery C.C. (1776–90).
Smith, Wm. (1800–4).
Smith, Wm. (1803–10).
Smith, Jas. (1790–1815).
Smith and Asprey (1817).
Smith, George (1820).
Smith, William (1823).
Smith, John (1825).
Smith and Co. (1825).
Smith, T. W. (1820–30).
Smith, B. (1830).
Smith, G. (1823–30).
Smith, J. (1825–30).
Smith, Thos. (1820–35).
Smith, J., and Son, Clerkenwell (1835–42).
Smith, John (1842).
Smith, Joseph (1842).
Smithyes, Wm. (1740).
Smitton, Peter (1820–35).
Smoult, Thos., Lancaster (1708); Jas. (1739).
Smyth, Joshua (1690).
Sneeberger, Michael, Prague (1605–20).
Snell, George, C.C. (1688–1700).
Snelling, Thomas, C.C. (1680).
Snelling, Henry (1769–75).
Snoswell, William (1835–42).
Snow, Jno., London (1630).
Soar, Jas., Finsbury (1842).
Soffleur, Thos., London (1680).
Solomon, Hy. (1775).
Solomon, S. C. (1794–1804).
Solomon, Moses (1810–30).
Solomon, Henry (1835).
Solomon, Henry, and Co. (1840–42).

Solomon, P. (1840–42).

Solomon, J. (1842).

Somersall, George (1750–79).

Somersall, Richard (1776–1804); livery C.C. (1786).

Sommersal, John, C.C. (1708).

South, Joseph, C.C. (1709).

Southan, Saml. (1790–94).

Southwarth, John, C.C. (1689).

Southworth, Peter, C.C. (1664).

Sowerby, Jno. (1817–1830).

Sowerby, Thomas (1830).

Sowter, John, C.C. (1683).

Sparkes, Nicholas, C.C. (1659).

Sparrow, Thos. (1790–94).

Sparrow, Jno. (1815–18).

Speakman, Thomas, C.C. (1685).

Speakman, Edward, C.C. (1691).

Speakman, John, junior, C.C. (1706).

Speakman, William, master C.C. (1701); (1690–1715).

Spear, Jacob, musical clockmaker (1835).

Spencer, Thomas, Strand, C.C. (1682–85).

Spencer, Arthur, C.C. (1732).

Spencer and Perkins (1775–94).

Spencer, J. (1820–30).

Spiegalhalter, G. (1835–42).

Spink, Marshall (1772–1842).

Spittle, Richard, C.C. (1699–1720).

Spitz, Gaspar, Schwartz (1590).

Spratnell, Sam. (1793).

Springer, Sam. (1810).

Spurrier, John, C.C. (1684).

Spyer, J., and Solomon (1793–1825).

Stables, Thomas, C.C. (1685).

Stacey, John, C.C. (1683).

Stacey, William (1750).

Stafford, John, C.C. (1708).

Stafford, T., Chelsea (1810–20).

Stainton, Matthew (1772).

Stallard, Philip (1793).

Stamp, J. (1775).

Stamper, Francis, C.C. (1682–1700).

Stamper, John (1772).

Stanbury, Henry, C.C. (1709–20).

Standish, William, C.C. (1668).

Stanes, Jeffery, C.C. (1686).

Stanger, Hugh (1835–40).

Stanley, John, C.C. (1732).

Stanton, John, C.C. (1692).

Stanton, Edward, C.C. (1662–96).

Stanton, Joseph, C.C. (1703).

Stanton, Samuel, London, C.C. (1714).

Staples, Jas. (1788–94).

Stapleton, Thomas, C.C. (1694).

Staptoe, William, C.C. (1703–10).

Starey, John (1770–94); livery C.C.

Starkey, Joseph, C.C. (1706).

Starr, Robt., C.C. (1667).

Startridge, Roger (1750).

Stauffer, Robert, and Co. (1830–42).

Stauffer, Robert, Son, and Co. (1830–42).

Stauffer, Julius (1830–42).

Stayne, Thomas, C.C. (1654).

Stedman, J. (1790).

Steele, F. (1825–33).

Steers, Jno. (1793).

Stegar, John, C.C. (1699).

Steibel (or Stebbell), Christopher, Augsburg (1635–60).

Steinmann, Daniel (1840–42).

Stephens, Francis, C.C. (1632).

Stephens, Joseph, C.C. (1721); master (1752).

Stephens, Joseph, master C.C. (1776); (1760–90).

Stephens, Thomas (1823).

Stephenson, Benjamin (1774–77).

Stephenson, William (1793).

Stephenson, Thos. Sam., livery C.C. (1810).

Stephenson, D. W. (1820–30).

Sterck, William (1760–93).

Sterck (Sterk), William (1772–90).

Steuart, James (1790).

Stevens, Samuel, C.C. (1680).
Stevens, Daniel, C.C. (1661).
Stevens, George, C.C. (1673).
Stevens, Thomas, C.C. (1700).
Stevens, Nathaniel, C.C. (1702).
Stevens, Samuel, C.C. (1706–18).
Stevens, Richard, C.C. (1715).
Stevens, Joseph, master C.C. (1745–94).
Stevens, Samuel (1780–93).
Stevens, W. (1835).
Stevens, Ezek. (1840–42).
Stevens, William, junior (1840–42).
Stevens, William (1840–42).
Stevens, D. (1842).
Stevenson, Adam, livery C.C. (1786).
Stevenson and Farrow (1810–24).
Stevenson, J. (1835).
Steward, Jno. (1793).
Stewart, Joseph (1842).
Stiebel, B. (1823).
Stiles, John, C.C. (1704).
Stiles, Nathaniel, C.C. (1725–70).
Stiles, Richard, master C.C. (1770–90).
Stiles, William (1835).
Still, Francis, C.C. (1699).
Stimner, Richd. (1780).
Stimson, —, London (1710).
Stirling, John (1788).
Stirrup, Thomas (1652).
Stock, Jabez (1700).
Stockwell, Hy. (1793).
Stoddart, Robert (1815–42).
Stoddart, J. (1835–40).
Stoddart, James (1825–86).
Stogden (Stocten), Matthew, (1712); C.C. (1717–70).
Stokes, Henry (1586).
Stone, Andrew, C.C. (1699).
Stone, William, C.C. (1700).
Stone, Roger, C.C. (1710).
Stone, Samuel (1820).
Storer, Robert (1721–1865).
Storey, James, C.C. (1703).

Storey, Charles (1743–60).
Storey, J. (1830).
Storie, W. (1810).
Storr, Marmaduke (1760–74).
Storr, William (1765); C.C. (1794).
Storr and Mortimer (1830–42).
Story, William (1760–72).
Story, Hy. (1820).
Stracey, John (1790).
Strachan, Andrew (1691).
Strachan, A. and J. (1830).
Straiton (or Straton), Archibald, Edinburgh (1780).
Stratford, George, C.C. (1704).
Stratton, Richard, C.C. (1720).
Stratton, Jno. (1816–25).
Stratton, Joseph (1810–35).
Street, Richard, C.C. (1680–1716).
Strelly, Francis, C.C. (1665).
Stretton, Sarah, C.C. (1710).
Stribling, Benjamin (1700).
Strigel, William F. (1760–75).
Strigel, George Philip (1760–88); C.C.
Strongfellow, John, C.C. (1691).
Stroud, Elizabeth (1835–40).
Stubb, Thos., London (1690).
Stubbs, Gabriel, C.C. (1675–77).
Stubbs, Joseph (1793).
Stuk, William (1781).
Style, Nathaniel, C.C. (1725–70).
Style, Richard, livery C.C. (1764–96).
Sudbury, John, C.C. (1686).
Sully, Henry, C.C. (1704–1728).
Summer, William, C.C. (1662).
Summer, Francis (1790–94).
Supple, John (1783).
Sutherland, D., Leith (1775).
Sutherland, Thos. (1793).
Sutor, Wm. (1712).
Sutton, Isaac, C.C. (1662).
Sutton, Wm., and Co. (1790–93).
Swale, Jaques (1668).
Swannell and Co. (1790–94).

Swannick, G. (1820).
Swanson, Robert, C.C. (1730).
Swanson, William (1790).
Swearer and Son (1820).
Swearer, J. (1840–42).
Sweeby, John, C.C. (1671–1700).
Swift, M. (1793).
Swinden, Francis Charles (1824–25).
Sword and Sons (1838).
Sydenham, H. and J. (1800–4).
Sydenham, J. (1816–23).
Sylvester, John, C.C. (1693).
Symes, Robt., London (1800).
Symonds, Thomas (1770–88).

Taber, Thos., Clerkenwell (1825).
Tailour, Edward (1629).
Tallans, Gabriel (1720).
Tallibart, Louis (1842).
Tallis, Aaron, C.C. (1722).
Tanner, Joseph, C.C. (1682).
Tapp, Francis (1775–85).
Tarman, J. B. (1825).
Tarleton, Wm., Liverpool (1790).
Tate, Ruth, East Sheen (1790).
Tatum, Jno. (1817).
Taylor, John, C.C. (1702).
Taylor, George, C.C. (1703–15).
Taylor, Charles, C.C. (1723).
Taylor, Richard, C.C. (1724).
Taylor, Jasper, C.C. (1729–70).
Taylor, Jno., Lancaster (1772).
Taylor, Benj. (1793–1800).
Taylor, Samuel, C.C. (1788–1810).
Taylor, Edward (1822–25).
Taylor, Joseph (1825).
Taylor, John S. (1809–40).
Taylor, Kennard and Co. (1822–30).
Taylor, David (1842–64).
Taylor, Jas. (1835).
Taylor, Robert (1835).
Taylor, Charles (1840).
Teams, John (1790–94).

Tebball, Benjamin, C.C. (1683).
Temple, Thomas, C.C. (1720).
Templer, Charles, C.C. (1673).
Tenant, Leonard (1617).
Tennant, Thomas, C.C. (1668).
Terrier, James, C.C. (1694).
Terrier, Thomas, C.C. (1694).
Terrier, Mary, C.C. (1713).
Terrot, P., Geneva (1730).
Terrot and Thuillier, Geneva (1750).
Terroux, l'aîné, Geneva (1770–85).
Terry, Isaac, Clerkenwell (1835–42).
Terry, —, Thoralby (1730).
Terry, —, Yorks. (1820–50).
Teulings, C. (1793).
Thacke, Philip, C.C. (1685); (1685–1700).
Thead and Pickett, Ludgate Hill (1758–65).
Thitchener, W. (1835–40).
Thitchener, J. (1835).
Thitchener, Thomas (1840–42).
Thomaque, Abraham, C.C. (1675).
Thomas and Evans (1793).
Thomas, Jno. (1810).
Thomas, Richard (1793–1817).
Thomas, Thomas (1825).
Thomas and Son (1825–69).
Thomas, F. L. and J. W. (1821–30).
Thomas, John (1835).
Thomegay, Mark (1768).
Thomlinson (1670).
Thompson, John, C.C. (1662).
Thompson, Robert, C.C. (1681).
Thompson, Isaac, C.C. (1699).
Thompson, John, C.C. (1720).
Thompson, Troughton, C.C. (1731).
Thompson, Ann, and Son (1790–94).
Thompson, James (1790–94).
Thompson, John (1765–94).
Thompson, W. (1790).
Thompson, Thomas, and Storrs (1817).
Thompson, E. (1835–40).

Thompson, John (1835–47).

Thompson, William (1840–42).

Thompson, Edward John (1829–96).

Thomson, Philip, and Son (1769).

Thomson, Adam (1830–60).

Thorlet, Jonas, London (1760).

Thorn, Thomas (1758–69).

Thorn, Robert (1760–68).

Thorne, Simon, London (1750).

Thorne, J. Travis (1760).

Thorne, John (1790–1818); John and Son (1820).

Thorne, James, Limehouse (1835–42).

Thorne, John (1842).

Thornton, Henry, C.C. (1699).

Thornton, John, C.C. (1731).

Thorogood, John, C.C. (1660).

Thorogood, William, C.C. (1660).

Thorogood, Richard (1783–90).

Thorowgood, L., London (1770).

Thuret, J., Paris; S.K.M. (1700).

Thwaites, Ainsworth, Clerkenwell (1740–80).

Thwaites, Jas. (1768–90).

Thwaites, John, master C.C. three times (1780–1816).

Thwaites and Reed, Clerkenwell (1817–42).

Tidbury and Son (1822–25).

Tilly, Joseph, C.C. (1703–20).

Tinson, Thos. (1793).

Tipping, George, C.C. (1674).

Tobias, Morris (1798–1800).

Tobias, Morris, and Co., Wapping (1804–12).

Tobias and Levitt (1816–42).

Tolby, Charles, C.C. (1720).

Tolkien and Dancer (1807).

Tolkien, George (1810).

Tolley, Charles, C.C. (1683).

Tollison, John, C.C. (1714).

Tomkins, William (1768–72).

Tomkinson, Humphry (1768–75).

Tomlin, Edwd. (1772–88).

Tomlinson, Thomas, C.C. (1647).

Tomlyns, Nicholas, C.C. (1647).

Tompion, Thomas, junior (1694); C.C. (1702).

Tompson, J., Clerkenwell (1842).

Toms, T. E., Minories (1820).

Topham, J. (1788–1800).

Torado, Francis, C.C. (1633–75).

Torin, Daniel (1766).

Torin, James Lewis (1738–80).

Torkler, Peter (1782–90).

Tothaker, William, C.C. (1703).

Toutin, Henry, Blois.

Townsend, Jno., forbidden to work by C.C. (1632).

Townsend, Samuel, C.C. (1702).

Townsend, Elizabeth and John (1760–69).

Townsend, Elizabeth (1804).

Townsend, William (1793–1842).

Towson, Jno. Thos., Devonport (1826).

Trail, Edwin (1835–40).

Trail, Edwin (1835–42).

Travers, Wm., Clerkenwell (1788–1810).

Travers, Adam, Clerkenwell (1783–94).

Tregent, James (1770–1804).

Trelegon, James, Strand (1775).

Trelegon and Ockley (1793).

Trembley, J. L., Geneva (1710).

Trenholm, —, C.C. (1728).

Trewinnard, Joshua and James (1790–1842).

Trewinnard, Joshua (1807–10).

Trewinnard, Edward (1825).

Trewinnard, James (1835).

Trewinnard, Joseph (1835).

Trewinnard, George (1835).

Trigg, Thomas, C.C. (1701).

Triggs, Thomas, C.C. (1708).

Trim, John, London (1790–1800).

Tringham, Geo. (1828–42).

Tripp, Job (1772).

Trippett, Robert, C.C. (1700).

Trippitt, William, C.C. (1706).

Triquet, Jas. (1768–72).

Tristle, —, Williton (1742).

Tritschler and Co. (1835–40).

Troughton, Nathaniel (1768).

Troughton, Joseph, Lancaster (1779).

Troughton, Bryan (1760–75).

Troup, Jno. (1822–42).

Troup, W., London (1760).

Trowe, Gilbert, C.C. (1722).

Tuck, J. and L.

Tudman, James (1697–1710).

Tuite, William (1761–75).

Tupling, B. (1820).

Tupman, Geo. (1790–1830).

Tupman, James, Bloomsbury (1816–42).

Turges, Josiah (1768–72).

Turmeau and Kettlewell (1793).

Turner, Joseph, C.C. (1717).

Turner, Thos., London (1745).

Turner, William (1760–72).

Turner, John (1788–94).

Turner, Wm. (1825–40).

Turner, J. and Charles (1830).

Turpin, Benj. (1835–42).

Turton and Walbancke (1793).

Turvee, Jarrett, C.C. (1688).

Tutet, Edward, livery C.C. (1766); master (1786); (1760–94).

Tuttell, Thomas, C.C. (1695).

Twhing, James, C.C. (1688).

Twycross, Stephen (1793).

Twycross, Stephen, and Son (1800–1817).

Twyford, Robert, C.C. (1770–82).

Twyford, Robert, and Co. (1790–1810).

Twyford, R. (1815–19).

Tyas, W. T. (1820–35).

Tyler, George (1715–1735).

Tyler, James Henry (1835).

Tymms, A. (1820).

Tymms, M. (1820).

Tyrer, Jas., Hy., Clerkenwell (1806–30).

Tyrer, Jas. (1842).

Udall, Thos. (1793).

Udall, J. (1819–22).

Uffington, Jno. (1793).

Ulrich, John Gottleib (1830–74).

Underhill, Cave, C.C. (1655).

Underwood, Wm., London (1720).

Underwood, John, and Sons (1758–63).

Underwood, John (1754–75).

Underwood, Robt. (1769–1810).

Underwood, Cæsar (1798–1820).

Uneman, John and William, Dutch clock-makers in England (1368).

Unwin, Edward, Paddington (1820).

Upjohn, James, and Wirgman (1769–94).

Upjohn, Peter (1783–1835).

Upjohn, J. and T. (1835).

Upjohn and Bright (1842).

Urseau, Nicholas (1553); on New Year's Day, 1556, he presented a clock to Queen Elizabeth.

Urseau, Nicholas, probably a son of the preceding (1572–90).

Usherwood, William (1830).

Vale, Samuel (1747).

Vale, Wm. (1770).

Vale, Howlett, and Carr (1754–90).

Vale and Rotherham (1790–1840).

Vale, Wm. (1776–94).

Vale, William (1816–40).

Valentine, Chas. D. F., livery C.C. (1810).

Vallance, Thos. (1820).

Van Ceulen, John, Hague (1660).

Vandenburg, J. (1830).

Vanham, Leonard (1737–40).

Vanscolina, Richard (1842).

Vardon, Samuel and Thomas, Soho (1783–94).

Vaslet, Andrew, C.C. (1717).

Vaucher, Fritz, Soho (1842).

Vaughan, Geo. (1816–28).

Vauguion, Daniel (1790–93).

Vecue, Thomas, C.C. (1632).

Vere, John Henry (1769).

Vernon, Christopher (1650).

Vernon, Samuel, C.C. (1649), master (1679).

Vernon, —, C.C. (1685).

Vesper, J. (1820).

Vesper, T. and W. (1835–42).

Vevers, Richard (1825–30).

Vickerman, Thos. (1760).

Viel, George, Soho (1842).

Vieyres, Anthony (1842).

Vigne, James (1770–94); C.C.

Villiscum, Stephen (1780–85).

Vincent, John (1840–42).

Vine, Jas. (1790–94).

Vine, James (1825).

Viner, Charles Edward (1776–1840); livery C.C.

Viner, Charles Edward, and Hopkins (1829–42).

Vines, James, C.C. (1708).

Vines, Joseph, Berks (1836).

Virgoe, Thomas, C.C. (1682).

Visconti, G. (1410).

Voght (or Vogt), Auty (1830–35).

Vogt and Co. (1830).

Vogt, Chas. and Fredk. (1836–42).

Voland, Elias, C.C. (1632).

Volk, P. (1835–40).

Vossière, Thomas, C.C. (1698).

Voughan, Edward, C.C. (1715).

Voughan, Daniel (1775).

Voughan, George (1820).

Vouloire, Matthew, C.C. (1692).

Voyce, Gamaliel, C.C. (1694–1700).

Vuille Brothers (1840–42).

Vulliamy, Justin (1730–75).

Vulliamy, Benjamin, C.C. (1781); (1775–1820).

Vulliamy, Benjamin Lewis (1810–54).

Vulliamy and Son (1793–1820).

Wade, Henry, C.C. (1728).

Wade, Jos. (1793).

Wagdon, Stephen, C.C. (1724).

Wagner, Johan Heinrich (1650).

Wagner, J. (1800–75).

Wagstaff, James (1835).

Waine, — (1774).

Wainwright, John, C.C. (1679).

Wait, Jno., and Son (1765–72).

Wakefield, Wm., Lancaster (1782); Timothy (1811).

Wakefield, John (1835–42).

Wakefield, T., (1835).

Wakelin and Taylor (1788–94).

Wakelin and Garrard (1800–5).

Waker (Walker?), Peter, C.C. (1663).

Waldoe, John, C.C. (1677).

Waldvogel, Anthony (1835–40).

Walford, John, C.C. (1717).

Walkden, Thomas, C.C. (1694).

Walker, Jas., C.C. (1632).

Walker, George, C.C. (1683).

Walker, Jonadab, C.C. (1687).

Walker, John, C.C. (1710–30).

Walker, Peter (about 1740).

Walker, Joseph (1790–94).

Walker, Wm. (1790–94).

Walker, D., and Son (1806–20).

Walker, John (1816–40).

Walker, Thomas (1820–30).

Walker and Blundell (1835–42).

Walker, Edwd. (1839–42).

Wallace, Hy. (1775).

Waller, J. (1790).

Wallis, William, C.C. (1715).

Wallis, Peter (1737–40).

Wallis, Henry (1765–68).

Wallis, Jacob, London (1780).

Wallis, Jno. (1825–40).

Wallitt, Richard, C.C. (1693).

Walton, Christopher (1823–35).

Warburton, William, C.C. (1693).

Ward, John, C.C. (1731).

Ward, Edward, C.C. (1731).

Ward, Robert (1762–85).

Ward, Richard (1790–94).

Ward, Henry, a well-known clockmaker (about 1770–90).

Ward, John, master C.C. (1797).

Ward, Benjamin (1790–1808).

Ward, John (1790–94).

Ward, Robert (1790).

Ward, Rich. (1826–42).

Warden, Thomas (1691).

Ware, Robert, C.C. (1701).

Wareham, John (1816–23).

Warfield, Alexander, C.C. (1692).

Warne, James (1760–75).

Warner, John, C.C. (1682–92).

Warner, John, C.C. (1696–1701).

Warner, John (1835).

Warnes, Robert (1822–5).

Warre, W. H., free of C.C. by redemption (1857), assistant (1863).

Warren, Richard, C.C. (1668).

Warwick, Wm. (1793).

Washboure, Thomas (1754–59).

Wassell, J. (1830).

Waters, John, C.C. (1646).

Waters, John, C.C. (1683).

Waters, Thomas, C.C. (1731).

Waters, John (1775).

Watkins, John, livery C.C. (1820–38).

Watkins, Joseph.

Watkins (1820).

Watson, William, C.C. (1691).

Watson, Samuel, C.C. (1692); inventor and maker of a curious piece of clockwork.

Watson, Walter, C.C. (1720).

Watson, John (1780–85).

Watson, Thomas (1785–94).

Watson, James (1788–1805).

Watson, Wm. (1793–1805).

Watson, W. (1820).

Watson, Edward (1820–42); livery C.C. (1820).

Watson, Wm. (1842).

Wattes, John, C.C. (1664).

Watts, Richard, C.C. (1680).

Watts, John, C.C. (1712).

Watts, James, C.C. (1720).

Watts, William (1770–75).

Wayland, Henry, Stratford (1835).

Waylett, Jas. (1793).

Waylett, John (1795–1810).

Weadon, William, C.C. (1695).

Weakman, William, C.C. (1661).

Weare, Robt. (1846).

Weatherley and Roberts (1800–5).

Weatherley and Son (1810–23).

Weaver, Cuthbert, C.C. (1682).

Webb, Charles (1737–40).

Webb, Peter (1753–68).

Webb, Benjamin (1778–90); hon. freeman C.C. (1787).

Webb, Arthur (1780–94).

Webb, Robert (1815–19).

Webb, Edward (1616–20).

Webb, J. (1820).

Webb, Wm., and Co. (1816–20).

Webb, William (1840–87).

Webber, W., Woolwich (1817).

Webster. Many generations of this family have carried on business in the City of London from 1675.

Webster, Robert, C.C. (1675).

Webster, John, C.C. (1695).

Webster, George, C.C. (1703).

Webster, Henry, C.C. (1709).

Webster, Thomas, C.C. (1709).

Webster, William, C.C. (1734), died (1735).

Webster, William, master C.C. (1755); livery (1766).

Webster, Samuel, livery C.C. (1766).

Webster, Robt., Whitby, Yorks. In 1772 patented a repeater.

Webster and Son (1781–1800).

Webster, Richard (1788–1840); livery C.C. (1810).

Webster, Richard (1642–82).

Webster, Charles (1835–42).

Weekes, Thomas, C.C. (1654).

Weeks, Thomas, C.C. (1688).

Weeks, Charles, C.C. (1713).

Weeks, John (1810–23).

Welborne, William (1800–13).

Welcome, John, C.C. (1631–49).

Welcome, John, C.C. (1705).

Welder, Thos. (1780).

Welle, Robt. (1825).

Weller, John, C.C. (1713)

Wellington, John, C.C. (1726).

Wells, Joseph, C.C. (1667).

Wells, John, C.C. (1682).

Wells, John (1758–68).

Wells, Matthew (1755–60).

Welsh, Robt., Dalkeith (about 1790).

Wentle, Jas. (1793).

Wescott, John, C.C. (1703).

West, William, C.C. (1697).

West, Samuel, livery C.C. (1766); (1750–67).

West, Thos. (1820–42).

Westaway, John (1840).

Westbrook, William, London (about 1730).

Westfield, Robt. (1813).

Westlake, John (1820–42).

Westmore, Robt., Lancaster (1761); Thos. (1779); Robt. (1785).

Westoby, John, C.C. (1677).

Westwood, Richard, C.C. (1691).

Wetherell and Janaway (1785–94).

Weylett, Jos. (1790–94).

Whaley, J. (1840–42).

Wham, — (1820).

Wheatley, John, C.C. (1668).

Wheatley, William, C.C. (1698).

Wheatley, John (1820–25).

Wheatstone, Sir Charles, inventor of a system of synchronous clocks; died 1875.

Wheeler, Thomas, C.C. (1655), master (1684); died 1694.

Wheeler, John, C.C. (1680).

Wheeler, John (1794).

Wheeler, Maurice, invented a rolling clock (1684).

Wheeler, Thos. (1793).

Whellan, Thos. (about 1680).

Whichcote, Samuel, C.C. (1724), master (1748).

Whichcote, Samuel, C.C. (1764), livery (1766).

Whiphan, Thos. (1775).

Whiphan, Thos. (1775); Whiphan and North (1793).

Whitaker, S. (1830).

Whitaker, William (1835–42).

White, John, C.C. (1648).

White, John, C.C. (1692).

White, Joseph, C.C. (1713).

White, Wm. (1830).

Whitear and Raves (1790–94).

Whiteaves, Richard (1804–40); livery C.C. (1812).

Whitebread, William, C.C. (1728).

Whitehead, Richard, C.C. (1671).

Whitehead, Robt. (1810–15).

Whitehear, Richard, C.C. (1648); (1640–60).

Whitehurst, John, a well-known maker, inventor of tell-tale clocks; (1713–88).

Whiterow, Jno. (1840).

Whitewick and Moss (1790–94).

Whitford, Thomas (1790–1823).

Whitford, George (1830–42).

Whitlach, Jno. (1652).

Whittaker, Edward, C.C. (1711).

Whittey, John (1842).

Whittingham, William (1688).

Whittle, Thomas, C.C. (1683).

Whitway, Saml. (1735–40).
Whitwell, Robert, C.C. (1648).
Wichell, Samuel (about 1710).
Wickes, John, livery C.C. (1786–1804).
Wickes, John Haughton, livery C.C. (1810–35).
Wickes, W. G. (1823).
Wickes, W. (1835).
Wickes and Netherton (1753–60).
Wicks, William, London (about 1800).
Wicks and Bishop (1820–25).
Wicks, W. G. (1836).
Wicks, Thos. (1835).
Wicks, Alfred (1842).
Wicksteed, Edward (1768–95).
Widdowson, Joseph (1830).
Wideman, Jacob, Augsburg (1680).
Widenham, Richard (1830–35).
Widenham and Adams (1840–42).
Wieland, F. (1835).
Wieland, Chas. (1835–42).
Wieland, R. and W. (1835–42).
Wieland, Fredk. (1842).
Wiggins, Thos. (1835).
Wigginton, Wm. (1806–20).
Wight, Jas. (1816–20).
Wightman, William, C.C. (1696).
Wightman, Thomas (1798–1818).
Wightwick and Moss (1775–1804).
Wigram, Thos. (1804).
Wilcocks, T. (1817).
Wild, Jas. (1790).
Wilder, Jno., C.C. (1790).
Wildman, Watkinson (1753–63).
Wildman, Samuel (1760–88).
Wildman, Chas. (1800).
Wilkins, Robert, C.C. (1670).
Wilkins, George (1810–25).
Wilkins, Samuel (1835).
Wilkinson, William, C.C. (1718).
Wilkinson, T. (1825–30).
Wilkinson, James (1830–35).
Willcocks, Richard.

Willerme, Pierre, C.C. (1648).
Willerton, Skull, and Green (1783–94).
Williams, Joseph (Ireland), C.C. (1685).
Williams, Jno. (1769).
Williams, Jas. (1794).
Williams, John (1800–4).
Williams, Geo. (1817).
Williams, E. (1825).
Williams, John (1821–31).
Williams, S. (1840–42).
Williamson, William, C.C. (1664).
Williamson, Thomas, C.C. (1668).
Williamson, John, C.C. (1682).
Williamson, Edward (1694–1720).
Williamson, Joseph, invented an equation clock in 1720; master of C.C. (1724), and died in office (1725).
Williamson, Timothy (1769–88).
Williamston, Christopher (1840–42).
Willin, Wm. (1800–11); livery C.C. (1810).
Willis, Mary (1822–5).
Willmot, Stephen, C.C. (1674).
Willmot, Thomas, C.C. (1715).
Willmot, John (1762–75).
Willoughby, John, C.C. (1686).
Willoughby, Benjamin (1708).
Willshire, James (1769).
Willshire, James (1781).
Willson, Thomas, C.C. (1659), assistant (1685).
Willson, George, C.C. (1692).
Willson, William, C.C. (1693).
Willson, John, C.C. (1714).
Willson, G. V. (1835–40).
Wilmot, George, C.C. (1670).
Wilmot, Stephen, London (1730).
Wilmot, J. (See Willmot.)
Wilmot, Richard, 1, Wilmington Sq. (1842).
Wilson, Joshua, London (1700); h.m. (1707).
Wilson, Jno., Edinburgh (1711).

Wilson, James, C.C. (1723).

Wilson, George, C.C. (1730).

Wilson, Titus, Lancaster (1779).

Wilson, James (1770–94); hon. freeman (1781).

Wilson, James (1804–1810).

Wilson, Jas., Askrigg (1786).

Wilson, G. (1820).

Wilson, W. (1829–42).

Wilson and Gandar (1855–65).

Wiltshire and Sons (1822–30).

Winch, Amos, C.C. (1677).

Windess, Lancaster; Thos. (1795); Stephen (1823); Thos. (1825); Wm. (1830).

Windham, Jas. (1840).

Windmills, Joseph, a good maker of clocks and watches; C.C.

Windmills, J. and T., master C.C. (1718); (1710–40).

Windmills and Elkins, London (about 1725).

Windon, Daniel, C.C. (1718).

Windsor, James (1835–42).

Winerow, William, C.C. (1718).

Wing, Mark (1816–42).

Winne, Hy. (See Wynne.)

Winnerl, Joseph T., Paris (1799–1886).

Winnock, Joshua, C.C. (1672).

Winnock, Daniel, C.C. (1707).

Winsmore, John, C.C. (1712).

Wint, — (1774).

Winter, Robt. (1817).

Winterhalter, J. (1840).

Wintle, David, London (1680).

Wintle, Thos. (1760–68).

Wintworth, Thos. (1700–40).

Wirgman, Peter (1775–94).

Wirgman, G. and G. (1804).

Wirgman, Thomas (1823).

Wirgman, G. (1825).

Wirgman, C. (1830).

Wirrall, Copley, C.C. (1648).

Wise, Luke, Reading (1686).

Wise (or Wyse); several generations among the early makers.

Wise, John, C.C. (1669).

Wise, Richard, C.C. (1679).

Wise, John, C.C. (1683).

Wise, Thomas, London, C.C. (1686).

Wise, Joseph, C.C. (1687).

Wise, Peter, son of John, C.C. (1693), master (1725); (1693–1726).

Wise, Luke, C.C. (1694).

Wise, Robert, C.C. (1694).

Wise, John, C.C. (1710).

Wise, Mark, C.C. (1719).

Wiseman, John, C.C. (1647).

Wiswall, Thos. (1800).

Wiswall and Co. (1810).

With, Thos., London (about 1790).

Wither, John, C.C. (1699).

Witte, Samuel, C.C. (1660).

Wogdon, Stephen, Greenwich (about 1730).

Wolfe, Joseph (1762–72).

Wolverstone, Thomas, C.C. (1650).

Wolveston, Thomas, C.C. (1670).

Wonnter, John, well-known maker (1770–1812); livery C.C. (1810).

Wontner, John, and Son (1804–12).

Wood, Thomas, C.C. (1691).

Wood, Robert, C.C. (1670).

Wood, John, C.C. (1701).

Wood, Henry, C.C. (1720).

Wood, Thomas, C.C. (1727).

Wood, F. (1770–90).

Wood, Robert (1785–1810).

Wood, John (1775).

Wood, Thomas Jas. (1822–30).

Wood, Robert (1820–35).

Woodall, T. J. (1804–10).

Woodall, F. (1817).

Woodhill, Jabez (1830).

Woodman, Mary (1835).

Woodruff and Son (1822–30).

Woods, Thomas, C.C. (1713).

Woods, C. R. (1842).

Woodward, J. (1835).
Woodward, Thos. (1835).
Woolard, John (1810–18).
Wooley, Thos. (1793).
Woolverton, Jas., C.C. (1677).
Woolverton, James, C.C. (1690).
Worboys, Arthur (1769–85).
Worboys, Jno. (1780–94).
Workman, Benj., portable sundial, B.M. (about 1700).
Worrall, John (1840–42).
Worsley, Thos. (1783–1805).
Wotton, Thomas (1690–94).
Wragg, Houblon, C.C. (1724); (1724–40).
Wranch (Wrench?), Jno. (about 1750).
Wray, Hilton, master C.C. (1785); (1770–86).
Wren, John (1780–85).
Wrench, John, died 1716.
Wrench, John, Chester, died 1751.
Wrench, Jno., Chertsey (Chester?) (about 1750).
Wrench, Charles (1780–1815).
Wright, John, C.C. (1661).
Wright, John, C.C. (1696).
Wright, Joseph, C.C. (1671).
Wright, John, C.C. (1700).
Wright, John, C.C. (1714).
Wright, Thomas (1765–75).
Wright, Chas. (1780–90).
Wright, S. (1820).
Wright, Elizabeth (1825).
Wright, Jas. (1820–35).
Wright, Thos. (1835–42).
Wright, John (1842).
Wright, William (1840–42).
Wrightman, James, C.C. (1670).
Wrightman, Thomas, C.C. (1701).
Wrightmark, Mark (1840–42).
Wrightson, Thomas, master C.C. (1737), (1734–38).

Wyatt, Anthony (1800–18).
Wyatt, Hy. (1840–42).
Wych, David, C.C. (1694).
Wyeth, John, C.C. (1655).
Wyeth, Lionel. (See Wythe.)
Wyke, R. (1825).
Wylder and Hall (1794).
Wymark, Mark (1816–42).
Wynn, W. M. (1804).
Wynn, William (1810–35).
Wynne, Henry, C.C. (1662), master in 1690.
Wythe, Lionel, C.C., a good maker (1646–62).

Yardley, James (1763).
Yates, Samuel, C.C. (1648).
Yates, Samuel, C.C. (1685).
Yates, Jno. (1800).
Yates, Thomas, Preston (1846).
Yelverton, Wm. (1780–94).
Yeomans, Ralph, C.C. (1722).
Yeriaf. (See Fairey.)
Yonge, George (1798).
York, Thomas, C.C. (1716).
York, John (1840).
Young, William, C.C. (1668), assistant (1695).
Young, Thomas, C.C. (1699).
Young, William, C.C. (1682–1700).
Young, Henry (1679–1775).
Young, James (1783); livery C.C. (1786).
Young, Hy. (1783–88).
Young, John, livery C.C. (1781).
Young, J. (1820).
Young, Wm. (1825).
Young, Jas. (1835).

Zachary, John, C.C. (1694).
Zech, Jacob, Prague; he invented the fusee in 1525; died in 1540.
Zollner, Martin, Augsburg; clock by him, Vienna Treasury (about 1580).

NOTABLE CLOCK DATES

(*From* BRITTEN'S FIRST EDITION)

	YEAR
The invention of weight clocks attributed to Gerbert about	990
Clock at St. Paul's Cathedral prior to	1298
Hall-marking powers conferred in the Goldsmith's Company at London	1300
Clock-tower at Westminster about	1300
Clock at Exeter Cathedral prior to	1317
Clock of Lightfoot at Glastonbury	1335
First Strasburg clock	1352
Clock by Henry de Vick	1360
Clock at Dover Castle	1360
Clock at Rouen	1389
Clock at Lübeck	1405
Clock in Piazza at Venice about	1495
Hele invented the mainspring about	1500
Watches first made about	1500
Stackfreed about	1500
Zech invented the fusee about	1525
Clock by Zech, Society of Antiquaries	1525
Anne Boleyn's clock	1532
Turret clock at Hampton Court Palace	1540
Paris clockmakers incorporated by statute	1544
Cruciform watches from about	1555
Skull Watches from about	1560
Octagonal watches from about	1565
Floral watches from	1570
Clock by Bartholomew Newsam in the British Museum	1580
Watchmaking in Switzerland said to have been introduced by Charles Cusin	1587
Clock by Isaac Habrecht at British Museum	1589
Glasses for table clocks first used about	1598
Clock at Lyons Cathedral	1598
Small oval or Nuremburg egg watches	1580–1640
English lantern chamber clocks first manufactured about	1600
Queen Elizabeth's watches	1571–1603
Watch-glasses introduced about	1610
Watches first worn in the pocket about	1625

YEAR

Clockmaker's Company incorporated	1631
Introduction of the pendulum about	1641
Loose outer cases for watches introduced about	1645
Balance spring invented by Hooke about	1658
Enamel decoration was occasionally employed on early watches, but cases adorned with enamel painting, executed by Toutin and other French artists of his school, became the fashion about	1660
The Virgule, a primitive form of duplex escapement, said to have been invented by Hautefeuille about	1660
Pendulum first applied to domestic clocks	1661
Fusee chain to supersede catgut invented by Gruet	1664
Watches with minute-hands about	1665
Huygens' pendulum clock with cycloidal cheeks about	1670
Watch clocks formed with the table of circular outline to protect the balance about	1670
Anchor escapement invented by Hooke about	1670
St. Dunstan's clock	1671
Rack striking work invented by Barlow	1675
Repoussé chasing applied to watch cases about	1675
Tulip pillars in watch movements	1676–1700
Plain enamelled dials for watches about	1680
Watches with balance arranged to appear as a pendulum about	1680
Enamelled plaques over watch bridges from about	1680
Long pendulum clocks about	1680
First keyless watch about	1680
Revocation of the Edict of Nantes, by which many French horologists were driven to England	1685
Repeating watches patented by Quare	1687
Equation clocks introduced about	1690
Dead-beat escapement for watches invented by Tompion	1694
Cylinder escapement patented	1695
Watch jewelling invented	1704
Caps applied to watch movements about	1710
Rack-work for winding repeating watches invented by Stogden about	1710
One-year clocks from	1690–1710
Dead-beat escapement for clocks invented by Graham about	1715
Mercurial pendulum invented by Graham about	1723
Pinchbeck alloy invented about	1725
Bells for repeating watches were used in England as late as 1800; wire gongs, at first more popular in France than England, are said to have been applied to repeaters by Julien Le Roy about	1750
Watch cases decorated by gold of various colors soldered on and chased about	1760
Harrison's chronometer taken on voyage to Jamaica	1761
The marine chronometer or timepiece for ascertaining the longitude	1761

YEAR

Second hands became popular after the successful trial of Harrison's watches in.. 1761

Lever escapement invented by Mudge about............................. 1765

Watch movement remodelled with a view to reducing its thickness, by Lepine,
about 1770

Helical spring patented by Arnold.................................... 1775

Spring detent escapement by Earnshaw and Arnold about.................. 1780

Duplex escapement patented by Tyrer..................................1782

Compensation balance by Earnshaw about............................. 1782

Rack lever escapement said to have been invented by Hautefeuille about 1722, but
patented and introduced by Litherland in........................... 1791

Duties imposed on owners of watches and clocks in........................ 1797

CLOCK AT ROUEN

INDEX

Allen, Clarence H., 46, 47.
America, 16, 18, 19, 20, 22.
American clocks, 14.
Anthony, Edwin P., 31.
Art, in clock cases, 18.
Astronomy, 12.
Atkins Clock Co., 47.
Atkins & Downs, 36.

Bagnall, Benjamin, 40, 53.
Bagnall, Samuel, 10, 39.
Bates, Francis E., 33.
Birge & Fuller, 38, 45.
Boston Clock Company, 44.
Brainard, Mrs. Homer, 5.
Britain, 16.
Britten, 5, 9, 54.
Brown, G. Winthrop, 30, 32, 53.

Chandler, A., 41.
Chandler, Timothy, 46.
Chetwood, Dr. Charles H., 32.
Chronometer, 16.
Claggett, Thomas, 38.
Claggett, William, 10, 30, 49.
Clapp, Preserved, 44.
Connecticut, 10.
Cookerow, Mrs. M. B., 41, 42.
Cornwall, Thomas, 46.
Creamer, Warren W., 33, 34.
Cummens, William, 33.
Cumming, Alexander, 48.
Curtis, 18, 35.
Curtis, Lemuel, 31, 32.
Custer, J. D., 39.

Dahl, O. I., 48.
David, Louis, 52.
Davis, Albert, 52.
Doolittle, Enos, 39.
Durfee, Elisha C., 31.
Durfee, Walter H., 6, 32, 34, 45, 49, 53.
Dyer, Elisha, 29.

Early clocks, 20, 21.
East, Edward, 52.
Edwards, Nathaniel, 33.
Essex Institute, Salem, 43, 44, 45, 46, 47, 48, 49, 50, 51.

Fales, Warren R., 54.
Faulkner, Edward, 39.
Ferguson, James, 43.
Fleureau, Esaye, 55.
Flower, Henry, 43.
Flynt, L. C., 53.
Ford, Henry, 39.
Forrestville Mfg. Co., 34.
French, 18.
Fromanteel, 30.
Fromanteel & Clarke, 30.
Fromanteel, Johannes A., 30.

Galileo, 9.
Gates, Z., 35.
Gould, Christopher, 40.
Grant, William, Boston, 33.
Gretton, Charles, 55.

Habrecht, Isaac, 20.
Halford, John H., 39, 40.
Hammond Collection, 43.
Harland, Thomas, 37.
Hatch, George H., 39.
Hoadley, 46.
Hostetter Collection, 52.
Huntoon, Mrs. Harrison B., 36.

Ingraham, Elias, 43.
Ingraham, Brewster &, 43.
Ingraham, E. & Co., 43, 44.
Ives, Joseph, 34, 38, 41.

Jackson, Benjamin A., 40, 41, 55.
Jerome, C. & N., 32.
Jerome & Darrow, 35.
Johnson, Philip A., 32.
Johnson, Robert C., 33.
Jones, Ezekiel, 45.

Keating, Mrs. Guy Metcalf, 29.
Knight, C. Prescott, 30, 31, 32, 33, 35, 37, 41.

L'Horlogerie, 20, 52, 53.
London, 9.
Lounds, Jonathan, 55.

Manning, R. T., 47.
Martin, John, 54.

Mayereffer, Archangelo, 50.
Metcalf, Stephen O., 54.
Metropolitan Museum, 37, 38, 39, 40, 41.
Miller, John M., 53.
Montague, William E., 33, 34, 35, 36, 39, 40, 45, 50, 52.
Moore, T. G., 54.
Moore, Thomas, 40.
Muller, Andreas, 52.
Mulligan, W. L., 29.
Mulliken, S., 41.
Mummery, 54.
Munger, A., 36.
Munger & Benedict, 36.

Nutting, Wallace, 40, 47.

Oakes, W., 49.
Old Garrison House, Trenton, 42, 46.
O'Neil, Mrs. L. F., 31.
Owen, Griffith, 40.

Parker, Thomas, 51.
Peacock, George, 54.
Pendleton Collection, 30, 33.
Pennsylvania Museum, 43, 51.
Perry, Marsden J., 31, 54.
Porter, Dr. Emory M., 29, 35, 38, 39, 40.
Prescott, William, 34.

Quare, Daniel, 51, 54.

Rambal, Joseph, 20.
Reed, Col. Isaac G., 34.
Rhode Island Historical Society, 30.
Rhode Island School of Design, 30, 33.
Rimbeault, Stephen, 54.
Rittenhouse, Benjamin, 40.
Rittenhouse, David, 10, 14, 18, 36, 40, 50.
Robinson, Leonard M., 29.
Rose, Daniel, 41.
Rosenbach Company, 49.
Russell, William G., 30.

Safford, P. H., 41.
Sawin & Dyer, 41.
Sawin, John, 31, 33, 41.
Schmidt, John, 45.
Shattuck, Mrs. George L., 36.

Smith, Edward, 48.
Smith, J. & Sons, 53.
Solliday, D. H., 45.
Soltykoff, 52, 53.
Steele, D. J., 33.
Storrs, N., 37.
Strausser, Jacob, 49.

Taber, E., 32.
Taber, S. M., 29.
Taft, Mrs. Emma A., 41.
Terry, Burnham, 44.
Terry, Col. William, 45.
Terry, Eli, 32, 33.
Thomas, Seth, 36, 44.
Timby, 47.
Tompion, Thomas, 53.
Turner, W. G. A., 41, 42.

Universum Clock Co., 43.

Vanderaam, J. B., 49.
Vaughan, C. Wheaton, Mrs., 43.

Wagstaff, Thomas, 48.
Washington Headquarters, Morristown, N. J., 35.
Wayne, Anthony, 37.
Wayside Inn, 39.
Weeks, Harry, 34, 44, 45, 48.
Wetherfield Collection, 52, 53, 54, 55.
Wharton, Susan P., 51.
Wheaton, Caleb, 29.
Wheeler, Richard E., 35.
White, Peregrine, 29.
Wilder, Joshua, 30, 31.
Willard, Aaron, 32, 34, 35, 38, 47.
Willard, Aaron, Jr., 34, 42, 43.
Willard, Benjamin, 29.
Willard family, 10, 18.
Willard, Simon, 10, 23, 24, 34, 36, 38, 39, 40, 43, 44, 45, 47.
Williams, Charles F. Collection, 43, 51.
Williams, David, 29, 39.
Willson, Joshua, 54.
Winkley, John, 42.
Wood, David, 34, 39.
Wood, John, 46.